THE BRENTFORD REVOLUTION

THE RISE FROM THE BASEMENT TO THE PREMIER LEAGUE

Published by
Legends Publishing

E-mail david@legendspublishing.net
Website www.legendspublishing.net

Born and bred in Hanwell, Tim Street has been a Brentford fan since the early 1990s. In 2004, having completed a degree in journalism at the London College of Printing and worked as a news reporter for three years on the Hounslow Chronicle, he landed his dream job as sports editor on the publication, covering the Bees as well as all other manner of local sport.

In 2009, following a company restructure, his job no longer existed, but he took his place on a newly created larger sports department, still covering Brentford but also many more sports clubs in West London, Buckinghamshire and Surrey.

Following numerous more company restructures, he also served as primary reporter for clubs such as Wycombe Wanderers (when they featured ex-Bees like Sam Saunders, Marcus Bean, Sam Wood, Paul Hayes, Myles Weston, Aaron Pierre and Alife Mawson), Luton Town and Cambridge United, while still helping out with Bees coverage.

Having been made redundant during the pandemic, he stepped away from sports reporting and now works as a journalist and sub editor in the hospitality industry, and enjoys being able to watch his beloved Bees purely for pleasure once more. Having kept up his passion for sports writing by penning articles for the Beesotted website last season, this is his first book, something he has wanted to achieve for many years, and which he hopes will be the first of many.

CONTENTS

INTRODUCTION BRENTFORD REVOLUTION

Brentford Football Club certainly aren't the first side in the modern era to rise from the bottom tier of English football to the top in little over a decade, and let's hope they won't be the last as the feat gives all smaller clubs hope that, against all the odds, it is possible to dream the dream. However, let's make no mistake, the Bees' progress is inextricably linked to the ownership of lifelong fan, Matthew Benham, who has revolutionised the West London club and made them the talk of a footballing world fascinated to understand how a forward thinking, fully sustainable small club has outthought and outfought big club traditionalists armed with parachute payments and large fanbase finances, rather than by out-and-out sportswashing.

Remodelling the fortunes of a failing lower league football club – alongside a protracted, complex, new stadium land deal in one of the most expensive areas of London – was never going to be an easy task. Many questioned the owner's sanity and often mocked the methodology for embarking on his quest to deliver success for Brentford, but they had completely underestimated Benham's professional nouse as well as the huge advantages his Smartodds data afforded him and his staff.

The success that was being delivered at FC Midtjyland, Benham's other football club, aided and abetted by shared executives and directors of football, was also rarely recognised, despite delivering Danish Superliga title wins as well as Europa League and Champions League campaigns. All the signs were pointing to a footballing visionary at work, yet large swathes of the sports media denied the reality provided by their own eyes. And, until fairly recently, even a segment of the club's supporters preferred to look backward rather than forward, with some even questioning the owner's motives.

It is undeniable that without Benham's acumen, statistical secrets, self belief and, importantly, the ability to make tough decisions and put his money where his mouth is at critical moments – despite remaining a selling club when the price met valuations to ballance the books – none of what has been achieved at Brentford would have been possible. Indeed, as you will read, in all likelihood, the club would have died without him. Instead, almost 80 years later, Thomas Frank's side are emulating the prewar achievements of the great Harry Curtis and his top flight heroes of yesteryear. What a journey the past 12 years has been for Brentford, and long may the good times continue. Ivan Toney's selection to the England squad, as well as 'second season syndrome' dispelling demolitions of Manchester United and Leeds certainly point to a bight future.

In writing The Brentford Revolution, we have enjoyed unrivalled access to the men at the coalface – the movers and shakers central to the club's metamorphosis – including managers and head coaches, directors of football, players, executives and, thanks to Bees United, an interview with the elusive owner himself. We also have contributions from Brentford supporters, all of whom have shared the rollercoaster ride to the top and provide even more colour to an already vivid picture.

Of course, not everything has gone to plan in the past few years and this book certainly does not paper over the cracks when there have been knock-backs and upsets – but by the time you read the last words of the final chapter you wlll realise, too, that the club's top flight status was achieved because of the hard lessons and the new Gtech Community Stadium sits on stronger foundations because of those experiences – even though they hurt like hell at the time.

It is also important to underline that although Brentford continue to establish themselves as a Premier League football club, contributing so much at the highest level, that nothing is taken for granted. A unique sense of self awareness and humility permeates from everyone we have spoken to whilst producing this book and that simple, well mannered, down-to-earth honesty, when combined with cutting edge data and a bold, exciting style of play, makes for a very special environment where good people can achieve great things.

I have been fortunate enough to have written and published many books about Brentford, a club I have supported for approaching fifty years, but instead of recounting yesterday's history, this one celebrates a quite remarkable journey to the top in the here and now. I have thoroughly enjoyed writing it with my good friend, and longtime local sports journalist, Tim Street, and we both hope you enjoy reading The Brentford Revolution as much as Bees supporters have enjoyed living through the era.

David Lane

CHAPTER ONE

August 13, 2021, a balmy Friday night. Brentford FC's shiny new stadium, squeezed almost impossibly into a parcel of former railway land surrounded by tracks heading in the directions of Brentford, Chiswick and Acton, waited to welcome a capacity crowd for the first time. The club's old Griffin Park stadium, its home for 116 years and the scene of so much triumph and despair, heartache and joy, over the years had, due to Covid, taken an inglorious last bow behind closed doors. The future lay in a new home, a mile or so away, in Lionel Road.

When this new stadium site had first been mooted, two decades previously, there had been talk of monorails ferrying supporters down the Great West Road to a new mecca of football. That was, of course, a pipe-dream. So too, it seemed at the time, was Brentford ever playing in the Premier League. Blimey, just getting back into the second tier for the first time since the early 1990s would have been enough for the vast majority of Brentford's long-suffering loyals.

But as the thousands poured into the Brentford Community Stadium that night – most for the first time (limited crowds had been allowed back in for two league matches between lockdowns the previous December, and for the home leg of the play-offs against Bournemouth five months later) – it was to watch their beloved Bees make their debut as a Premier League side. Indeed, their first foray in English football's top flight since the end of the Second World War. Their visitors were Arsenal, one of the English game's most famous names, and despite not being the force they once were, were still undeniably one of the country's top sides.

The atmosphere was electric. Everywhere, people were smiling and looking on almost in disbelief. What had seemed an impossible dream had become a reality. But what happened next took that dream into a whole new realm of fantasy. Just 22 minutes in, Sergi Canos picked up a poor clearance on the left hand edge of the area. The former Barcelona youngster cut inside, skipping past a challenge before rifling a shot past Gunners' keeper Bernd Leno. The stadium exploded with euphoric noise.

Seventeen minutes from time Christian Norgaard made the game safe when he nodded home at the far post, after the visitors had failed to deal with a Mads Bech Sorensen long throw from the left. The noise was deafening at full time. Sky pundits Jamie Carragher and Gary Neville looked on in awe, like school kids at a particularly impressive fireworks display, and couldn't help but join in with the delighted renditions of Hey Jude – that Brentford anthem of old – booming from the stands' impressive, club-like, sound system.

The Bees' rise has been one of English football's stand-out success stories in modern times – Brentford aren't another of the nouveau riche sides that have simply spent their way into the top flight, or a fallen giant returning to recapture past glories. This is Brentford, who for most of the previous five decades have been playing in front of a hardcore of around 5,000 fans, mainly serving up what could be best described as functional football, while flitting between the third and fourth tiers. So, in the words of David Byrne, in the Talking Heads' 1981 hit Once in a Lifetime: "And you may ask yourself, well, how did I get here?" Well, the answer is 'largely thanks to one man's vision and financial acumen.'

In order to properly understand the journey Brentford have been on since Matthew Benham got involved with the club, you have to first take a look at the financial situation the club found itself in at the time. Like many clubs of its size, the Bees had experienced numerous ups and downs on the balance sheet as well as on the pitch. Rare moments of carefree spending were interspersed by longer, leaner spells, as boom was inevitably followed by bust – almost literally.

A steady decline following the club's only previous spell in the top flight culminated in relegation to the Fourth Division for the first time in 1962. Heavy investment led by chairman Jack Dunnett – including an astonishing (for that level) frontline of three former internationals – won back a place in the Third Division, but when a return to the Second Division failed to follow, the purse strings were tightened and a financial crisis ensued. Infamously, this culminated in Dunnett attempting to sell Brentford down the river and put an end to the club in 1967 – then allow local rivals Queens Park Rangers to move into Griffin Park.

History was to repeat itself more than three decades later when Brentford, again finding themselves in the fourth tier, went about a spending spree unprecedented at that level, paying both a club and divisional record fee of £750,000 (although some say it was nearer £500,000) for Iceland international defender Herman Hreiðarsson from Crystal Palace, the former club of new owner and chairman, Ron Noades. Under Noades's management, the Bees spent their way to the Third Division title, but as before, with Brentford struggling to build on that initial success, the chequebook started to come out less frequently, less extravagantly and certainly less successfully. Noades quit as manager after an embarrassing FA Cup defeat at home to non-league Kingstonian but stayed on in the board room. However, the battle was just starting to heat up off the pitch, never mind on it.

Having failed to significantly grow the fanbase, with initiatives like Target 10,000 falling by the wayside, Noades's frightening vision for the club's future was to move away from Griffin Park. His reported choices for new homes were even less inspiring, with the likes of Feltham Arena and Woking FC's Kingsfield Stadium mooted as alternatives – whether or not his relocation plans were a bluff to force Hounslow Council to get behind plans to find us a new home in the borough, or he was looking to cash in, only he will ever know. Either way, it had become increasingly clear that Noades's previous heavy spending was not an act of philanthropy but in fact covered by an overdraft, which had risen to more than £4m. By the time he eventually relinquished control, the club he had taken over, financially in the black, was now millions of pounds in the red.

Supporters shook buckets inside and outside the ground, and some even bravely undertook sponsored walks to far-flung places like Hartlepool, Brighton and Stockport to give the coffers much-needed boosts. Against this backdrop, supporters' trust Bees United (BU), founded as a pressure group in 2001, was working hard to secure a future for the club. Launching a 'Back the Bees' campaign in the summer of 2005, which aimed to raise £1m to buy out Noades's shareholding in the club, it brought on board former BBC director general Greg Dyke. But as they toiled to raise the funds necessary to take up the option on the shareholding, BU chairman Brian Burgess delivered a bombshell when addressing the crowd on the pitch before a home game against Rotherham at the beginning of October 2005.

He said: "Yesterday was the day when the option to acquire our club expired. It's clear that we need more time. It's only recently become clear that the club is suffering a cash crisis and it would take even more cash than we originally thought to put it on a sound financial footing. Yesterday, we also arranged for two of our Bees United members, whose pledges are included in the £700,000 (that needed to be raised), to put an emergency loan into this club so that it could pay its wages and avoid going into administration today."

Those last five words rang around a stunned Griffin Park. Burgess later told The Hounslow Chronicle that the close call with the administrators had stemmed from the club's budget being changed without BU's approval, and that he felt "angry and utterly let down" by those running the club. Not only was securing the funds necessary for the takeover far from certain, but speculative incomes had not materialised, and £700,000 would need to be found to see Brentford through to the end

Bees United's Jon Bishop, Jon Gosling and Brian Burgess raising much needed funds which kept Brentford Football Club alive

of the season. With the club's spiralling debts thought to have reached around £8m, Brentford Independent Association of Supporters (BIAS), took to the streets before a home game against Bournemouth to hand out leaflets alerting fellow fans to the club's perilous financial situation.

By early November, the situation was being described as "critical", and Bees United were preparing a Plan B of talking to other interested parties should the trust fail to raise the funds for a takeover. But the New Year brought new cheer, with the takeover finally secured at the end of January 2006 in the shape of a 60 per cent stake in the club, although Burgess warned that "the battle starts here", with such a high level of debt to contend with. As the metaphorical champagne corks popped, Burgess said: "We now have to step up the efforts to help the club pay its bills. We had to raise £5.5m to finance the club's debts. We have to repay those debts, and have to pay back more than £1m over the next three years." The club may finally have been in the hands of the fans, but it was far from out of the woods, and there was much more financial uncertainty to face up to in the coming years. Indeed, within a week of the takeover, star striker DJ Campbell made a cut price transfer deadline day move to Birmingham City, as the Bees, in the words of BU supporter director Jon Gosling, "face up to our financial realities".

Campbell's departure undoubtedly blunted Brentford's promotion hopes, just as the deadline day sale of Nicky Forster to the same club had done nine years earlier. With a £600,000 loss for the season forecast and their fingers burnt once already, BU financial director Joe Bourke sounded a warning for the following season that "we are looking at closing the budget by cutting back across the board". He added: "Nobody has the answer as to when over-investment in the playing budget puts us in danger and when under-investment in the playing budget puts us in danger. Very few clubs in this division don't make a loss, but we don't have a safety net in the shape of a wealthy benefactor. As a supporters-run club, we have to face reality and only spend what we earn." Burgess added: "Tough decisions will be needed, but we are trying to break even from next season."

The result of the cost cutting the following campaign was, statistically, Brentford's worst Football League season on record, as they finished rock bottom of the third tier and were relegated by Easter Monday, the first Brentford team to have finished bottom of a division since joining from the Southern League in 1920. In a campaign in which the Bees lost a depressing 25 games, they also set a new club record for successive games without a win (18), least wins (eight), fewest goals scored (40) and lowest number of points gained (37).

There was, however, a hint of the philosophy to come when Leroy Rosenior, a manager renowned for encouraging the playing of football the right way, replaced his former West Ham team-mate Martin Allen in the Griffin Park hot seat. Thirteen years earlier, Rosenior had scored a final-day hat-trick for Bristol City to seal relegation from Division One for a Brentford side which then still had a reputation for playing somewhat agricultural football.

On his appointment, Rosenior said: "I was brought up at West Ham under John Lyall, who was perhaps the biggest influence on my career, so I like my teams to play good football. He taught me to play the correct way, to get the ball down and pass it quickly. I am not about holding onto a 1-0 lead, I like to play positive football with positive thinking players." They are words which could have come straight out of the Brentford blueprint for success a few years down the line. But when you're lining up with Brooker (arguably the most skilful player in that team) and Shipperley (unarguably the most heaviest player in the team) rather than Benrahma and Watkins, putting that philosophy into practice would prove somewhat challenging.

Rosenior also acknowledged the budget constraints he would be working under, saying; "every club you go to will have a problem with its budget... I can certainly work to the budget". However, after a promising start to the season, Rosenior was gone by the end of November, following a 4-0 home defeat to Crewe Alexandra. That same week, Bourke told a BU AGM that it was a "watershed season" and a "crucial period of time" for the club, adding that if attendances continued to fall, "retrenchment becomes the order of the day".

As Brentford slid towards relegation under Rosenior's replacement, Scott Fitzgerald, the club took a final gamble on a clearly overweight Neil

Shipperley. The experienced former Crystal Palace striker was bought with money raised by supporters, but zero goals from 11 games showed the gamble had failed to pay off.

The New Year did at least see a glimmer of a silver lining emerge from the dark storm clouds, and a glimpse of what was to come for Brentford. The first mention many fans will have heard of Mathew Benham came at the end of January 2007. Without much of a fanfare, he had, 12 months earlier, helped facilitate BU's takeover with a £500,000 loan, helped set up a shirt sponsorship deal with betting company, Samvo, as well as providing an emergency stand-by facility to help the club get through the season. Now, Benham was to accelerate his involvement, shelling out £3m to buy £2m worth of loans from Barclays Bank and £1m from Ron Noades, ending the former manager-owner's controversial involvement with the club, much to the delight of Bees fans.

A millstone had been removed from the neck of the club off the pitch, but chairman Greg Dyke, having admitted the club would have struggled to see through the following season, warned that its problems were far from over. He said: "This in no way solves our financial problems, but makes things easier. We're not out of the woods, but this is a big help."

Noades took a swipe at Brentford's fans as he left, claiming that he'd never said he'd fund the club with personal resources, and saying they were "fixated" by the £4.1m overdraft he was leaving behind. Whichever way he chose to frame it, having claimed in 1998 that one of the things which had attracted him to Brentford was that it didn't have any debts, his involvement with the club ended with millions of pounds still owed, despite Benham starting to douse some of the flames.

The man brought in to replace Scott Fitzgerald, and tasked with getting Brentford back out of the basement division, was something of a curve ball. While Rosenior had been all about the footballing philosophy, former England international Terry Butcher was all about pulling a team, lacking in any conviction or confidence, up by its bootstraps. Bees fans who had witnessed their side relegated so meekly were perked up by thoughts of a man leading their team who had once shrugged off a head wound so deep it turned his England shirt a bright shade of bloody red (during a World Cup qualifier against Sweden). They were delighted to see Butcher, not yet appointed manager but sitting in the dugout for the final game of the season at Tranmere, rise from the bench on a number of occasions to issue rollockings to players he wasn't even in charge of yet.

Butcher himself admitted that having spent the lion's share of his previous managerial career in Scotland, with Motherwell and Partick Thistle, he knew very little about the English lower divisions. The man entrusted to help fill the gaps in his knowledge was someone already very familiar to Brentford fans. Andy Scott had played more than 150 games in four years with the club in the late 1990s and early 2000s before leaving for Oxford United, then having his career cut short when, at Leyton Orient, he was diagnosed with the heart condition, hypertrophic cardiomyopathy. Having coached the Orient youth team after hanging up his boots, Scott jumped at the opportunity to return to a club he had formed a great affinity with during his playing days.

Scott, speaking to us at a salubrious Premier Inn hotel in Brentwood (not Brentford), said: "Coming back in 2007, the club had been through a really rocky time. A lot of managers had been there, the football wasn't great, the recruitment wasn't great, it felt as if the club's life had been drained out of it a little bit. There was no soul to it anymore. When I left (as a player), we had a vibrant group of players who went on to do really good things, but it felt like the club was going nowhere and just treading water.

"David Heath, who was my sponsor when I was playing, mentioned that they had appointed Terry Butcher as manager, but he didn't have any knowledge of players in League Two. They needed an assistant who knew the league and knew the club, to help Terry along. I loved my time at Brentford and felt it was my club, so the opportunity to go back and help revive the club was too good to turn down. Terry was an England legend, and to work with someone like that was an opportunity I couldn't miss either.

"The first time I met Terry was in a hotel near Heathrow. We chatted for a few hours about how he wanted to play and what he wanted to do, which was effectively him interviewing me to see if he could get on with me. That went well, but prior to that I'd had no dealings with Terry other than seeing him play for England. He's a really impressive guy and one of the kindest men you'll ever meet, a real people person you can't help but like, and we hit it off straight away.

"I gave him a list of players I thought we could recruit and we went from there. He did the main stock of the coaching and I did some bits, but I was the buffer between the players and the manager, the usual assistant manager stuff. I think we recruited alright but we lost out on a couple that year, like Charlie MacDonald. Terry wasn't over-enamoured with Charlie and the way he came across."

In scenes a world away from Brentford's recruitment methods of the future, MacDonald – who was to sign for Brentford at the second attempt a year later and go on to become something of a Bees legend – remembers that first involvement with the club well. He said: "It was a strange one really. I was at Gravesend & Northfleet at the time and had scored a lot of goals for them. I had three clubs speaking to me, one of which was Brentford in League Two. The others were Scunthorpe, who had just got promoted to the Championship, and Southend, who had just been relegated from the Championship.

Manager Terry Butcher and assistant Andy Scott explaining tactics to defender John Mousinho

"Brentford was the first I actually had a chat with, down at Osterley. I came into the office, and Terry Butcher – as a football fan watching Italia 90, and the bloody headband – you think he's a bit of a legend. The first thing he told me was he didn't know much about me, and said he knew a lot about Scottish football but not so much the English side. He said he didn't know any players but was going off Andy Scott's recommendations. As a player, hearing from a manager that you wouldn't be his signing, I was never convinced. I came out of the training ground knowing I wouldn't be going to Brentford at that stage."

Nevertheless, the squad put together by Butcher made a steady, if unspectacular, start to the season. One who was impressed was local boy John Mousinho, a fringe player under Allen and Rosenior, who suddenly found himself one of the longest-serving squad members. "It's a lot more professional here than last season," he said after firing in the winner against Barnet to secure the first three point haul of the campaign in mid-August. "Training methods, attitudes, a winning mentality – just small things, but things which make a huge difference."

For all this apparent new-found professionalism, results soon started to go south, and as the Bees embarked on a miserable run of five defeats in six games, things were not looking any rosier off the pitch. Just five weeks into the campaign, the club was already dipping into the £500,000 emergency loan fund set aside by Benham for the season. Chief executive, Keith Dickens denied it was a cash crisis but warned: "I think it's safe to say this facility has been set up to use, and to use in total. We will have to use it again unless we beat the budget by getting better crowds than the forecast average of 4,250 through success on the pitch."

He went on to say the loan was essentially another overdraft, but "at a far more agreeable rate than with a bank or previous owner".

It was also not clear, at that stage, how far Benham's involvement would go. As the club continued to stumble on and off the pitch, BIAS called for more leadership from key figures like Dyke, Dickens and Burgess, with chairman, Tony Cross, saying: "I am concerned they have put all their eggs in the basket with Lionel Road. But what if it doesn't happen – will Matthew Benham keep coughing up the cash if we stay at Griffin Park?"

The misery continued on the field of play with a run of five successive defeats, including a 1-0 defeat at Macclesfield in which Brentford failed to muster a single shot on target, an embarrassing 7-0 drubbing at Peterborough, then two uninspiring home defeats to Morecambe and Grimsby in the space of four days. Butcher had stood defiant throughout, saying he would take the flak but wouldn't throw the towel in. After the Grimsby defeat, it was a decision which was taken out of his hands. There had been an internal board target of four points starting from the Grimsby match but, as Butcher's side lost and could not get to four points, he was fired. That same week, Bourke stepped down as BU finance director, warning that being in League Two made the club's "massive debts" more of a problem, and that breaking even was "no more than an aspiration", as the club faced continued losses of £500,000 a season without exceptional income from cup runs or transfer fees. Following both men out the door was chief executive Keith Dickens, with a club insider giving the Hounslow Chronicle an insight into the haphazard way the club was being run off the pitch as well as on it. "We had a farcical situation where if Joe Bourke had been run over by a bus, nobody would have a clue about the club's finances, not least the chief executive," it was claimed.

The man tasked with reviving the team's fortunes would be Butcher's assistant, Andy Scott, who was given the manager's job on an interim basis before an impressive run of form, dragging the Bees away from the League Two danger zone, landed him the job permanently. Looking back at the Butcher era, Scott said: "I felt we had a good mix of younger and experienced players but it just didn't work, it just didn't click. I don't think Terry could get his head around players at that level not being able to do things he had found it easy to do. He tried, but I think he over-thought things – changing formations and systems, trying to be too clever. I was trying to impress on him that League Two players need structure and needed to know their roles and their jobs, and be drilled into doing it on a daily basis.

"At the end of November, we got beaten 7-0 at Peterborough – you know when things go wrong and they just seem to keep going wrong, and you think this isn't going to work. At the end, there was an inevitability about it. Terry found it hard to cope with the fact we were losing and things weren't going well. He took it to heart and took things personally, he's a very emotional man. Everyone could see the writing was on the wall and Terry struggled with it. I'm a loyal person and I'll back who I'm working with and working for, but unfortunately, the way it worked with me being offered the caretaker role, Terry thought I'd gone behind his back. It couldn't be any further from the truth. I had been out there with him facing the music 7-0 down at Peterborough.

"The fact of the matter is I was 33 or 34 at the time, just retired from football and didn't have too many coaching qualifications, and when Terry went it was either take the caretaker role or be on the dole, so you do it. I never had the aspirations to manage as a player, but when you have a heart condition and have to retire straight away you have to rethink these things and I started doing my badges. I was plonked in position and had to get on with it, you don't know how long you will get. We went to Wrexham having not come from behind or won away all season, so it was a tall order. We were going down and I needed to stop the slide, get some confidence into the lads, and fortunately things turned around. I simplified it a bit really, went back to 4-4-2.

"I probably had three days coaching before the Wrexham game and we just broke it down into the back four, then put the midfield in, then the front two. We decided what their roles were and how we wanted to play. We went behind but came back to win, which gave us impetus and helped the players believe in me a bit more. It was a massive game for me in my career, looking back. I probably wouldn't have become a manager if I hadn't won that game, or shown that we were progressing and the players were with me. They were great lads and responded brilliantly, they were just a bit lost."

Scott eventually led the Bees to a comfortable mid-table finish and was rewarded with a five-year contract. Another perspective was provided by Craig Pead, who somewhat surprisingly, and despite having had a very average season, made it into the League Two Team of the Year, as he had the season before with Walsall. He said: "A club like Brentford needs to be up there going for promotion, or at least the play-offs. I couldn't really put my finger on what went wrong (under Butcher), but it was a whole new team put together, with new players and formations, and it just didn't work." Of Scott, he added: "He's a young manager in his first job, but the new deal shows they want him to do it for the long term."

Brentford had thankfully eased away from the non League trap door, but there were certainly times where dazed Brentford fans had been concerned that the worst could happen. If the Bees had got relegated that season, it would have likely been the death of the club as we knew it. It was hard to imagine a way back from that fate.

CHAPTER TWO

Although Brentford were far from out of the woods, there was suddenly a much-needed air of stability emerging on and off the pitch – although Benham remained very much a man in the background. It was evident he wasn't one to simply throw bags of cash at a problem – Brentford wouldn't be buying their way of the bottom division this time – but on the other hand, the club no longer had the wolves howling at the door. Scott said: "I don't think we'd ever heard Matthew's name at that point. Obviously I wasn't involved in the board meetings, but Matthew wasn't really involved or talked about. We just knew we didn't have to carry buckets around to keep going any longer. When you're working at a club, you don't want to have to worry about whether or not the players will get paid, which is a massive problem at a lot of clubs."

Recruitment was still also very much, in a more traditional manner, left down to the management team, and Scott, together with assistant Terry Bullivant, set about putting together a side full of the kind of characters needed to thrive in the bottom division with a £1.3m budget. Players like Charlie MacDonald (signed at the second time of trying), Marcus Bean, Alan Bennett, Mark Phillips, John Halls, Adam Newton, David Hunt and Nathan Elder formed the cornerstone of a side that would, in fact, see Brentford do more than just thrive, holding off challenges from Exeter, Wycombe, Bury and Gillingham to secure the League Two title. Scott said: "We had a budget that was probably mid-table. The key was bringing in Terry Bullivant, who had worked at Brentford before, with Ray Lewington and Ron Noades. I knew he was an excellent coach and the players would respond to him. The second thing was we did early recruitment. Marcus Bean was training with us for the last four weeks of the season and we got Charlie Mac done early – two key players. We got Ben Hamer in early too, he had a good stature and was a good personality. Straight down the spine of the team, good characters – players we felt had the ability and character to get us promoted.

"We also got some players out who I felt were holding us back. The January after I got the job we went to Spain, and I wanted to test a few players to see if they were with me or not, and that was a real eye-opener for me. The group then ran itself. When things don't come back to you as a manager and they're being dealt with by the players, you know you've got a good dressing room. Players like Halls, Newton, O'Connor, Bean, MacDonald – they were my managers in the dressing room. We wanted to be competitive, but knew we had to over-achieve to get anywhere near promotion, and that mentality, of fighting for each other and the club, galvanised us.

"Their attitude and application was outstanding every day. We never set targets, but wanted to maybe get into the play-offs. We were a tight group on and off the pitch and never put pressure on ourselves or each other. Before we knew it we were in the top three, but even then there were no thoughts about promotion, nobody spoke about it. We knew we had to be on it each game and we didn't smash teams, they were all tight games. We were always in a game, and if a team was better than us we still gave them a game – that was our attitude."

One player who could have been added to the roster that summer was Michail Antonio, who has since gone on to become one of the Premier League's most feared strikers with West Ham, and having been called up by England once – only missing out through injury – decided to become a Jamaican international instead. Back then, Antonio was a raw teenager with non-league Tooting & Mitcham, when he turned out for the Bees in a pre-season friendly at Staines Town. Seen by Brentford as one who got away, Antonio joined Reading a few months later instead. Scott explained that such was the fragility of the club's finances at the time, gambles like Antonio couldn't be taken unless they were going to produce a guaranteed return.

"Michail came late in pre-season and played at Staines in a friendly," said Scott. "I really liked him but money was so tight that we couldn't afford to bring someone in on a couple of hundred pounds a week who wasn't going to start. We didn't have enough time with him, I don't think he even trained with us, and 45 minutes is difficult to judge. He went to Reading a few months after, it happens, but the key thing at that point was we needed to strengthen the first XI, and he wasn't going to get in the first XI straight away. When you look back, when you bring someone in on trial you have to give them enough time to impress and give them an opportunity, and it's something we did a lot. But Tooting would only let him play one game and wouldn't let him train."

Another example of the fragility of Brentford's recruitment situation at the time can be demonstrated by the club being forced to shelve plans to restart its reserve team at the start of that season – it was a conveyor-belt supply of loan signings which saw them through when injuries hit or extra legs were needed. This was especially important during the run-in, when a series of injuries meant that Billy Clarke and Sam Williams were the only strikers left standing with the Bees striving to secure the title. Scott said: "We were always out watching games. Look at the injuries we had to our strikers at the end of that season – if we didn't have that pool of players we could go out and get, we wouldn't have got promoted. Charlie MacDonald, Jordan Rhodes, Nathan Elder and Damian Spencer had all got injured. If anything was going to go against us, it seemed to, but we had a good supply of loan players we could recruit from, and they got us over the line. The key was every single player who came in on loan fitted in straight away, and their personalities were incredible. All of them bought into what we were doing, and our players, being who they were, allowed me to bring those players in."

Scott's views were echoed by striker Charlie MacDonald, a key player in his side who would go on to impress at the level above too. He said: "Andy put together a squad which was hungry, would fight for each other and had fantastic work rate. He put in place the work ethic, that if you want to win, you work hard. For example, Glenn Poole started the season really well with goals and assists, but as the season went on he was not so much brushed aside, but became a bit-part player because Sam Wood came in, and his work ethic and defensive duties in that position were vital. That was the foundation Andy built the squad upon. In the end, it worked, because we kept a lot of clean sheets and always knew we'd score goals at the other end. There was a lot of self-belief within the group, a lot of players who had played at a higher level and hungry players coming out of non-league – Andy got a really good mix of players in."

Another interesting perspective is provided by Marcus Bean, the midfield general of that side, who then returned to Brentford as consultant scout in the summer of 2019 before progressing into a role as the club's head of emerging talent. Marcus is therefore well placed to compare the Brentford he played for to the Brentford he returned to seven years later. He said: "The rise has been amazing. When I left (in 2012), I could see the difference in the way the club was going and the direction it was going in, you could see it had big potential. Not just with the new stadium, but the difference at the training ground from my playing days is amazing – we used to eat dinner with tiny partitions with the gym work happening next to us in a tiny pavilion – the facilities have improved so much.

"When I first arrived there was no real structure, it was just Andy Scott and Terry Bullivant, that was it for the scouting department really. Now there's a very clear structure and a clearly defined philosophy, which everyone is working towards, and that's the hallmark of any good organisation.

You need principles and a philosophy you stick to, and that's what we've got now. There's nothing that has stood still and the club is always evolving, which is great. Yes, it was a surprise to see us make the Premier League, but when you look back at all the things being put in place at the early stages, it's not too surprising as we've got such clever people involved."

Bean would cement his status as an all-time Brentford favourite with his performances in the middle of the park during that title-winning season, not least in a famous Bank Holiday win at Bournemouth in April 2009, in which Billy Clarke scored the only goal of the game. Bean seemingly covered every blade of grass on the pitch in that victory which, although it was still not guaranteed, clinched promotion in the eyes of many Bees supporters. In a performance which typified the team under Andy Scott, the ten men of Brentford (Darren Powell having been sent off for fighting his own team-mate, Karleigh Osborne) scrapped for everything and showed exemplary team spirit to pull off a fantastic result against the odds in the blazing sunshine, cheered on by a packed away section of sunburnt Bees fans.

"Bournemouth was a crazy day for many reasons, one of those season-defining matches in terms of going through the kind of adversity we did and pulling through," Bean said. "It was a really special day, one of my better performances to be fair, but as a team, to do what we did was pretty impressive. Karleigh and Powelly were all right in the end, it's the one and only time I've seen that (two teammates fighting) in my career, it was a strange, strange day. When I first joined, with the club having had a season like they did the year before, and with lots of new faces, I came without any expectations of challenging at the top of the table. What became clear quite quickly was what we did have was a fantastic team spirit, and that's what dragged us through to be honest."

Looking back at that day, Scott speaks with a certain amount of pride and with a glint in his eye. "It was the first time I thought we could get promoted," he said. " It's the best game I've ever been involved with in terms of the drama – we had a player sent off for fighting with our own player. I know the club's in the Premier League now, but I know for the fans who have followed the club for a long time, the performances of our players that day will go down as some of the best they have ever seen. We were up against it, took an amazing following, the sun was shining and it was a culmination of everything we put together – the players' attitude, work rate, fitness, desire, unity – my proudest moments as a manager were seeing my team respond in adversity, when they're up against it and the pressure was on – to pull out that result made the whole day perfect.

"The fact Powelly was sent off made it even better in some ways, as belief kicked in and nobody could stop us after that. It was a beautiful feeling. Straight after the whistle, Powelly apologised to Karleigh and everyone else as he knew he'd let everyone down, but we didn't scapegoat people.

If someone got sent off we put another ten per cent in to make up for it. There was no blame or finger-pointing and we never castigated Powelly, he was still involved in the group. Powelly's an emotional guy and he simply wanted to win. It spilled over, it was the wrong thing for him to do and they should both have dealt with it better. But you can't let those things define your season, we dealt with it there and then. Karleigh was fantastic as he could have held a grudge. But the group rallied round and handled it."

After swatting aside Accrington Stanley 3-0 the following weekend, Brentford travelled to Dagenham & Redbridge for a midweek fixture knowing a win would seal promotion. In the event, a Daggers side, inspired by future Bee Sam Saunders, put a dampener on the celebrations by storming into a 3-0 lead, and although Damian Spencer pulled one back late on, the damage had already been done. Instead, the Bees would have to wait four more days before wrapping up both promotion and the title with a 3-1 win at Darlington, again dragging out a result in the face of adversity. After just two minutes, Brentford lost one of only three fit strikers left at the club when Spencer was taken out by the elbow of Darlo's Alan White, who was duly sent off. Although Sam Williams came on as the replacement, it was strike partner Billy Clarke who sealed the deal for the Bees, scoring either side of half time, following Alan Bennett's opener, to take the champagne off the ice and start the party.

Brentford fans' loud celebrations echoed around the sparsely populated Darlington Arena, which had become a complete white elephant for the club and a monument to failure and bad management by rogue owner George Reynolds. Opened in the summer of 2003, as the new home ground of Darlington Football Club, following the decision to leave their previous ground, Feethams, and with a capacity of 25,000, the arena rarely attracted more than 3,000 supporters. The cost of the arena caused the club to go into administration three times and would have been seen as an example to Matthew Benham, and any other owner with half a brain cell, of how not to do things at Brentford going forwards.

"Darlington was another really good away performance, really professional, and we got the job done," said Bean. "There were some fantastic scenes on the coach on the way home, it was a really special year – one of my best in terms of the fact we were unfancied, so to win the league was amazing. None of us got into the division's team of the year, which we found funny – it was probably because we weren't fancied to do it and people were a bit jealous of us. Scotty showed he was good at recruitment even then, some of those loans he brought in were fantastic, and if you look back now, you think how the hell did we get them? Bully (Terry Bullivant) too – I see him on the circuit all the time and he's a top, top scout with a real eye for a player. Between them, their recruitment was immense that season."

Andy Scott and captain Kevin O'Connor are League Two champions – Brentford could now start to plan for a brighter future under Benham

For Scott, it was an emotional culmination of two seasons worth of hard work, pulling the club back from the precipice and getting it heading in the right direction again. Following a mammoth journey back from the north-east, Scott and his players joined an impromptu party outside The Griffin pub – one of the famous four on the corners of Griffin Park. "We went up to Darlington with the attitude to get the game won," he said. "Damian was taken out with a really bad tackle early on, but again the lads thought we've got to battle here. Damian came in and fitted in straight away, and we saw it as one of our players being wronged, we're going to show them. Billy Clarke was incredible that game and Sam Wood had so much energy, it's crazy how much he ran. Ryan Dickson too, nobody could run like our team. They're characters you want alongside you, and I'd gladly go out for a drink with every single one of them now. You knew nothing would faze them.

"We won the game, and (kit man) Dave Carter came up and said 'we've done it'. I said 'I know'. He said 'no, we've won the league', Wycombe have lost. The fact we were so far away from home and knew we had that long journey home, it was like it was meant to be. Poor Damian was laid out injured on the top deck of the coach, while we stopped off at a Tesco and loaded it up with drinks to have a party on the way home. We got back to Griffin Park and there were thousands of people waiting on Braemar Road. Two years on from when the club had been on its knees, to have brought the club together and revived it was really important. Seeing so many deliriously happy people and the impact winning had had on the fans showed we'd done something to make their lives better – it was amazing."

Charlie MacDonald, a player who contributed so much to that season but had to sit out the climax with a dislocated shoulder, is in agreement with Marcus Bean that Brentford had been unfancied that season, but showed incredible hunger and determination to get the job done. And when you consider his strike partner, Nathan Elder, was also injured, Brentford's title win was all the more impressive. MacDonald recalls; "The expectation was to push for the play-offs rather than going on to win it," he said. "After a disappointing opening day at Bury, I made my debut at home to Grimsby, and I felt after we beat them, one of the favourites, there was a lot of self-belief within the group. Andy Scott got a really good mix of players in, a lot of players who had played at a higher level and hungry players coming out of non-league. Utilising the loan market at the end of the season when it mattered was massive as well.

"It was a very frustrating end to the season for me as I had scored 17 goals, and six weeks away from the end of the season I was looking to push on and compete for the golden boot, so to be sitting there watching the lads, but not being able to play a part and help the boys get over the line, was very frustrating. But thankfully, they stayed strong and, in the end, we were worthy winners."

For the fans, moving back out of the bottom tier was a cocktail mixed with equal mixtures of jubilation and relief. It is true to say that at several times in the preceding seasons the very survival of the club had been questioned, with many dark days having been endured. The celebrations witnessed in the streets surrounding Griffin Park – following a mad dash back to West London from Darlington – ran long into the night, with players and supporters sharing pints, songs and happy memories. The club was, in the grand scheme of things, simply back to where it had spent much of the previous three decades – the familiar territory of the third tier. However, Scott and his team had stopped the rot, there is absolutely no doubting that achievement, as well as injecting some much needed pride back into the club's veins.

According to life-long Brentford supporter and reporter for the Middlesex Chronicle for many years, Jim Levack, the side's defeat in build up to the Darlington promotion clincher remains as memorable as the party scenes that followed – which underlines the nervous nature that all Brentford fans share until promotion is a mathematical impossible to blow. Jim recalls: "It was the game four days earlier that I recollect just as vividly, when a certain Sam Saunders broke the deadlock for Dagenham in a first half Brentford no-show that eventually saw us roll over to a 3-1 defeat. There'd been weeks of calculating promotion permutations, so for Brentford to disappear that night in East London was a hammer blow... but 'there's always Saturday' was the consensus as we headed home.

"Saturday came and an early red card for Darlington defender Alan White calmed even my cynical nerves, and when Alan Bennett rifled home from the edge of the box just past the half-hour, I had a feeling everything would be fine... it was his first and only goal for us. Omens and all that. Billy Clarke, an Ipswich loan player I really liked, then smashed in another two either side of the break and it was a brand of pandemonium that not even a consolation goal response from the home side could dampen. It felt like the football gods were with us that day, a little bit like the Championship play-off win at Wembley in 2021. Party time for a whole half! The prize might not have been the same, but it didn't feel like that at the time. In hindsight, it's days like those, that make Premier League days like these, all the sweeter."

Another life-long Brentford fan who'd celebrated promotion up in the North-East that late-April 2009 afternoon, Martin Holland, was just as happy that the Bees were out of the basement; "When the final whistle blew at Darlington, I celebrated like we had won the league – it had been achieved with our band of lower league pros, misfits and loaners. But it was League Two. Did I think that was the first step towards the top flight? Did I think it was part of some bigger master plan? Did I f**k! It was us getting back to where, at that point, I thought we ought to be, to where we belonged. Any bigger vision than that was in the minds of others, not in mine, or any of the fans' there that day I doubt. It proved to be a pivotal moment. But only in hindsight. We came back to Griffin Park and drank the pubs dry. It's unlikely anyone even mentioned the Championship that night, let alone the Premier League!"

Another important development was to come a few months later, when Bees United, the Supporters' Trust, accepted Matthew Benham's offer to plough £5m into the club over five years, with an option to pay him back at the end of that period, or let him take over as majority shareholder. However, to the vast majority of club supporters, Benham remained somewhat of a mystery figure.

In fact, there was not even a recognisable photograph of the new, low-key, investor that could be used in press reports, which prompted the Brentford fanzine, Beesotted, to produce a hand drawn sketch with spoof copyright restrictions on its use. The magazine joked: "Benham, who is prepared to invest £5m into the club over a five year term, made his first 'public appearance' at last night's Bees United meeting. Benham was smuggled into the venue under a pile of coats and spoke only through a vocoder behind a back-illuminated screen. We thought for one minute that it might be former Eastenders actor Dean Gaffney, but we cannot confirm this rumour."

But all jokes aside, without that investment lifeblood, Scott would have been handed an even smaller transfer budget to build a squad expected to survive in League One than he would have received for getting out of League Two. Benham was certainly becoming a lot more talked about around the club – even if few people would be able to pick him out successfully in an identity parade. Ambitious talk was circulating about Benham already having aims of seeing Brentford step up to the Championship, with Scott saying at the time: "The deal with Matthew has been going on behind the scenes for some time and I have met him several times. The most important thing is his plans bring some stability to the club and make me able to plan for the future."

As Bees United members voted on Benham's investment offer, he sent out a statement promising that although he hoped to be able to use his expertise in the world of football data analysis to assist Scott, he would not be seeking to become a Ron Noades-style real-life version of the computer game Championship Manager. He said: "Final responsibility for player recruitment, team selection and tactics will remain the responsibility of the manager, and no players will be signed without his approval. I believe I may be able to bring expertise to help the manager identify players of potential value to Brentford. As a result of my business experience, I have amassed considerable experience of football strategies as well as a broad knowledge of players both in the UK and internationally." Although still remaining hands-off to a large extent, it was a first sign for supporters of what Benham would eventually bring to the club above and beyond financial investment – a whole culture change and a whole new way of operating. Was this development the first sign that a Brentford Revolution could be plotted? Undoubtedly.

The voting process to accept the proposed business agreement took place just as the Bees team were about to embark on life back in the third tier, after a two-year absence, with a campaign curtain-raising trip to Carlisle United – Brentford won 3-1 thanks to a brace from new signing Myles Weston. Also arriving that summer were fellow winger Cleveland Taylor, plus former top-flight strikers Carl Cort and Steve Kabba, while Alan Bennett's loan from Reading was made permanent. In a triple swoop on the Dagenham & Redbridge side, which had tore Brentford apart and put their promotion celebrations on hold a few months earlier, the Bees also brought in Sam Saunders, Ben Strevens and Danny Foster. Looking back, Saunders said: "Dagenham did really well that season, just missing out on the play-offs, and we were players on form and at a good age. Strevs and I were the first to come – then Andy Scott actually asked me which full-back I'd like to work with, so as I combined really well with Fozzy, Andy thought that was a good option too, so he came in as well!"

Considering it was Brentford's first season back in the third tier for two years, there were some impressive performances that season, especially early on, when relegated Norwich were beaten 2-1 at Griffin Park, while fellow fallen giants, Southampton, were held to a 1-1 draw down at St. Mary's – Cleveland Taylor's headed equaliser was probably his stand-out moment in a disappointing spell with the Bees.

Another Bee to have his stand-out moment with the club that season was Strevens, a player who never really nailed down a starting place in the side, but who sent a noisy travelling Brentford army into raptures when he gave his side the lead at Elland Road in early March – only for Jermaine Beckford to grab Leeds a point. Games against the likes of Leeds, Norwich and Southampton would become commonplace in years to come, but at the time, Brentford were going toe-to-toe with some big fish – clubs who had fallen into a small pond – and the minnows did themselves proud.

Another memorable game that season occurred on a freezing December day in Milton Keynes. Any new Brentford fan looking back in the history books would be forgiven for thinking there would have been nothing special about a 1-0 win at MK Dons in League One, but it has gone down as one of the ultimate smash-and-grab raids against a very good Dons side. The Bees barely had a sniff up front, but at the back, led by immense performances from loanees Wojciech Szczesny and Pim Balkestein, they repelled everything thrown at them. Conjuring up the spirit of that Bank Holiday in Bournemouth eight months earlier, nothing was going to get past the Bees that afternoon, and when Charlie MacDonald grabbed a late breakaway winner with pretty much Brentford's only chance of the game, it made for another famous day for Scott's side.

"MK Dons away I will always remember," Scott said. "The pitch was frozen, rock-hard. Pim, bless him, didn't have a clue what was going on. He'd come from Ipswich and went up for a header and came down on a solid surface. He was a bit melodramatic was Pim, and he came in moaning at half time, but Bully just said to him you either sort yourself out and stay on or you're coming off. I think it was the first time he'd had someone tell him to just get on with it, and in the second half he was brilliant. Wojciech was just a joke, that was probably the best individual goalkeeping performance I've seen in one game. He saved about eight one-on-ones, and then Charlie Mac only needed one chance at the other end. We were completely up against it, but that was what we could do. We were never beaten and never thought another team was better than us. To have a group of players you knew would give you everything, every game, just typified it really."

Matchwinner Charlie MacDonald also looks back fondly on that day, saying: "You have to give the boys credit for how we dug in that day, although Szczesny at the time was unbelievable between the sticks. They were doing everything but score, hitting the post and hitting the bar. MK had a good side at that point and were expecting to beat us. I remember it like it was yesterday, one of the coldest games I've been involved in. The ground was rock solid, and to be honest, we were surprised the game was on. In the end, I don't think it was just my only chance, I think it was our only chance as a team. Luckily it fell at the right time for me and I managed to get decent contact on it, and at the final whistle we were a little bit embarrassed shaking hands as it was daylight robbery. But the changing room was buzzing because in football you talk about stats and possession percentages, but the only stat that matters is obviously the scoreline, and we took the three points."

Szczesny, who had signed on a season-long loan from Arsenal, before maturing into one of the world's top keepers with Juventus and Poland, was one of several impressive temporary signings that season, alongside Balkestein (Ipswich), James Wilson (Bristol City), Toumani Diagouraga (Peterborough) and Lewis Grabban (Millwall) - once again the Bees had made good use of the loans market. Another, highly-rated Spurs prospect John Bostock, announced his arrival with a brilliant brace against Millwall on his debut, including one direct from a corner, but he never lived up to that early hype with Brentford, or anywhere else unfortunately.

It was a campaign which would ultimately see Brentford finish in ninth place, which Scott, looking back now, feels – despite the new investment – was a good showing in a division featuring big, recently top-flight, clubs. He said: "We had a great year. That league had Leeds, Norwich, Charlton, Southampton, Sheffield Wednesday – clubs with real pedigree. We found it tough in some games, but had some incredible performances against some big name clubs. We kept the majority of the side and the spirit remained the same. Matthew was still in the background, although his name was being mentioned more and he came down to the training ground a few times, but there was no real relationship. I had a bit more of a budget, but didn't want to bring in players on more money than those already there and put their noses out of joint. That was really key, and probably where I went wrong the year after."

The summer of 2010 also saw Benham begin to unveil more of his long-term visions for the club, with the announced setting up of an academy – and despite it being scrapped several years later in favour of a B team model, after the likes of Josh Bohui and Ian Poveda were cherry-picked by Premier League clubs Manchester United and Manchester City (respectively) for scant financial reward – it did at least bare some fruit. Losing those two players, however, would trigger a total rethink in youth development strategy, as well as a fair deal of controversy further down the line, but back then, the new indoor academy structure and facilities, to be housed within the grounds of Uxbridge High School, was undoubtedly an exciting and positive proposal.

Andy Scott shares a moment of celebration with the Griffin Park faithful

Having an academy enabled the club's U15s to be invited to play in the prestigious Northern Ireland Youth Soccer Tournament, the NI Milk Cup. "This is a signal of both Brentford FC's and Matthew Benham's personal ambition," said Bees United chairman David Merritt at the time. "Having an academy is almost unique for a League One club, and it's certainly something Brentford wouldn't be able to do without Matthew's money. I believe the idea will be to bring more home-grown players through Brentford's ranks, something Matthew is very passionate about."

Meanwhile, following a solid first season back in League One, Scott was busy putting together a side he felt would be capable of challenging to push for the next level. At a meeting with Benham, Scott was asked what budget would get him the play-offs – £3.5m was the answer – so Benham gave it to him. One of those he bought in was former Bees striker Nicky Forster, who returned to the club hoping for an Indian summer some 13 years after leaving Griffin Park to join Birmingham City for £700,000 in January 1997. Forster noted that the club he was coming back to had moved on drastically from the one he had left, saying at the time: "It's a very different club now, and one showing huge potential to move forward. But if it was the same Brentford, I wouldn't have come back. I wanted a new challenge, not to go over old ground again, and to be part of the new Brentford is an exciting challenge."

Also arriving that summer was goalkeeper Richard Lee from Watford; defenders Craig Woodman from Wycombe Wanderers, Michael Spillane from Norwich City and David McCracken from MK Dons; winger Nicky Adams from Leicester City and striker Gary Alexander from Millwall. Pim

Balkestein and Toumani Diagouraga, who had impressed on loan the previous season, returned on permanent deals. But there were signs that all was not well in a 5-0 pre-season hammering by Fulham, which was played as a testimonial game for long-serving Bee Kevin O'Connor. Lee remembered: "I think it's safe to say the first month was a nightmare. That Fulham game in particular, I was far from being match fit. Without making excuses, I was terrible, and I just remember feeling miles off it and wasn't at it. There were one or two other issues too and it took me a while to get going. Those first few weeks were a real baptism of fire, but fortunately I was able to turn things around."

The team itself, however, was struggling to do the same following a poor start, with only one win in the opening nine league games not what the doctor had ordered. The only respite during that time was a memorable League Cup run, which saw Brentford knock out Championship side Hull City before, on a famous night at Griffin Park, putting Premier League side Everton to the sword. It wasn't a scratch Everton side either, with Leighton Baines, Seamus Coleman, Sylvain Distin, Phil Neville, Leon Osman, Marouane Fellaini and Yakubu all starting, while Mikail Arteta, Stephen Pienaar and Jermaine Beckford all came off the bench. After Gary Alexander had cancelled out Coleman's early opener, Charlie MacDonald missed a penalty for the Bees, taking the tie to extra time and penalties, where the hosts triumphed 4-3.

"They were special nights under the lights at Griffin Park," MacDonald remembered. "Everton had some big players on show and bought more off the bench as they had to. Missing the penalty in normal time was hard to take, but I thought we matched them, and I remember Myles Weston giving Seamus Coleman a torrid time as well. We were definitely worthy of taking it to penalties, and I had no doubts whatsoever about stepping up again. Even the best players in the world miss penalties, and you can't let it affect you. Being a striker and having a selfish edge, it's a free shot from 12 yards, so if you offered me another one, I'd 100 per cent step up and take it, and luckily for me I managed to stick that one away." Richard Lee, who saved Beckford's penalty in the shoot-out before Jagielka hit the post to send Brentford through, added: "Looking back at that first season, it was my favourite time with the challenges it brought, particularly the Everton match. It was one of those games where I just felt so in the zone, and even now I can picture the moment where Jagielka hit the post, running up and down the touchline and the pitch invasion – it's a memory that will live with me for the rest of my life."

Joyous as that cup run was – it finally ended the following month with a very unlucky penalty shoot-out defeat at Birmingham after Brentford had been seconds away from winning in normal time – it only served to paper over the cracks. "The Birmingham one was really annoying because we should have won that game," Scott said. "They got a last-minute equaliser, and Robbie Simpson slipped over because he had moulds on rather than studs, which really annoyed me. That's probably the most frustrated I've felt because we really deserved to win, we played really well against a Premier League side. We had some good moments, but I never really felt, with the issues we had at the start of the season, that we got any momentum going. It didn't feel like we had that power of the group we had before. When you're on thin ice, when you have adversity, it breaks, and it's hard to get it back."

Results picked up in October, with four league wins out of five, but there remained hints that all was not right when, the following month, Scott addressed the media after a dismal 1-0 FA Cup defeat at Aldershot – during which some of the travelling support had called for his head. Scott's unexpected post-match reaction was to announce that his team would be "closing ranks". Clearly annoyed that former Bees boss Martin Allen was being linked with his job, Scott said: "People can talk about being negative, but look at what we have done these last two seasons. I'm sick of it, we're closing ranks. It's about us, what goes on in the changing room, our squad, our management staff. They believe 100 per cent in each other, and that is all I care about."

For Scott, looking back now, the problems that season started with the recruitment – a process which was still a world away from the one he would become immersed in when returning to the club as chief scout, then head of recruitment, in 2016. There was a hint of what was to come as Scott admits he abandoned his old methods of bringing in recruits of proven character and experience in favour of more technical players, but it failed to pay off. Following that Aldershot defeat, Scott seemed to have turned it around with four successive league wins, including an impressive 2-0 victory at Southampton in the Bees' final game before Christmas. However, a run of six defeats in seven at the start of 2011, which saw the club slide alarmingly down the League One table, ultimately spelt the end of Scott's time in charge.

"That year, there were a lot of mistakes from myself in terms of recruitment," he recalls. "I felt that because we'd finished ninth we needed to change things and move things on, get in what I thought were better players. I wanted to be more technical, but we brought the wrong players in – players with the wrong attitude who, personality-wise, broke the group. Three or four players just didn't work out and weren't much better than what we already had. I thought we had to try to move it forward, but the group, which had been so tight and solid, started to resent those players coming in, and me for not trusting in them.

"The second thing was, throughout August, we had probably four situations with players with personal issues that were horrendous,which, as a manager and a person, I had to deal with and look after them. The board didn't know about them, only myself, Terry Bullivant and the players. That affected me and changed my focus a little bit. When it's family, children, relationships and things like that, you need to look after your players. That impacted the individuals and the whole group, without a shadow of a doubt. It dragged on well into September and October, all really difficult situations. Maybe I should have let the board know about what was going on, it may have bought me a bit more time, but my relationship with the players was important to me and I didn't want to break their trust by making their issues public knowledge and risk it getting out. There was a lot going on behind the scenes which was no fault of the club or anybody else – situations that happen to everybody in everyday life, but when you have these things happening you can't control how it affects you physically and mentally and you can't perform."

Of the post-Aldershot rant, Scott said: "It was a bit of everything really, my naivety as a manager. It was the first really tough spell I'd had to endure, plus certain managers were on my shoulder in the press and starting to be a bit more visible, putting pressure on me. But I had no experience, it was the first time I'd been through it and didn't know how to deal with it. My frustration with the players we'd brought in came out – we'd had some meetings about players we wanted to bring in and it never really happened. There were things going on behind the scenes – obviously Mark Warburton came in quite quickly after I left, and I knew there was something going on. I didn't have the ability to deal with it. I was still a young manager, and rather than drive through it, I let it affect me."

A 4-1 defeat at Dagenham & Redbridge on 1 February proved to be the final straw, and for Scott, the character of players he had brought in were front and centre of the problem. He said: "We had a couple of games where things just didn't go right, like when Terry (Butcher) was in charge. We hadn't had that before, where we'd make a mistake and concede and never come back, it was a sign that we didn't have the strength or mentality to come through it like we did before. That's the thing I look back on, where I let the players down who had got us promoted. The players who were brought in weren't any better and were worse characters, and it feels like it tarnished my relationship with the players who had done so well for me. We didn't have the right types of people, and when things start going wrong, it's those people that are the ones who start stabbing you in the back.

"The fact we had to play Simon Royce in goal at Dagenham – I wanted to bring another keeper in and wasn't allowed, which makes you start questioning whether something is going on. Roycey let one trickle under him and Karleigh (Osborne) scored one of the best headed own goals I'd seen – sometimes you're on the touchline and things go in slow motion – you can see it panning out, how it's going to go. The fans were really brutal that night, a new type of fan that I hadn't seen before. I wasn't stupid, I felt the writing was on the wall. Nothing happened the next day, but I was driving into the training ground on the Thursday morning and got a call from (chief executive) Andrew Mills, saying he needed to see me. The chairman, Greg Dyke, should have done it – it shouldn't have been left to the chief executive – I deserved that at least. He (Dyke) had waited until he was getting on a flight out of Heathrow. He could easily have done it on Wednesday, or seen me early Thursday morning. I didn't like that.

"I hadn't dealt with that sort of situation before, so it was tough, but looking back, it was my own fault due to the players I brought in – players I found subsequently were very vocal in wanting to get me out. The ones I had previously wouldn't have done that. I felt I deserved a bit longer for what I'd done for the club, but it's Matthew's club, and he's entitled to run it how he wants. We've had a great relationship since then as that's the natural progression of football – people get sacked and people move on. It was a learning curve. I was grateful for the chance and loved every single moment of managing the club, it was a major part of the pathway to where I am now."

Marcus Bean, who like Scott later returned to the club in a recruitment capacity, agreed with his former manager's assessment, saying: "There is a tendency to sometimes rip things up. Yes, you need to tinker, but wholesale changes don't necessarily work. You just need to add a bit and keep that momentum going, and one or two players he brought in perhaps weren't the right fit. We were in a rut we couldn't get out of, and it was probably the right decision at the time as it didn't seem we could get ourselves out of it, and sometimes a fresh face is needed. But Scotty will go down as a legendary Brentford manager for what he achieved in getting us promoted, then keeping us up."

Charlie MacDonald, another of Scott's trusted generals during the promotion campaign and first season back in League One, commented at the time that he didn't think everyone was giving 100 per cent for the manager, saying: "It's hard to say if some had stopped playing for the gaffer, but there were players trying against Plymouth (the following game which the team won 2-0) who haven't been trying in recent weeks. I always gave 100 per cent for Andy, but I don't think everyone can say the same these last few weeks. As a group, we have definitely let him down."

Looking back at that period, MacDonald recalls: "I don't think he lost the dressing room, and I've no bad words to say about him, but after the Dagenham game we were aware the chairman wanted to make a change. It was disappointing because Andy lifted the team back from being on its last legs really, but you have to look at where they are now and it's all part of the process – off the pitch the club is run unbelievably well. You see a lot of football clubs that win promotion with a set of players who will run through brick walls for the club, and all singing off the same hymn sheet, then there's a bit more in the budget to bring in players on more money and perhaps bring in a bit of ego with them. Can you control that? Will it be harmonious in the dressing room? It's a fine balance really. I get that now as a manager (MacDonald manages Isthmian League North side Barking) – other managers don't ask me what players are like as players but what they're like as characters. It's massive, and if you can get the dressing room right, you're halfway there."

For Sam Saunders, who was signed from Dagenham & Redbridge immediately after promotion, in July 2009, but only really flourished under later managers, Brentford were already thinking ahead in terms of recruitment and football culture by the time Scott left. He said: "You don't like to see anyone lose their job, but I think it was more the style of play rather than anything else. Matthew had it already in his mind how he wanted to play and how he sees football, and Andy wasn't quite doing that. He was obviously very successful in getting Brentford out of League Two, but I think it was a clear shift in how Brentford go about their business, including the type and the age of players they bring in, because there was a real change from when Scotty went to afterwards in terms of personnel brought in and the style of play.

"They play a lot different now to how they did back then. It was all 4-4-2, balls into the box and getting crosses in, and that wasn't the player I was or the player they signed, so it was quite difficult to get a run of games. Since then, I've had discussions with Andy, and maybe things could have been done differently. I've got a good relationship with Andy and we probably get on better now than when we worked together. It was nothing personal, he just didn't think I was going to help his team, and that's football."

Rumours had circulated at the time, however, that suggested Matthew Benham had used his contacts at several Champions League clubs around Europe to arrange visits for Andy Scott to learn first-hand how elite level coaches prepared training sessions and to inspire the then Brentford manager. Some say there was a reluctance, even an arrogance, in Scott's outlook back then, which meant that somebody with a more proactive mindset would be a better match for Brentford going forwards.

Goalkeeper Richard Lee, in his book *Graduation: Life Lesson of a Professional Footballer*, admits he was one of the players who perhaps didn't see eye to eye with Scott. Looking back at what he saw as being behind the decision, Lee said: "I have to be careful what I say, but Andy did a reasonably good job for the club, and I think it just got to the point where they wanted to move forward and felt his way of playing wasn't quite in line with the way they wanted to take the club."

A final word on the saga goes to Mark Chapman, who served on the Brentford Football Club board as a Bees United representative between

2010-12, and was in a unique position to observe the end of the Andy Scott era and provides the following recollections.

"Relations with the board had deteriorated over the months prior to the dismissal. Andy's attitude in board meetings had won him no favours. He looked put out by being asked to attend them or answer questions from board members. If he'd played the game a little bit more he might have won himself a few more matches of support. Having said that we were a proxy for Matthew by then; it was his club in all but name.

"I was standing next to fellow director Alan Bird in the Daggers' boardroom after the game when his mobile phone rang. I noted the caller was 'Matthew Benham' on the screen. It didn't take a genius to work out Andy was in trouble. Shortly after, chairman Greg Dyke ushered us into a side room (I think nine directors attended that night, which was a big number compared to normal away trips). Greg said: "It's been decided there's going to be a change". Matthew said he wouldn't put in more money with Andy still in charge.

"I learned afterwards Matthew snapped after listening to the match commentary, which had several mentions of our right-back, Stephen Wright, being turned inside out. He had not really approved of this signing and had decided enough was enough.

"Andy was called to the Petersham Hotel in Richmond, with coach Terry Bullivant in attendance too, on the Thursday after the game. Finance director Alan Bird, and if I recall the then CEO Andrew Mills, met them both. Greg wasn't there as he left the country on business the day before."

"It was a pretty fractious encounter. Andy did not take the news well, but Bully had been in the game longer so knew the score. Andy was told specifically not to go to the training ground after the meeting to speak to the players but did so anyway, which made it an extremely difficult day.

"I did not enjoy the experience and had a few sleepless nights after. Ultimately you are whipping the legs away from someone who had put a lot of effort into building his squad and then dumping him on the dole, and in a very public manner. Andy's the only person to have won a championship medal as a player and manager for Brentford. It never sat well with me, despite it being the correct decision at the time.

"I never agitated for his dismissal but there were others on the board that did, even after the first few games of the season. I'm pretty sure Andy would have approached the final chapter a lot differently with the benefit of hindsight and it's good to see his success in the game after his departure."

CHAPTER THREE

With Scott pushed out of the picture, Brentford were to take their time with the next appointment – one which would be 'Benham's first appointment' and one that would hopefully see his long-term vision and strategy for the club start to take root. Before that, however, there were still the final three months of the season to negotiate, and the man handed the reins was veteran striker Nicky Forster, pulled off the training ground the morning after Scott's departure and given the keys to the manager's office in a caretaker's role.

In another nod to the future direction of the club, Mark Warburton was brought in from his position with Watford's academy to assist Forster off the pitch – more on him later. Things began well for Forster, starting with an unbeaten run of six games, including four wins – one in the second leg of the JPT semi-final to book a place at Wembley – to dispel any lingering thoughts of a relegation battle. Another sequence of four wins from five followed in March, but a damp squib of a Wembley final (more of them later too) ended in a 1-0 defeat to Carlisle United, after which the season petered out with just one win in Brentford's final seven league games.

Warburton had become a foreign exchange trader in the City after his football playing career had extended no further than spells with non-league Enfield and Boreham Wood, before reinventing himself once more – he was working as Watford's academy director when Benham made his call. Warburton had been introduced to Benham by a mutual acquaintance, film producer Justin Andrews, and had actually first approached Benham to see if he would be interested in investing in a pre-Gino Pozzo owned Watford, who were experiencing financial difficulties. "Obviously, his love for Brentford runs deep, so I broached the subject not knowing how deep that love was, and that was really our first coming together," said Warburton.

Nicky Forster follows Sam Saunders away from the gantry after losing at Wembley with chairman Greg Dyke looking perplexed

Of his partnership with Forster, Warburton said: "I was a very basic Conference player and never had the pedigree of a Lampard or a Gerrard, so I wanted to push really hard in the youth and academy area. Nicky was obviously a player who had never coached a session in his life at the time, so he was the figurehead, but I was doing all the coaching. Brentford were 18th in League One, and we put a different structure in. Senior players are the same as youth players, they need structure and they need to enjoy coming to work. They were really receptive, and really quickly, we saw what we could do by laying a structure down. That's not being critical of Andy in any way, it was just something different to mix it up a little bit.

"You have to give people belief. Again, nothing critical about the previous manager – I would never do that, but sometimes it just takes a different environment – looking at things you can do immediately, like changing the food at the training ground and cutting the pitches a little bit tighter so the grass is better. Just small details the players notice. Making the hotels we stayed in for away games the best you possibly can, for example, and it worked because we had a good run of results. Belief started to grow, fears of relegation started to ease and we were in a much better place."

Perceived logic amongst Bees fans has always been that the JPT final, in which Forster angered supporters by dropping popular veterans Marcus Bean and Kevin O'Connor for two loan players who failed to make an impact, was Forster's failed dress rehearsal for the job. O'Connor said at the time; "This was my chance to lead the team out as captain, so I'm extremely disappointed, although I don't blame Fozzie [Forster] personally." It doesn't explain a very odd team selection however.

Speaking to the Evening Standard after the final defeat the Bees' interim manager confessed; "It took a while for them to get used to the occasion... As much as you try to prepare them, it's a unique atmosphere, and we didn't get to grips with it in the first half. In the second half we moved the ball a lot better and got at them but, in all honesty, we didn't get enough quality into the box and we didn't test their keeper. But I'm proud of the lads, they have worked very hard to get here today." But would victory at Wembley really have made a difference to his long-term managerial chances at Brentford?

In fact, it becomes clear when speaking to those around the club at the time that the job was always going to go to someone else – Forster simply didn't have the experience to be trusted with the crucial next phase in the club's metamorphosis. From the outset, the chief executive at the time, Andrew Mills, talked of an "interim stage" and not putting a timescale on Forster's reign, and of a "full and proper process" in which the position would be "considered fully and thoroughly".

Yes, Forster would be part of the process, but despite Mills saying "the man in the seat is probably in the best position", he would always be an outside candidate. From the outside looking in at least, that could perhaps be seen as surprising considering Forster was a well-spoken and intelligent footballer who many observers could easily see fitting into the club's new forward-thinking culture. Then again, with the sum parts of Forster's subsequent managerial career being failed spells at non-league sides Dover Athletic and Staines Town, perhaps those running the club knew what they were after – and it wasn't him.

Warburton said: "I don't think Nicky had taken any coaching badges, and that's not being derogatory of him, but a factor that was always going to be difficult for Nicky, because Matthew is such an intelligent individual with a clear vision for Brentford and was looking at the next stage of the club. From that point of view, I didn't think Nicky would get the job and I don't think Nicky did either. He was a good guy – very media friendly and speaks very well – and I think he wanted to see where it would go. But he knew deep down you have to get the badges and qualifications to deal with the trials and tribulations of the men's game. I think he knew."

Richard Lee recalls that Forster was popular with the players and would have been a welcome choice had he been given the job. He said: "Nicky was actually pretty popular, and it was quite a successful short period of time with him and Warbs working together. But I got the impression that they wanted to bring in a bit more of a name, or someone with a bit more experience. I remember at the time, it was one where the lads would have been happy had Nicky got the job, as there was a good feeling between him and the players. But a lot of clubs go for that bit more experience, especially a project like Brentford was at that time."

Charlie MacDonald, who in a three year stay at Griffin Park scored 40 goals in 111 games for Brentford, also believes the writing was already on the wall, saying: "When you look at who was putting their name forward for the job and who they gave the job to – somebody with a bigger name in terms of who he was and what he's done. It was disappointing for Nicky as it was the route he wanted to go down. But it's a tough one, fine margins, and I don't think that route has worked out for him really."

Marcus Bean is still quick to highlight his former teammate's qualities and suitability at the time, but clearly appreciates inexperience was a key factor in Forester not getting the job on a permanent basis: "Nicky is a very intelligent, thoughtful, football man with some good ideas as a manager, but the less said about that little period the better. My overriding experience from that is, as a manager, you've got to be your own person and stick to your guns, you can't let other people influence your thinking, and I think Nicky did. He should have stuck to his principles and his beliefs but got slightly misled, and the rest is history."

Sam Saunders, who earlier admitted that he and previous manager Andy Scott hadn't seen eye to eye in terms of playing time and style, felt the shackles were off under Forster, and believes he helped introduce the football culture Brentford would soon be entrenched in. He said: "Fozzy did really, really well, but it looked like the club already had a plan in place. He got us playing a good style and slightly changed the system to one which suited me, so personally, I really enjoyed it. Mark Warburton came in to assist him and gave really good training sessions. For me, it was an improvement, and the club has gone from strength to strength. We brought in loan players from clubs like Sunderland and Leicester, and it showed the players a different way of playing."

Having become far more invested in the Brentford project – both financially and time-wise – Mathew Benham was clearly relishing the opportunity to name his own man, rather than simply handing the job to whoever happened to be in situ. Nicky Forster not getting the job as full time Brentford manager was without doubt the correct decision, one that cleared the way for another stepping stone to be put in place. Somebody to spark the Brentford Revolution.

Brentford's next appointment is somebody who has been credited by those playing under him as the man who really kick-started Brentford's culture change on the pitch, but was certainly a left-field choice as far as English football was concerned.

Former East German international Uwe Rösler's playing career, which included spells in England with Manchester City and Southampton, had ended when, after a brief time playing in Norway, he was diagnosed with lung cancer after a tumour was found. Having made a full recovery after chemotherapy, Rösler took his coaching badges and landed a succession of managerial jobs in Norway – with Lillestrom, Viking and Molde – with varying degrees of success.

He took a Lillestrom side, which had finished seventh in each of their previous three seasons, to successive fourth place finishes – they are yet to finish higher – in Norway's Tippeligaen, as well as guiding 'The Canaries' to their first and only Royal League final, and first Norwegian Cup final in 13 years. Following on from there, Rösler took a Viking side, who the previous year had just avoided relegation, to a third place finish – although the ninth and tenth placed campaigns which followed were less well received. Most impressive, however, was the half-season that Rösler spent at Molde in 2010. Before his arrival the club were heading for relegation after collecting just 20 points from their first 22 matches – a tally which, under Rösler, they matched in their final eight games. Molde then brought in their former player, and future Manchester United boss, Ole Gunnar Solskjær, as head coach, with Rösler returning to England to start a new chapter in his own life.

Looking back at his time in Norway, and how his move to England came about, Rösler said: "I was working in Norway after my playing days had finished out there. I started my coaching career and had six great years, culminating in a successful job with Molde. At that stage we decided to go back to the UK – one of the reasons was the prospect of managing in English football, but also we wanted to bring our kids to a private school in Manchester as our youngest was a good footballer we hoped would make the Manchester City Academy (Norway U21 international Colin Rösler would spend nine years at City, and after failing to break through, moved to NAC Breda, then one of Uwe's former clubs, Lillestrom).

"I had been asked to stay on at Molde as interim manager before Solskjaer, but the team was struggling and I was asked to help keep them in the league. With six wins and two draws, we achieved that, before I joined the family over in England. Finding a job in football became a frustrating process, without much feedback from my CV, but then I got a call from Brentford asking if I'd like to have an interview, which of course, I was delighted about. I remember the contact to apply was Matthew Benham at NextGen. Brentford had found out about my availability through Ole and Molde, who were being lined up to take part in the international club U19 series Matthew had created with Mark Warburton. Molde had put a good word in for me.

"There were five interviews, which was the longest process for a job I've ever had. It was very unusual, but you could see they meant business. One meeting was obviously with Matthew, then the CEO, then

Uwe Rösler and assistant Alan Kernaghan are animated as Shaleum Logan prepares to take a throw-in against Bury in April 2012

with Mark Warburton, who had also applied for a job. Then I met with Matthew again and was offered the job – I was very, very happy. I saw a lot of potential, especially the passion in Matthew and Mark Warburton's hearts, as well as their vision. I brought in my own expertise from watching so much League One and League Two football during the six months I had been looking for a job. I had compiled a list of players to bring in when I arrived, the likes of Jonathan Douglas, Clayton Donaldson and Shaleum Logan. All three proved to be instrumental in the following three years. The timing was right, the people were right."

Sam Saunders was one who particularly thrived under the new manager, finally becoming the player Brentford fans had seen destroy them while playing for Dagenham, but never quite managed to become, until that stage, at Griffin Park. He said: "At the back end of the previous season we were playing some really good stuff under Nicky, with more responsibility and freedom, and when Uwe came in he'd obviously watched some games at the tail end of the previous season and seen the same in me as Nicky Forster did. I had a good run of form under Uwe, performing to what I felt were my capabilities.

"Different types of players were coming in too. We brought in some foreign players alongside young lads like Harlee Dean, Adam Forshaw and Jake Bidwell, so the recruitment was changing too. We were suddenly bringing in young players from Premier League clubs we could potentially keep hold of rather than just older players, so there was clearly more of a plan in place – develop young players and sell them on, which has come to fruition in the last five or six years. The foreign players coming in and the German tactics made a big difference – we had never really been coached in that manner of detail in and out of possession before, particularly out of possession. Uwe was quite studious in what he did, sometimes perhaps too much on the opposition and not enough on us, but he really kick-started the professionalism of the club."

Marcus Bean echoed those sentiments, despite only playing one season under Rösler before being released and joining Colchester United. "When Uwe came in you could see a complete change in the standards being set, and it's kicked on since then," he said. "Bringing in Uwe was really the change in the football club, I think. Tactically, he's one of the best managers I've played for in terms of his attention to detail, tactical knowledge, work ethic – he lived and breathed football. His intensity was, at times, a bit too much for some – but he's one of those people you appreciate more when you leave the club and maybe the management isn't as good elsewhere, and you realise he was actually brilliant. The more time went on, the more I appreciated my time with him. I think he took the club to another level, drove the standards up and demanded high levels of achievement.

"His man-management might not have clicked with certain people, especially with different cultures in play, but for me, he kick-started the revolution. It was immediate – he had an influence on everyone and transformed a lot of the boys in the team in terms of their play. By the time I left, the club was bringing in another level of player, recruiting better and better. It became evident the owner wanted to see the club get out of League One. Whereas before it has been about surviving, it then became about thriving. The kind of players coming in, you could see the club really meant business."

A later arrival under Rösler was the tough-tackling Irish midfield-slash-right-back enforcer Alan McCormack, a player that really excelled in that period for Brentford. McCormack says of his former gaffer: "I wouldn't say Uwe was strict but he was very, very thorough in what he wanted the players to do. He was on at players to make sure that standards were met every single day in training, let alone in games, and if you weren't on it, he'd let you know about it – but you knew exactly what you had to do. The style of football was possession-based, fast attacking football, and he was the catalyst for the way Brentford have been playing these last few years – it was like a domino effect. The culture was there, and it was able to build through Uwe's tactics, ways of playing and the players he brought in."

Richard Lee, who was Rösler's number one goalie during the 2011-12 campaign, making 42 appearances, before being replaced by Simon Moore after Lee was unable to start the following campaign because of a persistent shoulder injury, admits that he had a lot of time for Uwe and how he communicated: "Uwe was very upfront and honest about how he saw things. He would tell you to your face, and I appreciated that. That was important to me, and I think most players like a manager to talk to them and tell you how they see it. He certainly wasn't afraid of confrontation and had that winning mentality, that strength of character and doing whatever it took to find a way to win. You could see on the sidelines the passion he had. There was a certainly a shift in mentality once he came in, and I think you saw it that first season."

One who wasn't so impressed was Charlie MacDonald. Having initially expressed excitement at being coached by, and learning from, a former Premier League striker, MacDonald soon realised that he wasn't the sort of player Rösler wanted going forward. "When I saw his name come up and what he'd done in the game, I thought he was someone who I could work with and improve as a striker. Surely he can teach me a thing or two, but it didn't work out that way. We didn't hit it off and it seemed I wasn't part of his plans. At the age of 30, I needed to play and wasn't happy sitting on the bench being a bit-part player. Pre-season and training was different from what Andy Scott implemented. When you bring in foreign managers, they're used to more ball work in pre-season and not so many long runs, so in that respect it was a good pre-season, but not in terms of actual games.

"As a player and a manager you have to have that relationship, and me and Uwe didn't have one from the get-go. He rubbed me up the wrong way in terms of my preparation for games, which he tried to interfere with. It was just a clash of heads really, and it was never going to work out. It came to a head when he took me to Exeter away and I didn't even get on the bench. I knew the writing was on the wall for me. I didn't want to leave as Brentford was a massive part of my life, probably the best years of my career, but for the sake of my football I had to."

By chance, barely a week after leaving Brentford and signing for MK Dons, MacDonald came up against his old club in a Football League Trophy tie at Stadium MK, opening the scoring in a 3-3 draw before Brentford won 4-3 on penalties. "It all happened so quickly," said MacDonald. "A move to Notts County under Martin Allen was more or less done and dusted, which would have been financially better and longer term, but once MK Dons came in for me, with the style of football they were playing at the time, it was definitely the right place to go. Playing against Brentford in the cup a few days after making my debut was strange, I managed to escape Marcus Bean and get a header in from a corner to score. The Brentford fans had always been great to me, so I was never going to celebrate out of respect, and I think they enjoyed the way I carried myself whenever I went back."

MacDonald may have been on his way out, but he was, however, impressed by the calibre of players suddenly coming in. He said: "Several of the signings they made that year – Jonathan Douglas, Toumani Diagouraga, Shay Logan – you're looking at them thinking something could be happening here. Did I think Brentford would do what they did as quickly as they did? Probably not, but what the owner has put in place, by recreating Brentford Football Club, is fantastic."

A key signing that summer was indeed Jonathan Douglas, with the former Blackburn, Leeds and Swindon midfielder going on to become a real catalyst in Brentford's rise. His arrival – along with the aforementioned Shay Logan and Clayton Donaldson then, later in the season, loanees Harlee Dean, Jake Bidwell and Adam Forshaw – signalled a significant improvement in the club's recruitment quality. Upon signing, Douglas also gave an interesting insight into the new manager, new culture and what had attracted him to the club.

He said: "Apart from last season when Swindon went down, I've always been in teams going for promotion from League One – and that's why I came here, to do the same thing. We have a squad capable of matching the best teams in this division. You need a lot of experience to mount a promotion challenge because it's a difficult division to get out of, and a lot of togetherness as a squad. You also need to try to play some football, get the ball down and play it, and that's what we're trying to do here. The manager wants to play football the right way. He wants us to keep the ball, and we have the players capable of doing that. It was the manager who sold Brentford to me. Everything he said was positive, and everything he was saying, I wanted to be a part of."

Rösler was quickly earning the respect of his squad, with Kevin O'Connor, having just been re-appointed as club captain after ten years of first team football for Brentford, saying: "There's always a buzz at the start of a new season, but there's something a bit more there this year. The way the gaffer has got us playing and the results we've been getting has got confidence flowing through the side. Uwe has been excellent. He talks to everyone and is very black and white in what he says, which is what you want in a manager." Sam Saunders, who was branded his very own David Beckham by Rösler after a brilliant brace of free kicks shot down Leyton Orient in August, added: "The way we are playing definitely suits my game more. But to be fair, we have been playing better football since Christmas, as we played some good stuff under Nicky Forster and Mark Warburton too."

It was certainly a culture change for Brentford fans. "Pass them to death," yelled Rösler from the touchline during Brentford's pre-season friendly against Stoke City in July 2011, a month after joining the club. His Bees side had also put 16 goals (in two games) past non-league sides Tonbridge Angels and Hampton & Richmond Borough, but the Bees' first real test was against Stoke. And not only did they beat the Premier League side in Rösler's first match at Griffin Park, but they did it taking their new manager's cue to keep the ball on the deck. The wheels were being greased, but had the Brentford Revolution really started? While banks of stats and data were still an alien concept to Bees fans, the brand of football their team were trying to play was certainly a welcome change and created a real buzz on the terraces.

Brentford fan and regular Beesotted Pride of West London podcast commentator, Matt Allard, looks back at the immediate on-pitch changes that were witnessed by Uwe's arrival. "Rösler brought a more modern influence to the team tactically. Initially this meant playing out from the back and not just lumping it forwards quickly. I'm never quite sure who was more confused by this, the fans getting frustrated, shouting 'get it forwards' or the luckless centre-backs who were being asked to do something alien to them. Somewhat surprisingly Rösler's fellow countryman Marcel Eger looked no more adept than the likes of Karleigh Osbourne and Leon Legge. Uwe also tried various systems including a horribly narrow diamond in midfield, which still gives me nightmares. My initial thoughts were Rösler did have a plan but he was struggling to find players that could execute it, so in some cases, he was having to revert to more tried and tested lower league methods to get results. But you could sense his arrival was a sea change and, despite the initial resistance, Rösler was going to drag us forwards towards a more modern approach."

Rösler had arrived in TW8 a month earlier, pledging to push for the play-offs and "take the next step". He also warned, however, that it would not all be about playing attractive football, adding: "The most important thing is to win football matches. We will find a strategy that suits the players, but we must have a balance. We need a Plan A and Plan B, (more on that later in the book) and it also depends on the opposition we're facing. We want to dominate and control games, but you can't do that if you don't have the ball."

In the years to come, Rösler would find out just how difficult getting out of League One would be, but he was in no doubt about the size of his task from the outset, saying: "The level in League One compared to when I was a player has increased dramatically and it's a very tough league to get out of. It's not going to be easy, even when you're at a club with financial backing, so you have to make the right decisions and have lady luck on your side. I achieved everything as a player through hard work, and I want my team to be the same. We have a budget which is solid, but not on the same level as the top clubs."

Looking back at the summer following his arrival, Rösler said: "We set about reshaping the team, which included shifting out 16 or so players, because we wanted to improve the style of play as well as the profile of the club. The plan was to compete with a mid-table budget, but to fight in the top half of the table. That meant we had a lot of young prospects who Mark had identified from running the NextGen tournament, and his great contacts in football academies – for example, at Everton with Adam Forshaw, Jake Bidwell and Conor McAleny. That mix of exciting, ambitious energy, combined with players who had been around the block more, like Kevin O'Connor and Clayton Donaldson, started to make that difference.

"Although we had a very ambitious squad of players, they probably didn't believe in the beginning what could, and would, happen in the future, but step by step we went in that direction. We started to try to play out a little bit more from the back, but obviously, even with good players and good coaches, they are adjusting to the situation, and we also needed to win football matches. What has been instrumental in our philosophy was the high press – to win the ball back as high as possible, work coordinated as a team to press, not in singles. When we are in possession of the ball, to play fast, play on the ground, with a lot of fast, forward passes, with plenty of crosses into the box. Obviously, later on, the better the squad got, the higher quality we got, and we started to build up from the keeper."

Although Brentford would become synonymous with a stats-based approach to recruitment – even though Benham was starting to play far more of a part in the club than just writing out the cheques – bringing players in was still a simpler process back in the summer of 2012, according to Rösler. Asked if there was any talk of data analysis at that stage, he said: "No, definitely not in the first two years. We had weekly and monthly meetings where we would tell Matthew and the board our plans, but they gave us freedom and they trusted us, which was very nice to see. And when we came close to a signing, we always gave Matthew the names so he could check up through his models.

"We worked on a three-stars system when names came back to us – three stars meant we should make the signing, two stars maybe sign, and one star they weren't good enough for Brentford. So, in the time I was at Brentford, it wasn't the case of Matthew proposing his players. But you must also remember that, in parallel, he went on to run FC Midtjylland, where he could try out certain things there that he would later on introduce into the regular set up at Brentford.

"Back in that first year, Matthew set up a three-year plan. He said to me: first year we want to see an improvement in our league position and improve the quality by implementing a new style of play, to introduce more young players and more value into the squad. Second year, he said he wanted to get promoted or fight for promotion. The third year, you have to get promoted."

Not everything was going Uwe Rösler's way, but he had made great strides forward in the quality and style of play

A promising pre-season fed into a fine start to Rösler's first campaign, with five wins from their first seven league games, including a 5-0 hammering of Leyton Orient, which had the home crowd purring. But Rösler was not getting carried away and told his team afterwards that they were still some way off being a top League One side. Indeed, within a month, the Bees had suffered back-to-back defeats at Griffin Park, including a 4-0 drubbing by Huddersfield. This came after a 3-1 home defeat to Preston, after which Rösler admitted his side's shortcoming, saying of their victors: "They have powerful, strong, experienced players, who might not be as skilful as some of our players, but know what it takes to survive in the Championship or get promoted." There was, clearly, still work to be done.

Leon Legge, about as uncompromising a defender as they come, was nevertheless impressed with what Rösler had brought to his game, saying at the time: "It's a new philosophy the gaffer has brought in, he likes a passing game. He is encouraging both centre halves to bring the ball out of defence, just like the rest of the team. It's something I definitely want to add to my game, but it wasn't really encouraged when I joined the club. For the last few years, we have been told to concentrate on just defending, rather than bringing the ball out of defence."

By December, under-fire from the fans after Brentford were knocked out the FA Cup by non-league Wrexham, Rösler revised his targets and warned against raised expectations, saying: "Our form in pre-season raised expectation, but everybody should realise the budget we're working under and the size of the club. I said from day one our target is to finish in the top ten. We want to make the next step, but we've changed personnel and the style of play."

If all was not going quite Rösler's way in his first job in English football, at least he had a trusted guiding hand in the background. Mark Warburton was obviously disappointed not to land the top job following Forster's departure, but instead, contented himself with being appointed as the club's first sporting director.

"I was disappointed as, not in an arrogant way, I felt I could do that job," said Warburton, looking back at that summer. "As it turned out, being a sporting director, I got on very well with Uwe. I hadn't done the job before, but with my background working with teams and in the City, I knew of certain parameters and areas I should be heavily involved in and where not to cross over with Uwe. I was in charge of the first team and academy, with medical sporting science thrown in. I was very lucky to be able to create the right environment very quickly. Uwe had an outstanding playing career but was also passionate about the game and about learning about improving. He can be very volatile at times, but you quickly get to know how he works, and he calmed down quickly. He brought in a style of play, and I think the fans saw his passion – fans need to see the passion and need to see the manager cares.

"We had the squad reconstruction going on with certain players coming in to compliment it through the loan market – the likes of Jake Bidwell, Adam Forshaw, George Saville – boys who are comfortable playing with the ball. But you have to slowly transition – you can't simply take 18 out and put 18 in – it takes time to do that, and that was my job with Uwe. Matthew is a Brentford fan who, at the end of the day, wants to enjoy watching his team play. He's highly intellectual and has a clear vision for the club, but at the end of the day, he wants to enjoy it too. I think that was obvious from the style in which we played."

Although Warburton was Brentford's first sporting director, a model which was only just gaining recognition and acceptance in the British game, it wasn't a set-up completely alien to Rösler, who said at the time: "The model is common abroad. The manager is in charge of team selection and transfers, and the sporting director will be there to provide support. We will have discussions and work closely together, but I have the final decision." Looking back at how the two men dove-tailed, Rösler added: "I never asked, but I knew Mark applied for the job. Obviously I got the job and he was appointed sporting director, so we worked very, very closely. After about a month it was clear the trust and confidence in one another was growing – we also had good support from the board. Then later on, there was more of a direct line into Matthew – especially during the second year."

Despite a promising start and signs of what was to come football-wise, Rösler's first season fizzled out into a disappointing ninth-place finish. A run of seven games without a win through December and January was ended in emphatic style with a 5-2 hammering of Wycombe Wanderers, inspired by a Gary Alexander hat-trick, while the arrival of loanee Saido Berahino provided a springtime spark, the West Brom striker bagging braces in a 4-0 win over Carlisle and a 2-0 win over Exeter. A run of three successive defeats in March was followed by four wins in a row, and then a further four games without a win as Rösler's side struggled for consistency, before ending the campaign on a winning note with a 3-2 triumph at Chesterfield.

However, the building blocks had been put in place, and the summer of 2012 saw more significant changes. Other veterans of Scott's side, players like Marcus Bean, Sam Wood, Myles Weston and Gary Alexander, trod the same route to the exit door that Charlie MacDonald had a year earlier, while back came Harlee Dean and Adam Forshaw on permanent deals, with the likes of Stuart Dallas and Marcello Trotta also arriving.

Perhaps more significantly came the news in June of that year that Matthew Benham was taking over the majority shareholding of the football club two years earlier than had been originally roadmapped. Five years after re-emerging on the Griffin Park scene – having originally stood on the terraces as a supporter in the 1980s – Benham was now the new owner rather than just the principal financial backer after Bees United members had voted in favour to sell him the trust's majority shareholding in the club. The overwhelmingly supported decision ended the agreement, struck in 2009, that would see the club ownership transfer to Benham if Bees United weren't able to pay back his loans, which had saved the club from a slow death. The news was hardly a surprise in all honesty. Many supporters felt there was an inevitability that the Supporters' Trust had to stand aside and allow Benham to crack on with a project that was already bearing fruit – Bees United had done everything they could to ensure survival, they now had to hand Brentford over to the right man. That man was clearly Matthew Benham.

Bees United chairman David Merritt echoed those sentiments, saying the world had become Brentford's oyster and Championship football was now within the club's reach, but also warned that Benham's investment would continue to be steady, unlike the so-called 'financial doping' where some clubs simply use money to attract better players, pay more than their competitors and, if necessary, also buy their rivals' best players. It could be argued that Brentford could be seen at a similarly-sized club in the shape of AFC Bournemouth, who were also just starting a transformational journey, under Russian businessman Maxim Denim.

Only three years had passed since Brentford and Bournemouth had been battling it out in the Football League's basement division, however, both had embarked on a steady ascent which would see the pair plant their flags on the Premier League peak. However, it's a sign of the Bees' under-the-radar growth spurt under Benham that commentators would see the West London club's rise as more of a scientific experiment than a footballing fairytale. Nobody could deny Brentford were a more financially stable club than ever, one that would soon see levels of investment their supporters could only have dreamt of whilst shaking buckets outside the ground and on fundraising walks to Hartlepool. But as Merritt warned, Brentford weren't about to start lighting cigars with banknotes just yet. Instead, Brentford's growth was to be more organic, with a heavy focus on buying, developing and selling on young talent, or under-appreciated players, from the lower league or abroad – and infamously by using cutting edge statistical analysis. And boy, would stats rattle some cages!

"The club board decided what the budget is going forward, and it will be up to Matthew if he funds it, but this deal only allows the budget to run at the same levels as it has been, we won't suddenly be awash with cash," Merritt said. "It's all about continuity. We have been splashing the cash by the club's standards since the partnership with Matthew began, and it can now continue at this level. When I first got involved with Bees United, we were worried about the solvency of the club and whether we could finance through a season."

Looking back ten years later, Benham admitted in an interview with Bees United that the more money he was putting into the club, the more natural it felt that he should have more of an element of control. "The thinking for the first few years was to just put a bit of money in, but not be involved day-to-day, just peek behind the scenes... I was anonymous for a little while, described as a 'mystery investor', and then it gradually got to the stage where as I put more and more money into it, I naturally wanted more of a say in how things were run and were going to be run." This came three years after Benham had bought out Ron Noades's interest in the club and pledged to pump £1m a year into the club over the next five years. "I think at that point (2009), it was more towards the sort of charity end of the spectrum," he added. "And as the sort of investment grew over the years, it gradually became more to the business end."

CHAPTER FOUR

Benham had barely made himself comfortable in the owner's chair before making a commitment to another huge financial investment – buying the land necessary to kick-start Brentford's bid to build a new stadium at Lionel Road. It had already proved to be a very testing project, which had been on and off, then on again, for the best part of a decade. However, the new stadium dream had been declared dead in the water in 2011 when the economic downturn caused development partners Barratt to back out – Benham's investment in the project allowed the plans to go back to the drawing board – putting in place another central building block for the club's future development and ability to truly grow in physical stature, not just simply improve their league position. Spurning the idea of having the stadium, or a stand, named after him, Benham said: "I've been lucky enough to be able to help the club I support, and that is enough." This was no vanity project for Benham.

It was typical of the notoriously publicity-shy man who now owned the club. Indeed, despite his reluctance for public speaking, Benham gave an interview to the Hounslow Chronicle in July 2012 – the same week in which another foundation block was laid with the Football League's approval of Brentford's Category Two Academy. He admitted his peak support as a fan had been "a few hundred games" in the mid to early 1980s before gradually drifting away, then being tempted back, having made his fortune through his sports analytics businesses, to help guide the club away from the threat of financial oblivion to a more sustainable future. He said: "I have always remained a Brentford fan, but as my work life got busier, it became more difficult to watch matches. My initial involvement with the club was pretty much 'no strings', and my involvement in terms of financial support was a pretty 'light touch'. I certainly didn't think I'd be involved at that time in owning the club, although as I put more and more money in, the seed of the idea started to grow."

Looking back, Donald Kerr, a BU Board member for many years and who served as the club's deputy chairman, remembers that "Dave Merritt and Chris Gammon were the key people on the Bees United team. My overriding emotion when BU members approved the takeover by Matthew was relief. Success in those days was survival as a club, and I thought the greater financial stability, which the deal offered, may at the very least secure our long term Football League status. How terribly pessimistic and unambitious that now seems, but perhaps the years since the late Seventies, when I adopted Brentford as my local team, had conditioned my expectations."

Benham's modest, introverted persona would set the tone in those early stages for events that would unfold in years to come, especially when it came to dealing with big news stories. The expectations of what a football club owner should be, and how they should react and communicate, challenged traditionalists and those unable to tune in quickly to the same frequency as a new-world football visionary. It is true to say that there was also a degree of unease, even mistrust, in some quarters of the club's support and the club would, at times, be ridiculed for doing things Benham's way, even by their own fans.

Thinking outside the box, changing ingrained patterns of thinking and footballing perceptions, was not unanimously embraced for myriad reasons among the Brentford faithful and, in truth, it would take promotion to the Premier League before some fans would concede to the evidence provided by their own eyes. But as Bees fan Andy Cooper explains: "We'd thought David Webb was going to be a saviour when he became Brentford owner, then Noades showed his true colours... those men had scarred us, so when we were rattling buckets, begging for spare change to help Brentford and Bees United, we at least knew that true fans were involved."

With regard to Benham, Cooper added: "We didn't really know who this 'controlling stake' guy was, so naturally there was a level of concern about being done over again. There was a good deal of joy and relief when Bees United took control of the club, but not perhaps as much realisation about how difficult it would be to keep the club afloat. I think a lot of people didn't realise."

Jon Restall, another lifelong Brentford supporter forced to endure the worst concerns brought on by the Webb and Noades regimes, shares similar sentiments. "Brentford were in danger of going out of existence. Match days were punctuated by rattling buckets and occasional moments of skill, or the brief hope that our young substitute might turn into a superstar (they didn't). So you would have thought we would appreciate a saviour. But after Webb and Noades (the latter literally played a real life game of Football Manager with our money but not his own) we had been burnt. How could you trust another owner?

"Rumours seeped out that a mystery man had been quietly investing. Someone who was a Brentford supporter at heart. We feared another Michael Knighton at Manchester United – a ball juggling chancer. But Benham preferred then, as he does now, to remain in the shadows. The revolution was slow to start – two steps forward and one step back – but stability started to come to both our finances and our footballing intent. Gallows humour was tinged with optimism, although it's always the hope that kills you."

And from the national press' perspective, their journalists were racing off down to Blockbusters to hire out the DVD of Moneyball for future reference. All in all, the summer of 2012 was a sunny one for Brentford Football Club both on and off the pitch... Benham's takeover, plus exciting new signings, important training ground improvements, the academy, not to mention the new ground project being back on track, certainly heightened expectations. Club captain Kevin O'Connor said at the time: "It shows the club want to push on to the Championship and are getting the structure behind us first. Everyone around the club is brimming with optimism. All these things are hopefully going to help the club achieve what we want to."

Another impressive pre-season was followed by a mixed start to the 2012-13 campaign, the highlight of which was a 5-1 home hammering of Crewe Alexandra. The football was good, but something was still missing, and when Brentford travelled to Doncaster in mid-October and comprehensively outplayed their hosts before throwing away a lead to lose 2-1, Rösler called his team "too nice" and ordered them to get more cynical and aggressive. Yes, the football was indeed nice, but Brentford had to learn how to "win scrappy" if necessary. Rösler's men responded with a 13-match unbeaten run, including an impressive run of seven wins in eight games between November and New Year. Clayton Donaldson and Harry Forrester were both in hot streaks of form as the Bees saw out 2012 with the scalps of Portsmouth, Carlisle, Swindon, Sheffield United, MK Dons, Notts County and Colchester in that brilliant winters' run.

It was a run which saw Brentford fans start to harbour serious thoughts of promotion, but when Donaldson and Paul Hayes put goals past former Bees keeper Paul Smith against Southend, to earn an FA Cup fourth round glamour tie at home to Chelsea, the Bees' league form tailed off as a result. Between beating The Shrimpers in the third round replay and bowing out 4-0 in a fourth round replay at Stamford Bridge, following a thrilling 2-2 draw at Griffin Park, Brentford won just one of their five league games, perhaps having had their eyes collectively taken off the ball by the Chelsea ties.

Nevertheless, the home game against the Blues showed just what Rösler's Brentford were capable of, and how far they had come since his appointment. A Chelsea side crowned Champions of Europe just eight months earlier were given an almighty scare at Griffin Park, twice falling behind to the Bees and coming within seven minutes of being on the end of a humiliating defeat. Marcello Trotta put the hosts in front with a fine finish after Forrester's shot was half-saved just before the break, and although Oscar equalised ten minutes into the second half, Forrester restored Brentford's lead from the spot 17 minutes from time. A famous upset looked well and truly on the cards until Fernando Torres levelled once more for Chelsea seven minutes from the final whistle.

There was neither luck nor pluck in Brentford's performance, however. They had gone toe to toe with their illustrious neighbours in every aspect of their performance, even outplaying them at times. One standout moment came when centre back Harlee Dean left Torres flummoxed as he dummied past the Spanish international striker to bring the ball out of defence and start an attack. "Chelsea struggled to cope with the wind in the first-half and we had some good opportunities on the counter-attack," said a proud Rösler after the game. "We were very good and worth our 1-0 lead.

"They came at us in the second-half, had a lot of play but didn't create many clear-cut chances. To lead 2-1 five minutes before the end, I'm slightly disappointed we never won the game. But overall, my players did fantastic and earned the right to play at Stamford Bridge. It will be another great day for everyone at the club."

As with many such FA Cup ties, the underdogs' real chance of a giant-killing comes in the first game – the giants rarely allow them a second shot at an upset. Ahead of the replay, Rösler underlined that outlook: "The surprise factor has gone. We had the chance to beat them because they underestimated us the first time around, but they won't do that again. They were seven minutes away from getting knocked out but got away with it, so they will take us more seriously this time around." And so it proved, as the Bees bowed out 4-0 at Stamford Bridge, but with some fantastic memories from that Griffin Park game to savour for years to come. There would be better afternoons at Stamford Bridge for Brentford fans.

A disappointed Rösler, nevertheless, praised Chelsea after the game for showing his side due respect by putting out a strong side, just as Everton had in the League Cup three years earlier. But unlike that occasion, a giant-killing was beyond Brentford this time. Rösler said: "I think Rafa (Benítez) showed my players a lot of respect by putting out a very strong team. There were certainly a few names out there I didn't expect to be playing. It was a very physical team they put out, with the likes of Demba Ba, David Luiz, Frank Lampard and Branislav Ivanevic. For the opening goal, we did well to deny (Juan) Mata the space to receive the ball, and it was from a long ball forward that he finally got the chance,

Jonathan Douglas in full battle mode with Chelsea's Frank Lampard

and from that it was always going to be very difficult for us to come back. After the first goal we got too loose too early rather than doing the things which had served us well up to that point. Our plan had been to bring Harry Forrester on and go for the win."

Brentford's league form didn't so much take a dive after that, but there was a feeling that their FA Cup exploits had taken something in terms of spark and energy out of the side. Between the two ties, the Bees had won only one of their three league games, and Rösler had to warn his side not to take their eyes off the ultimate prize, saying: "We don't want to be the nearly men. We want to get back to our league campaign and push it over the line, and it is important we have our minds back in the right places."

After recovering from back to back defeats to Stevenage and Carlisle in March by beating Swindon, Preston and Notts County in quick succession, the Bees only won two of their final seven games to leave their automatic promotion hopes hanging by a thread. The Bees showed fantastic spirit in an astonishing game at Bramall Lane, in which Brentford were reduced to nine men as Clayton Donaldson and Tony Craig (plus future England captain Harry Maguire for United) saw red, with ten yellow cards also shown. Brentford earned a valuable point through Bradley Wright-Phillips' last-minute equaliser to spark wild scenes at the away end before the travelling Bees made the long, midweek trip back to London.

Four days later, without the suspended Donaldson, the nerves started to jangle further as Brentford could only draw 1-1 at already relegated Hartlepool United, after which Rösler said: "We are where we want to be, and I now have a week to find the right plan. We are the challengers and we have to attack – we have to win. But I loved being in that position as a player. Nothing has changed, even if we had lost today. It is still in our own hands – we have worked very hard for it to still be in our own hands." Indeed, main promotion rivals Doncaster had slipped up too, losing at home to Notts County, which set up a last-day winner-takes-all tie, but with Rovers two points ahead, they were in the driving seat to claim automatic promotion.

Going into the final game of the season, at home to Doncaster, the Bees still had a chance, fate was completely in their own hands. The maths were simple, nothing less than a win over their promotion rivals would do to secure second place and a first promotion to the second tier in more than 20 years. In the run up to the match, Rösler tried his hand at some Fergie-style mind games, in an attempt to put the pressure on Doncaster. "They have been leading the league for months, and according to their manager (Brian Flynn), they are the best team in the division," he said.

"They had a chance last weekend and didn't take it, so now they've given us an opportunity. It's a final for us, but we are the challengers, the underdogs. We have overcome so many obstacles this season. We've had to deal with injuries and suspensions to key players at important times, but we've coped with the pressure. We have the best home record in the division, which is an achievement in itself. We're full of confidence and going out with the mindset to attack them. We have to make it happen. There's not much between the teams and I don't think it will be a high-scoring game. We have shown this season we will fight until the last whistle, which we have done on many occasions."

It was a match which proved to be a defining step in Brentford's journey to the top. As they say, before the joy comes the pain... and the pain Brentford put their fans through on 27 April 2013 was like nothing before. Total agony in fact. An unsurprisingly, tight and uninspiring game was played out, which only really came to life deep into injury time at the end, when the referee, Michael Oliver, awarded Brentford a penalty for Dean Furman's high boot on Toumani Diagouraga.

An unseemly exchange followed, during which young loanee Marcello Trotta wrestled the ball from regular penalty taker Kevin O'Connor, with other players intervening on both sides. However, Trotta eventually emerged with the ball in his grasp. The Italian then smashed his spot kick against the bar, and as Brentford players sank to the ground in despair, Doncaster raced away to score the winning goal virtually unchallenged. The following match report appeared on the Brentford Beesotted website and paints an even more vivid, raw, picture of those anarchic final moments that late April afternoon at Griffin Park.

"So the season had come to this, all boiling down to a minute of mad, twisted, sick drama at Griffin Park. The referee, who had shown he was totally out of his depth all afternoon, stunned everyone inside the stadium by awarding the Bees a penalty deep, deep into injury time… The Bees HAD to win to achieve automatic promotion, and here it was on a plate, Championship football, just ONE KICK away… But it was all too much for some fans to take… Men, women, children, all tearful; the magnitude of the moment was palpable…

"Dark clouds were gathering overhead, but surely this ONE KICK would send the stadium into delirium… This ONE KICK would eradicate all those Bees heartache moments and consign the club's previous failures to a dark corner of our memories that we'd not have to revisit again… This ONE KICK would transform the history of our football club."

"But the players were arguing about who should take it… never a good sign… Marcello Trotta, the Fulham loan player who had been on the pitch for less than ten minutes, had grabbed the ball and was clearly in no mood to hand responsibility to anyone else… He WANTED it… He'd scored a penalty at Sheffield United, when Sam Saunders had missed, so why shouldn't he? Sam clearly DIDN'T want it, or knew it had been tasked to another… But what about Kevin O'Connor… The Brentford legend? Kev is club captain, an experienced penalty taker, the man who it had apparently been AGREED would take penalties against Doncaster… he wasn't happy… Words were exchanged… But Trotta was adamant, he looked confident. Bees fans looked sick with worry.

"I looked to the heavens and asked a question… Okay, I am not a man of faith, but this seemed a moment where, if a God does exist, he might just be in the mood to grant me a little favour… after all, I'm not a bad fella at the end of the day. I asked him: "Please, just this once, for me and for my son, and for all my mates that are here, and for all the Bees fans everywhere…" One little prayer, ahead of one big kick. ONE KICK.

"The Italian stepped up purposely and absolutely leathered the ball… It was not one of those nervy, half-hearted, poor excuses of a penalty kick, this was a manly wallop… The thousands standing behind the Ealing Road end goal visibly recoiled as the ball was struck. In that moment Brentford were about to be promoted, Doncaster stripped of their automatic place by a last gasp, cruel twist… Nine months of achievement, a large proportion of which had seen Rovers lead the table, was to be snatched away. This was our fate, our destiny, all our dreams, and the fantasy finish to a fantastic season… This was OUR time. ONE KICK.

"But what happened next was plain sick… SICK. Trotta hit it hard alright, so hard that he helped set up a goal for Doncaster. As the ball

Time stands still as Marcello Trotta's penalty hits the Doncaster bar

cannoned off the crossbar, 11 thousand hearts broke... it was simply too much to take, for most to comprehend, let alone cope with... Especially the players, many of whom had started to drop to the ground... Like they'd been taken out by a Donny sniper.

"A green flare was let off in the away end by a Rovers fan who obviously didn't care about a ban from Griffin Park, they were going up again... But they weren't JUST going up were they? No, they had scored... They had scored from OUR penalty... And now they were friggin' CHAMPIONS. I've never heard anything so perverse in my life.

"That shit doesn't happen in the real world, in fact I'm not sure that twisted shit happens in the fantasy world either. Has any team ever won the title with the last kick of the season from a rebounded penalty kick AGAINST them? That's impossible, right?

"And my last impression of the afternoon as I left the stadium, with my young son bawling his eyes out, was of a giant police horse taking a giant piss on the centre circle... the centre circle where I should have been standing with him, watching the Brentford players held shoulder high. An ironic and poignantly surreal image if ever there was one."

Rösler blamed nerves for the defeat after the game and refused to blame Trotta for the heartbreaking finale, saying responsibility would be shared amongst the players, despite admitting the Italian was not his choice of penalty taker. Looking back, he admitted it was something he had overlooked in the run-up to the game (Brentford's most recent previous penalty, in the 2-2 draw at Sheffield United a fortnight before, had been missed by Sam Saunders, with O'Connor on the bench) – and something he has put down as a harsh lesson learned.

Looking back at the aftermath, Rösler said: "When we were awarded the penalty, I saw that everyone was celebrating on the bench, which I knew was bad. But honestly, I was furious watching my players celebrating. We lost our calmness, and I had to try and settle everyone down. Normally, our penalty taker was Kevin O'Connor, who had a fantastic rate of converting spot kicks, but he hadn't played much leading up to that game, and all the penalties prior to the last league game had been taken by Marcello Trotta. But now he was back in the frame, for me personally, it was absolutely clear Kevin should take the penalty, because he was the penalty taker at the club. Marcello should have known that, but it was my mistake, I hadn't put it up on the wall in the changing room – something I have never, ever forgotten to do again!

"So that explains the confusion as to why it wasn't clear who should take the kick, and why Marcello hadn't automatically handed the ball over. But Kevin was also very clever, he stepped back and didn't escalate the situation. He asked Trotta if he was sure, and apparently he was, so Kevin stepped back. That was the best thing Kevin could have done. And then came the bad luck. I mean, five centimetres lower, the ball goes in. But I have to also take responsibility. I should have made sure everyone knew before we went on the pitch, 100 per cent sure, that Kevin was to take penalties. I learned from that very, very harsh lesson, I can tell you!"

The Bees would barely have time to recover before an emotionally charged two-legged play-off semi against Swindon – O'Connor exorcising a few ghosts by netting a venomous last-minute equaliser from the spot in the first leg at the County Ground. There were no arguments over who should take it that afternoon. The second leg tested Brentford's resolve to the limit once more, throwing away a 3-1 lead and conceding deep into injury time as the game ended in a 3-3 draw, and then somehow having enough left in the tank to scrape through on, yet more, penalties. It had been mentally and physically exhausting for the players and supporters alike, but a medium sized pitch invasion at the end of the game showed the fans still felt in a positive, celebratory mood, despite having been dragged through the wringer.

Rösler remembers: "It was one of the most difficult situations for me as a coach, to pick the team up, as well as myself and the staff – then to go into the semi-finals against a very strong Swindon team. From my own perspective, it was my family that helped me through that time. I felt a lot of people from outside the club wanted us to fail – because of Matthew with this new system, which was about to succeed. I think, in a short space of time, we created an 'us against the rest of the world' mindset. First of all, I had to pick Marcello up, as I was harsh to him back in the dressing room, but we had some very good dialogue and he was ready to go again. Kevin was back in the team anyway and did really well.

"Although I knew penalties could prove to be the deciding factor once again, I tried to keep training as normal as possible going into the second leg because I think when you emphasise something you normally wouldn't have in your training process, you risk creating some sort of fear with the players. Again, I've learned from that, and incorporate penalty taking into my training sessions every week. I just made sure we had the best takers in place when the time came. We had eight names lined up and the players knew who should take the first, second, third etc – so that was the change I made.

"I also knew that the crowd at Griffin Park would be an advantage and we had to get them right behind us. Of course, you pick up on the 'we always lose in the play-offs negativity', and it's true that if you allow your mindset to be 'we always lose', then the higher the possibility is that you will lose. That was the mindset of the whole club, including the supporters, when it came to play-offs. That was very, very tough. But that first leg at Swindon helped us enormously – we lost our nerves then. In the second game, we played well and took a comfortable lead. But then we let Swindon come back into the game. Again, we got nervous, the crowd got nervous. But there was a god up there who made sure we got through."

Through to Wembley they went indeed, however, was it any wonder, after all the team had been through in such a short space of time, that the Bees failed to show up for the Wembley final? Losing 2-1 to Yeovil, in another underwhelming performance on the big stage, certainly felt like an upset, but should anyone have really been too surprised that PTSD (Post Traumatic Stress from Doncaster) was still clearly a problem? Rösler said at the time that the semi-finals had seen his boys grow into men, and that getting through in such circumstances had been "psychologically massive" but he would later admit in the wake of the Wembley defeat that his players had been overwhelmed. Once again, Rösler felt that the club's past failures on the big stage (three Football League Trophy final defeats and two play-off final losses – soon to become three, and later four, before the curse was finally broken) were weighing heavily on his side.

"I mean, I would be lying if I said it wasn't something I had to deal with," Rösler states. "Whoever I spoke to at the club mentioned it, whenever I looked in a newspaper, or took questions in a press conference, or was interviewed by a journalist, or spoke to supporters, or went to the pub to have a beer in my spare time – everyone told me about that record of failures. But I think when you are in that zone with the players, I was focused on preparing the team in the best possible way for the final.

"I think we were a bit overwhelmed by the occasion and underperformed in the first half. In the second half we came back strongly, scored and created other good chances, but unfortunately that wasn't enough to turn the game around. It wasn't to be. I think we were devastated about not winning the final, but we were still probably more disappointed about the Doncaster game because we had promotion handed to us on a plate – that was still haunting us. I knew that, statistically, the odds were against us succeeding in the final because of the way the season had ended, with us having to settle for third place, but I didn't want to accept that. I think we'd shown a tremendous improvement from the year before, in the football we played, and the run we had been on, so I didn't want it all to end in failure."

But that psychological aspect Rösler mentioned post-Swindon – that strength in the face of adversity and coming back stronger – was a theme which the club would return to that summer. There was a hint of it from Harlee Dean, who shrugged off the play-off final disappointment by saying: "We've had some massive setbacks this season. Every time we've got ourselves back up, we get knocked back down. It'll stand us in good stead for next season. We've got to be positive, get it out of our system and go again."

There was similar optimism among some of the dejected supporters who trudged away from Wembley Stadium and tried to put on a philosophically brave face. Andy Watson was one of them, who said straight after the match: "What can you say, it's heartache again, but we'll come back, you mark my words, we're bigger and better than we have been before, we'll do it next year." However, nobody could blame those supporters who simply wanted to curse the footballing gods and head back to the pub to drown their sorrows... they'd seen it all before.

It's often been the case that teams who go so close and fall at the last hurdle, especially in such dramatic fashion, struggle the following season. Brentford themselves had suffered similar fates – from a play-off semi-final defeat in 1995 to 15th place the following season; from a play-off final defeat in 1997 to relegation the following season; from a play-off final defeat in 2002 to 16th the following season; from a play-off semi-final defeat in 2006 to relegation the following season. This time, it seemed different. Heart-wrenching as the Doncaster defeat and subsequent play-off final failure was, there was indeed a sense that, this time, it was only a temporary blip in Brentford's inevitable progress rather than another deep depression that would roll over into the next campaign.

One who noticed that vibe straight away was summer signing Alan McCormack. The former Southend midfielder, who would become a key figure in Brentford's eventual promotion by providing some of the steel and backbone needed to compliment the silky skills, arrived to find a club not suffering from the trauma of losing out on promotion in such a cruel fashion, but one ready to banish the bad memories and determined to make it count next time. He said: "I remember it very well.

They had a very traumatic last day of the season, missing the penalty for automatic promotion and then losing the play-off final. A lot of clubs may have gone the opposite way to what Brentford did that year, but when I met Uwe and other people at the club, I knew straight away this was a determined club, and as a soon as we went in for the first day of pre-season, the talk was never about devastation or being upset or a hangover from last season – it was all about this will be our year.

"The people who came in with me were like wow, we're going to be a part of something here – the boys who witnessed that never wanted to experience that again. Sometimes you need that in your life, that big upset and heartbreak to become a better person and turn it into a positive. I remember coming in thinking I've got to be on my game this year because these boys are at it. It started the year before, but they got unlucky with a couple of situations. Thankfully I was a part of the success that was to come.

"A year or two before, people may have looked at Brentford as a nice little club with a nice little ground who can be beat, but the whole set up of the club, with the players it was bringing in, was starting to change. The dressing room controlled itself, and the manager never really needed to tell us off for anything. Everybody worked for each other, there was never any selfish individual. It's hard to get 20 players like that, but they managed to recruit very well. There was this focus amongst the group which stemmed from the previous year. To go through that heartbreak made the players very wary of things which could go wrong at that stage – so you keep going and never relax."

McCormack's view was one echoed by Sam Saunders, who drew comparisons between the heartache of that Doncaster game and the extra-time play-off final defeat to Fulham seven years later. Just as Brentford bounced back to win promotion the following season after Doncaster-gate, so too did they after the gutting defeat to their West London rivals at Wembley, coming back stronger to claim a place in the Premier League nine months later. Saunders said: "You look at what happened with losing the play-off final to Fulham and then coming back the next year – sometimes it makes you stronger and more ready the second time round, and that's what happened after Doncaster. When we got promoted to the Championship we hit the ground running, and we did the same in the Premier League, so maybe building again and being stronger and better than the year before means you're better equipped when you do go up rather than going up, getting relegated and ending up back at square one.

"It's about characters and sticking to the trusted systems and methods. They don't panic when things don't go right because they're trying to do the right things, and you can see year on year that the club improves. As players and professionals in football there's always disappointments, but it's how you deal with them – you keep moving forward and use them as a fire in your belly to do even more the next season. We came back in pre-season in 2013 and said our objective was still to get promoted, and we managed to do it. I won't dress it up, it wasn't ideal, but we had our words and we moved on. You can't hold grudges in football, especially as the games come thick and fast. The next game was against Swindon, we got a penalty and scored it – so we'd moved forwards."

Richard Lee added: "The second season under Uwe had that disappointing finish with the final day and the play-off final defeat, but whereas a lot of teams go from nearly being promoted to struggling, huge credit to the lads. I don't think you'll see that often, to have such a blow and come back the following season galvanised by it."

An important part in this philosophy, of looking forwards rather than backwards, came from the owner himself, as Rösler revealed. Not only was Benham's new Brentford going to be different in so many ways – it was also not going to tolerate moping over any failures.

Benham had made his fortunes by betting without emotion clouding his position... just because a team loses a match, it doesn't mean they will lose the next, the team have to concentrate on doing the right things again, playing the right way again, creating more quality chances than the opponents, week in week out. It's a simple philosophy really. However, for many, it's hard to keep that steely-eyed focus when there are big set-backs. Rösler recalls: "What was crucial in Brentford's promotion into the Championship was Matthew Benham's reaction following the devastation after the Yeovil defeat. Matthew came into the dressing room after the game and re-energised the players for the following season. A lot of people saw that we had faded away, with the Trotta penalty situation, then losing in the play-off final. But he came into the dressing room and announced he would be increasing the budget for the next year and we all should get ready to go again. That was what everybody needed to hear, including myself, and especially the players in that critical moment.

"Right after that setback, he had shown his ambition and belief in that team. It was an example of great leadership, I will never forget that. That is leadership, that is how clubs should function. When you talk about how leadership should be structured at a football club, it should flow from the top and filter down from there. Then you can overcome situations like that defeat, that is how we came back in the third year to win promotion. We didn't do it by simply throwing money around and buying the most expensive players in the league, we just continued doing things our way."

CHAPTER FIVE

As Brentford recovered from the double blow of "Donnygate" and another play-off final defeat in the summer of 2013, there was also a sea change in Benham's thinking. Having been pumping money into the club for several years to plug the gaps and keep them afloat, he now saw the possibilities thrown up by distortions in the transfer market prompted by the new Premier League TV deal. Worth £3billion over three years, it increased the top flight's income by a staggering 71 per cent, changing the landscape of British football forever. As more and more money flooded into the game, Benham saw the value in developing players with the potential for a high resale value, a theory which Brentford's upwards trajectory came to be built on.

"For a long time, I bought into the common view that a football club can't possibly be profitable, so therefore it's about keeping things ticking along and trying not to lose too much money," said Benham in his 2022 interview with Bees United. "But in the summer of 2013, there was a new Premier League TV deal, and it became apparent to me that it would actually be possible to run a club sustainably, at break even, just on the football side, because there was so much money flowing into the game. And there was probably going to be inefficiencies in transfers.

"We were in League One, and I know that it's fashionable now for clubs in League One and League Two to say, 'Oh, the Premier League, they're killing us', but at the time, I took the view that this was going to be a good thing for us, because indirectly, we'd be getting our hands on some of that money, because there'd be a lot of money spent on transfers. It seemed that money going into the transfer market would help shrewd lower League clubs. Dwight Gayle was transferred from Peterborough to Palace in the summer of 2013 for a very big fee, and I remember thinking wow, that's crazy. This TV deal has really distorted the market, so there's potentially going to be some opportunities here.

"I think that across all markets, you always have a period where things are so inefficient, and what is generally accepted as true by the media and the public isn't necessarily true. Then things get progressively more and more efficient, and we've seen that massively in betting, where the markets are way, way, more efficient than they were 20 years ago. We've seen that in the football transfer market as well – it just gets more efficient every year."

At the time, Brentford were struggling just to get out of League One, but as far as Benham was concerned, the new money flooding into the game was his club's route into the Premier League, never mind the Championship. "We want to get into the Premier League and see how we can go from there," he said at the time. "The interesting thing about the television deal in the Premier League is it levels the playing field, because even the bottom club gets so much television money. In most other top leagues, the size of the club determines how aggressive they can be, so if you're a big-name club you get lots of commercial revenue and so on. So, if we get into the Premier League, let's see how far we can go."

As well as Alan McCormack, other key signings that summer included David Button and Jake Bidwell (his loan turning permanent), as Brentford's promotion-winning squad started to take shape. Striker Will Grigg also arrived from Walsall – but flopped massively – and fan-favourite Harry Forrester left for Brentford's conquerors the previous season, Doncaster Rovers. Meanwhile, promising young keeper, Simon Moore, was snapped up by Cardiff City. "We made the transfers of Adam Forshaw and Jake Bidwell permanent to ensure we locked the value from those young player's development to Brentford – that was a big change in the club's recruitment process which has evolved further for many years," said Rösler. "With less of a reliance on loan players, if they are your own players, you can sell them on." Kevin O'Connor, embarking on his 15th season with the club – a campaign that ended with him passing the 500-apperance mark – had been part of many squads in that time, but reckoned the class of 2013/14 was something else altogether. "This has to be one of the best, if not the best, squad I have seen here," he said after the opening day 1-1 draw at Port Vale. "The quality is there, and once we start clicking, we will be hard to resist."

However, after a steady, if unspectacular, start saw Brentford remain unbeaten in their first five league games, but only win two of them, a 4-0 drubbing at Bradford precipitated a run of four defeats in six games. All of a sudden, it seemed the ghosts of the previous season would be harder to exorcise than first imagined and it all came to a head after a particularly depressing 2-1 defeat at Stevenage's Lamex Stadium in early October. Clayton Donaldson's early opener was wiped out by a Francois Zoko brace and, try as they might, the Bees just couldn't break down

Boro's stubborn defence – it looked as if the wheels on the Brentford bus were well and truly wobbling and about to come off.

As the gathered post-match press corps waited patiently by the pitchside and an increasingly gloomy Hertfordshire night set in, it became evident that something was amiss. It took Rösler two hours to eventually emerge from the dressing room, still fuming, and it soon became obvious that a clear-the-air meeting had broken out, and was still taking place long after the home team had gone home for their suppers. At the time, Rösler said: "We had a good chat in the dressing room. I wanted some answers, and the players were very open and honest. All the cards have to come onto the table, and everybody in that dressing room now knows what the score is and what our ambitions for the next game are. At times you think things are clear, and in truth, it's not always like that."

Looking back, approaching a decade later, Rösler further reflects on that situation and what had brought it to a head that particular evening: "Everybody had written us off completely before the new season started after what happened. And we started slowly, there is no question about it. But although we always felt we were not so far away, we struggled a little bit to find the right rhythm and formation. The season before, the formation was absolutely clear, but then Harry Forrester left, so we had to replace him. Although the nucleus of the team was still there, the changes needed time to gel and settle, which was becoming frustrating.

"So, after the Stevenage match, I said okay, we need to put everything on the table, from all sides. From the players to the coaches, and from the coaches to the players. This took us two hours post-match at Stevenage, and from then onwards, we were all clear in our minds about which direction we were going and what it would take to get back where we wanted to be. And all those wins that immediately followed were a testament to that."

Alan McCormack agreed that the clear-the-air meeting had the desired effect: "It got heated in a good way. It wasn't people digging each other out, it was a heated debate about our standards and where we wanted to be. We knew we were good enough, Uwe knew that as well, and he didn't like the way we performed that day. He let everyone know he wasn't happy and wanted everyone to understand, and as players, we took it on board and took responsibility for what we had to do. Sometimes you need that in a dressing room when you have a bunch of honest players. It was needed and was a massive benefit."

Richard Lee agreed: "There were quite a few of us senior members having our say, and it ended up being quite a heated discussion. We were frustrated as we knew it was such a good team. There may have also been rumours regarding whether Uwe would stay or go too. That was probably the key moment, and the best thing that could have happened as a few home truths were told. We then built some momentum, which always baffles me. You talk of psychology – how often do you see teams win seven in a row and then lose seven in a row? Often there's very little rhyme or reason, but things like a feel-good factor, a bit of belief, and with each win, confidence grows – suddenly it's a nicer place to be."

Mark Warburton disagreed that there was any talk of Rösler's job being under threat, saying: "I don't think Uwe was ever close to being replaced, and that's one of Matthew's big strengths – the loyalty he shows to managers and coaches. There was frustration of course, and Stevenage was a low point, but certainly you can't fault Matthew's loyalty and communication with his coaches." Sam Saunders added: "Like anything, you sometimes just have to clear the air and get to the core of the problem. If you dwell on things and hold grudges, you're not going to last too long in football. We used that to motivate and improve on the training pitch. Soon the belief comes back and the principles the gaffer put in place come back, and then you get on a run like we did."

Indeed, Brentford's response to that lengthy exchange of views in Stevenage was spectacular. A run of seven wins from the next eight games – the only points dropped being in a goalless draw at champions-elect Wolves – saw Colchester (3-1), Bristol City (2-1), Shrewsbury (1-0), Crawley (1-0), Crewe (5-0), Peterborough (3-2) and Notts County (1-0) put to the sword. It not only put the Bees right back into promotion contention, but brought Rösler to the attention of Wigan Athletic. Back then, a division above Brentford, in the Championship, the Latics were looking for a new manager after parting ways with Owen Coyle. Strong press rumours circulated and social media was full of unconfirmed talk regarding Rösler's probable departure, which was confirmed on 6 December.

Wigan's Chairman at the time, Dave Whelan, told the BBC that afternoon: "I've had a good look around and I've had very good reports on Rösler... He's the type I'm looking for and I'm determined to get an agreement... I'm told he's mad keen to come and I have to say, Brentford have been very good in their dealings. They are obviously reluctant to lose him but they've been very, very helpful."

It proved to be a truly emotional evening for Brentford Football Club and its supporters as, despite the juxtaposition of losing their manager, the club finally received planning permission from Hounslow Council for their new stadium at Lionel Road. Indeed, one of the most significant landmarks in the club's history. For years, the club had been something of a political pariah in local authority circles, with many councillors ignoring or even objecting to the presence of a football club on their patch. But the magnificent work of the ABeeC campaign in getting Bees fan Luke Kirton elected as a Brentford ward councillor in 2003, and changing the perception of the club within the walls of the Civic Centre, changed all that. Ten years on, the councillors, after a meeting lasting four hours, finally gave the green light to Brentford's stadium plans.

Brentford fanzine, Beesotted, captured the significance of the council ruling at the time, reporting: "Brentford's new stadium bid organisers, and the hundreds of fans who had turned up to the Hounslow Civic Centre to witness the councillor's questioning and final decision, faced a gruelling Thursday evening, but thankfully, just before midnight, Brentford Football Club were handed the news that their plans for a new stadium had been given the green light. Few Bees fans present would have ever witnessed an event such as this, with local politicians split almost totally down party lines – Labour councillors voted for Lionel Road, and, all but one Conservative councillor voted against the development. But, after listening to some mind-numbingly petty, naïve accusations and concerns from opponents – who wandered so off track from voicing legitimate concerns they made themselves sound irrational at times – common sense prevailed and the Bees won the day. There were scenes of weary celebration at the end of the mammoth planning meeting, with fans and club officials mixing to congratulate each other on this pivotal evening in the club's history." From that day onward, the Brentford Revolution could be geared towards meaningful business expansion plans and forecasts could be made in the knowledge that the club would not always be tied to the limits of Griffin Park.

After the meeting, club chairman Cliff Crown said: "The support we have received from many sections of the local community and our fans throughout this process has endorsed our belief in this need for change. This is a once in a generation chance to create a vibrant new stadium and adds to the buzz that is going on around Brentford." Crown could barely have dared imagine the buzz and vibrancy which took hold of the new stadium once it was finally built and allowed to be packed to the rafters with fans – as the opening paragraphs of this book testify.

For now though, Brentford were presented with a strange situation – the euphoria of that significant decision by Hounslow Council's planning committee, tempered by the loss of a manager who, after a difficult start to the season, had got them playing like promotion contenders again. Rösler was officially unveiled at Wigan the following day, leaving his assistants, Peter Farrell and Alan Kernaghan, to take charge of Brentford's 3-2 FA Cup defeat at Carlisle that evening, along with Warburton. The Bees had lost for the first time in ten games in what had proved to be a very eventful 24 hours... and they say a week is a long time in football!

Reflecting on his departure, Rösler said: "A lot of people asked me why I left the club, and the answer is for purely family reasons. Of course, Wigan were also an attractive proposition at the time, but travelling between Manchester and London, having to live away from my family, especially for me as a very strong family man, took its toll. My family are the most important thing for me, not money. I wanted to achieve so

Mark Warburton and David Weir kicked on after Uwe's departure

many things at Brentford, I worked so hard with all the people around me, so it was difficult to let that all go. I had an emotional relationship with the players, with the staff and with the board. But I had to make sure my family, with small kids, was alright.

"Brentford is a special place. I've been at several clubs as both a player and as a coach, but Brentford will stay part of me forever. We had started to build the base for a sustainable future and started the whole process of selling players to allow the club to grow. Identify young players, bring them in, develop them, then sell, but always with the next targets already in mind, and never really losing any quality. Added to that, making sure you keep the fantastic staff, make them feel welcome, make them feel appreciated, make sure they are happy. The team around the team is always important. Unfortunately, I was never in a position to take advantage of when the training ground really improved, that was always a big issue. Over the years, that too has developed fantastically, so it was clear to me that the club was going to have a healthy future.

"I wouldn't say that without me the club wouldn't be where it is today, as somebody else would have done the job, but I arrived at the right time, at the right place, to witness something special in English football. Not many people gave the club a chance back in the beginning, even though we always did well. They always found faults in the transfer policy, or on appointing a sporting director, or bringing in a coach from

Norway who had never worked in English football... blah, blah, blah, blah, blah. I'm very proud of being part of that process as we stuck to it, even in the difficult times, by working together.

"I never got the feeling there was a lot of politics within the club, or that people tried to backstab each other. Everything was very professional, and you could trust the guys next to you. Whether it was the players, or the staff, the board, the chairman, or the owner, I always had the feeling you could trust everyone. Okay, you maybe did not always agree, but there was always a very professional atmosphere at the club. And for me, as a German, who likes to be professional, that was a very, very, nice feeling! Yeah, I'm very proud to be a big part in the beginning of it, but I have to say that without Matthew Benham, Brentford's success could never have been achieved. When you are in that bubble, you concentrate on the job ahead of you and sometimes cannot see more than that. So, when Matthew Benham always talked about 'in three years we'll be a Championship club, then another three years we'll be in the Premier League', I thought what is he talking about? The Championship... I could see ourselves there, absolutely, but with massive efforts, really, really good recruitment, good coaching and good luck, yes, we might get to that point. But reaching the Premier League is a stunning achievement."

For the players, it wasn't much of a surprise that Rösler was on his way. Alan McCormack said: "It wasn't a shock as there had been rumours – we could see why due to the way we were playing and results we were getting – the way Uwe liked to play and everything about the tactics and preparation. Wigan were a bigger club at the time and wanted that too, so it was only a matter of time. Some things happen for a reason – we probably would have got promoted that season under Uwe, but you never know. We seemed to get better and better under Warbs and the style of play continued and improved even more. Maybe it was meant to happen."

Richard Lee said: "We knew about the interest from Wigan and that it worked geographically for Uwe. It was disappointing as things were going so well at the time, and you kind of hoped he might stay a bit longer. But there was never any ill feeling towards him, only gratitude for what he had done. Sam Saunders added: "The Wigan job was a big opportunity for Uwe and it happened at a fantastic time for us. We were playing Carlisle away then had our Christmas do up in Newcastle, so we all got together and there was a real good team spirit with two days on the piss. We got back home on Tuesday, buzzing from the weekend we'd had, and that helped deal with the fact that Uwe had moved on."

The choice of replacement was unanimous with the players too. Three years previously, Warburton had been left to lick his wounds after being overlooked for the top job and threw himself into the sporting director role instead. This time, the job was his, and without doubt continued the good work Rösler had started. "Mark has done an exceptional job as sporting director since taking that role and we are happy he can step into this new role seamlessly," Crown said at the time. "We believe it will help the players and staff to work with someone they know and respect, and we look forward to continuing success for Brentford Football Club."

If a seamless handover was what Brentford were aiming for, it worked a treat as that eight-game unbeaten League run under Rösler became 19 games under Warburton and, by the time the Bees lost 3-0 at home to a Wolves side, with one hand already on the league winners' trophy, at the end of February, they had won 16 and drawn just three of those 19 games. From the moment Jonathan Douglas scored an injury time winner at home to Oldham in Warburton's first game in charge, the Bees were only heading in one direction. Preston (3-0), Swindon (3-2), MK Dons (3-1), Peterborough (3-1) and Port Vale (2-0) were all seen off too as Warburton won his first six games in charge.

After then drawing with Walsall and Shrewsbury and beating Bristol City and Gillingham, the last match of that impressive unbeaten run before it was ended by Wolves, showcased Brentford's freedom and confidence under Warburton. A 3-1 win at Crewe featured three outstanding goals – two from Alan Judge and one from Adam Forshaw – which on their own would each have been worthy Goal of the Season winners.

Alan McCormack said: "Warbs was incredible, the way he dealt with players. If you went to see him, he made you feel like the most important player at the club. He had unbelievable man management skills and his training sessions were excellent, every day you went in enjoying training. The hardest thing as a manager is dealing with players who aren't involved, and Warbs managed that superbly well. It meant players coming into the side were always ready and kept the starting XI on their toes. We didn't see much of him out on the grass before, he was there to support Uwe and the players. Uwe took a lot of strength from that and could concentrate out on the grass. As soon as Uwe went, Warbs was in the right place as he knew all the players and knew the style of play. It was a good choice by Matthew to continue and keep everything the same."

Richard Lee concurred: "Huge credit to him. Coming in and not having the CV other managers had, it was always going to be difficult to win people over, but we got off to a good start and continued the good run under Uwe. The more we won, the more confidence and belief we had. He brought in some simple ideas. Fair play to him as it's always going to be tough if you haven't played at the top level or got any management games under your belt. There's always going to be a few question marks, but he's got that way about him that he won everyone over very quickly. People could see he knew what he was talking about, and it was a modern approach. We played good football and it was very process-driven, there was just a lot to like about that period of time."

Sam Saunders added: "Warbs helped with the recruitment of a lot of the players, so he knew what he was inheriting. He didn't really change too much, probably made us a little bit more offensive-minded, and because we already had the defensive principles put in place by Uwe, I think it was a really good mix. I had a bit more freedom in possession.

"Training was really good – lots of passing and possession, balls on the floor, quick tempo, high intensity, possession-based drills, looking to dominate the football, all of which suited me."

As we've already learned, Benham and Warburton had first been introduced a few years previously, by film producer and mutual acquaintance Justin Andrews. The trio worked together on setting up the NextGen Series, a European football club cup competition for U19 footballers, which ran for two years before being scrapped in favour of the UEFA Youth League, as European football's governing body sought to push their own version to the front of the stage. Warburton said: "I travelled around a lot and Justin knew some clubs through filming for Nike. He had the film connections, I had the football connections, and between us, we came up with this concept. Everyone we spoke to was saying there was a problem for youngsters progressing from very talented youth players to first teamers. The transition's too big, and everywhere you went it was the same, so we asked Matthew if we put together a tournament, would he be interested? His response was immediate, so the work began – Matthew had seen the benefits of where we could take it and it snowballed from there."

Having been brought to the club in 2011, first as Nicky Forster's assistant, when he "got a call from the owner at 1:30 in the morning, asking if I would come in to assist Nicky... I didn't know a lot about Brentford or know any of the players, so I stayed up for the rest of the night looking at player profiles", Warburton now had the role he coveted most. He said of Rösler's departure: "Wigan came in with an aggressive approach and Matthew's not one to stand in the way if someone wants to go. We had dinner, and it went very quickly from there as Matthew is very matter of fact. Discussions started and I made my point of view very clear. There wasn't a plan for me to succeed Uwe so to speak, but the fact was many of the squad I'd had a big part in recruiting. I had a good relationship with the players, knew the agents and the contracts, so it was an easy transition in that respect. I wanted it, no doubt about it, but I didn't know if I would get it or not. I was very pleased that I did though. I was going to an Arsenal game at The Emirates and got a phone call from Matthew saying you've got the job if you want it, and that was it. From that moment on, it was a very exciting time for me personally, as it was an opportunity to push on and do what I'd wanted to do for a very long time.

"You look at your weaknesses first of all. I knew I hadn't had the most illustrious playing career, so we brought in David Weir, who'd had such an outstanding playing career, and getting him on board made a big, big difference. Then it was thinking about how we wanted to do it, and I looked at the club environment – get that right and it's a big part of it. I had staff there like Neil Greig, Bob Oteng, Chris Haslam, Kevin O'Connor – really good guys who allowed us to crack on. When you have good players and they're receptive, and you can make the environment right and use the loan market well, the whole thing just went from there. I just felt the belief was growing. Guys like Dougie (Jonathan Douglas) and McCormack (Alan) were very important, you just sensed they were driven and in a good place. It was little old Brentford, and it was nice to use that by staying under the radar. Teams underestimated us the whole way through and didn't expect us to see it through. You had to use it as a weapon – coming to Griffin Park with tiny away dressing rooms, it's difficult, and we had to use it."

Brentford's superb unbeaten run under Rösler and Warburton, which stretched over five months, was finally and clinically ended by eventual champions Wolves at the end of February. But the Bees responded in style, with four wins from the next five games. One of them, a gutsy 1-0 win at Leyton Orient, who had emerged as Brentford's biggest rivals for the second automatic promotion place, has gone down in Brentford supporter folklore. Marcello Trotta completed his rehabilitation with the winning goal, nine months after that tragic final-day penalty miss, by scoring a superb winning goal, and although there were still 11 games left, that was the day the fans (and players – "nobody wanted to say, but we were all aware of what the win by Orient meant" – Richard Lee) knew their club had one foot in the Championship.

After the match the Orient manager, Russell Slade, made salty comments about Mark Warburton and the Brentford bench celebrating the win "like they had won the FA Cup" much to the amusement of the Bees fanzine Beesotted who produced and distributed 5,000 Cup shaped cut outs featuring Slade's face at the next home match which fans held aloft..

There were still a few nervy moments, like a run of three games without a win at the end of March which included a midweek 3-0 trouncing at an impressive Rotherham United side, and it wasn't until mid-April that the Bees would actually finally clinch promotion – Alan Judge scoring the only goal of the game from the spot at home to Preston on Good Friday 2014. The final whistle saw jubilant fans spill out onto the pitch, even though the Bees weren't mathematically up at that precise moment as the game at Rotherham, the only team who could still catch them, had not yet finished. McCormack said: "It was a bit embarrassing celebrating after the Preston game, with the players being carried off the pitch, because we got into the dressing room and Wolves and Rotherham were still drawing and we still weren't promoted. But thankfully Wolves helped us out that day." McCormack would later be found behind the bar at The Lord Nelson pub in Enfield Road, serving up pints to delighted fans. "I don't remember much of it, but we had an amazing celebration," he added. "You don't see that often nowadays, with fans and players altogether straight after the game in the local pub, having one hell of a good time. To see that happen that day was incredible. My pint serving was supposed to be quite good, so I'll take that!"

Kevin O'Connor, who would get a special presentation for reaching 500 Brentford games after a 2-0 win over Stevenage on the final day of the season, made sure some praise was reserved for Rösler. "Uwe got the ball rolling," he said. "We were a bang average League One side, but Uwe changed the mentality. Everything he did was Premier League standard, he did amazing, so we'll be saying thank you to him. Warbs came in and was tremendous too. He very rarely loses his cool and has got the respect of all the lads."

Warburton himself, looking back on that Preston game, said: "We knew what was at stake. It was about getting the minds right and staying focused, making sure we were in a really good place. The fans were also key. I've often called London clubs like Brentford working class clubs because they are. The fans work hard and pay money to follow their team, which is never cheap, so to just make sure they enjoy watching their team play and they enjoy the success is what we wanted. It was very much about celebrating with the fans, but we knew we had to keep on building."

At the same time that Brentford were celebrating promotion, Benham had one eye on yet another football club, hundreds of miles away in central Denmark. Brentford's connections with Norden countries would blossom and grow over the coming years, both in terms of playing staff, coaching expertise and culture. However, it emerged that Benham was looking, initially, for a club where he could try out some of his ideas before, perhaps, reimporting them to England. He settled on FC Midtjylland, a Danish Superliga side which had been founded just 15 years earlier, following a merger between two older Danish sides. With Benham having taken over as majority shareholder in July 2014, Midtjylland were also about to embark on an unprecedented period of success. In their first season under the new owner, Midtjylland won the Danish top flight title for the first time – a feat they would repeat in 2018 and 2020. And in another neat parallel, the season Brentford finally won promotion to the Premier League, Midtjylland also qualified for the Champions League group stages for the first time ever.

Those more familiar with Brentford's recent history may recall that Midtjylland's chairman at that time was a certain Rasmus Ankersen, a

Bees fans swarm onto the pitch following the Preston promotion victory

former player with the club, whose playing career had been cut short by a knee injury. Having gained his UEFA A Licence and taken up a post as assistant coach with Midtjylland's U17s, Ankersen then put his football ambitions to one side to research and write several books based around achieving a transformational mindset and personal and business development strategies. He wrote books including, *A Winner's DNA, Mid-level DNA, Education of a Winner, The Gold Mine Effect* and *Hunger in Paradise* before returning to Midtjylland.

However, Ankersen's involvement with the Brentford owner had actually begun earlier than Benham's takeover of Midtjylland –in fact he was already working in the background at the club while Rösler was still in charge. Rasmus recalls: "I was introduced to Matt through a common contact in the 2013-14 season. There were some issues with Uwe in that Matt couldn't get some of his points across and needed someone to translate his view into football language, so I started consulting with him, and we realised we shared a lot of views on the inefficiencies in football. I was almost coaching for Rösler in the background, helping him and communicating between him and Matt.

"This was when Matt was looking into buying another club, and I recommended he look at Midtjylland. We won the (Danish) Championship in his first season, and a lot of the things we tried around set pieces and some game principles that worked out well, we thought we could use here. With the success at Midtjylland, Matt wanted to change things up, and I remember we sat down and had some long conversations at SmartOdds discussing how we could make it work at Brentford.

"Phil (Giles) and I were given the jobs to get it done, so that's how I got more and more involved at Brentford. The Midtjylland experience had opened Matt's eyes to what was possible. Some Brentford fans were perhaps not happy about him owning two clubs, but the biggest impact it had was showing Matt what could happen and opening his mind to things, and he really went all in on ideas that could really make a difference. It showed him it was something which was possible and not just something we talked about. It's not a theory, we can actually have outcomes."

At the heart of Ankersen's philosophy was investigating ways in which to gain an advantage over competitors – Brentford couldn't out-spend big club rivals at that stage, but they could perhaps out-think them by using data analysis instead of irrational, subjective and emotional decision-making. Using statistical models to judge success rather than league tables, which don't take unsustainable factors like luck and randomness into account. By judging players over multiple viewings on video to widen the sample base and only watching them live to confirm whether they would fit in from a personality and psychological perspective. By encouraging better use of set-pieces through the use of specialists, having identified them as a widely underexploited aspect of the game.

The Danish game was certainly way more open minded than an English one steeped in its long-held traditions and old-school shackles, but even then, it helped with the acceptance of his ideas that Ankersen already had links with Midtjylland. That, and the fact that they were running out of money, which formed another parallel with Brentford, who as we know, were on their knees financially before Benham started plugging the gaps.

Benham said: "I'd met Rasmus in about March 2013 and we just hit it off instantly in this sort of football geek, nerd way. Some of the things he thought were music to my ears. At that time at Brentford, the general culture and environment across the entire club wasn't as receptive to new ways of thinking. So at that point, I was thinking I've got various ideas, some of which worked, some of which didn't work, and if I could, I would have put them in place at Brentford. The thing about Midtjylland was, they would have probably gone out of business if I hadn't got involved, so it was very easy to walk in the door, say I'm the new owner and you've got to try out all this new stuff. And let's face it, their culture is a bit more open minded. They have much less hierarchy, so anyone can state their opinions, whereas there's elements of English football which are more like in the 70s, 'know your place' and so on."

Although plenty of new ideas were being discussed in the background, for now at least, it was very much Warburton in charge, as Brentford set out to build a side capable of making its mark in the Championship. The last time the Bees were in the second tier, some 22 years previously, they had only lasted a single season. The club was in a very different place now, however. In what was to be the last summer operating under the more traditional manager-led recruitment model, the focus was very much on unearthing lower league gems. Striker Scott Hogan was brought in from Rochdale to lead the line, but suffered a season-ending anterior cruciate ligament injury in only his second game. Andre Gray, brought in from Luton as Hogan's understudy, was promoted to first choice and rose to the occasion brilliantly, finishing the campaign with 17 goals. Another lower league gem was Moses Odubajo, plucked from former promotion rivals Leyton Orient and converted from a right winger into a roving right back. Alan Judge's loan move from Blackburn was made permanent, Alex Pritchard signed on loan from Spurs and Jota, one of three Spanish arrivals, joined from Celta Vigo to complete an attacking line up which, sometimes joined by Stuart Dallas, took the Championship by storm.

Warburton said: "It had to start straight away – looking at players like the Pritchards of this world, the Hogans and the Grays, see what you can do with all these boys developing, the Tarkowskis, Deans and Bidwells coming on, it was making sure we had the weaponry and attributes to really impact the Championship. That's the key, you can't just go up and think naively we'll be alright. We had a good team and we added to it well, but we had a 21st place budget and were everyone's favourites for immediate relegation. I was getting loads of texts from good football people saying 'just survive this first year', but that stuck in my throat. How could I go to a group of football players and say just survive? It's like saying just do enough. The question to the Brentford players was, is that just where we want to be? Matthew and I, with our City backgrounds, then put together an aggressive bonus system for the players which they bought massively into – people underestimated us. By the time people realised we were good we were second to Bournemouth."

Opening the campaign with a draw against Charlton, then a defeat at Bournemouth, Brentford enjoyed a big psychological boost in the third game when they came from behind to win 2-1 at Blackpool – their first Championship victory. That win at Bloomfield Road kickstarted a run of three wins in four games, but September brought a reality check with three defeats from four games, including a 3-0 home defeat to Norwich and a 4-0 drubbing at Middlesbrough. October then saw mixed fortunes, with a win over Reading, followed by two draws and a defeat at Bolton, in which McCormack suffered a season-ending injury, which prompted Odubajo's conversion to right back. Brentford had shown they could be stylish as well as competitive, but things weren't clicking just yet. All that changed during a memorable November, where five wins in a row showed Brentford meant real business. It all started with Stuart Dallas' last-minute winner at home to Derby – again coming from behind – followed by excellent away wins at Nottingham Forest and Millwall. A legendary Friday night, under the evocative Griffin Park floodlights, saw the Bees again come from behind to win – Jota this time the hero and West London rivals Fulham the fall guys. The 4-0 hammering of fellow newbies Wolves capped a month which shifted the perception of Brentford as also-rans to potential promotion candidates, all while unashamedly playing their superb brand of attacking, expansive, football.

Warburton said: "We had the late equaliser from Tommy Smith in the first game, and then in games like Blackpool away, it started to fall into place. We started delivering performances and Andre Gray started scoring goals. We started showing teams we could play. We went to Bournemouth and lost 1-0, but it was a proper game of football where for the last 40 minutes we controlled the game and did everything but score, and that gave the boys massive belief. We showed a lot of people we were a good team, but by the time they all realised it was too late, we were out the blocks and running. The loan players came on really well and the players we had were developing. Jota came in and was outstanding, Judgey was flying and we had a real attacking threat. We had a real squad of around 14 or 15 – us and Bournemouth used the least players out of the 92 clubs – and we had a real tight-knit squad. It was working really well – right place, right time."

Alan McCormack, whose contribution to the season was cruelly cut short with that injury at Bolton, said: "We were confident we could stay up. It wasn't spoken about, just let's do ourselves proud, continue playing how we play and see where it takes us. Don't back away or change our ways. That's been the Brentford way for a long time now, and Matthew's a big ambassador of that. He doesn't like sitting on a lead, if you go 1-0 up, you go and attack again and get as many as you can. Going into it, we didn't have a great start and there was another dressing room inquest after we got beat 4-0 at Middlesbrough. Having discussions and driving each other on, keeping our standards up, and it just clicked again. We went on an amazing run and confidence was up, we knew we could beat anyone. I was gutted to get injured, but if you look at the way Mo (Odubajo) performed that season, maybe it was meant to be."

Goalie, Richard Lee, who was by that stage beset by injury and would make just one appearance, in the amazing 6-6 League Cup tie at Dagenham & Redbridge, was forced to retire at the end of the season. He was, however, still very much in and around the squad and recalls: "There was a quiet confidence when we went up. There's a general thing in football where teams that get promoted are underestimated and teams that go down are overestimated, and I think there was an element of that. There was a feeling quite early on that we were going to be alright, then results started getting better and better and belief built. We got a better idea of what the other players and teams were about, but also a growing realisation that we were a very good team. It was a real positive place to be, a real learning environment had been created, and to go as close as we did was extraordinary. There's always this notion of going into cauldrons of 30-40,000 and asking can we compete, but suddenly we're half an hour in and not only competing but dominating games. It again comes down to belief – the mentality shifted. Suddenly it's not about can we avoid relegation, why not keep pushing and see where we go?"

Sam Saunders, who was also destined to be more of a bit-part player that season, observed: "You never know what you're going to get stepping up a league. A lot of us had never played there before and relied on the experience of players like Jonathan Douglas and Tony Craig who had played at that level previously, and they said we could more than hold our own. We made some good signings, but team spirit and confidence helped us hit the ground running."

The good form continued into December, where Jota scored Goal of the Season contenders in successive games against Blackburn Rovers and Cardiff City. But the Bees were brought crashing back to earth with back-to-back defeats between Christmas and New Year, Saunders returning with a brace at home to Ipswich on Boxing Day, but the festive cheer ran short as the Bees lost 4-2. Warburton said: "We had the disappointment of a big game at Griffin Park against Ipswich when we let ourselves down, but in general we had the weaponry to go out and play with freedom. That was always the way, take teams on and be bold, be brave. When we played Ipswich away in the return game, they had a corner in the 88th minute and we left four up, so they had to bring five back, and it was that kind of approach that made teams wonder what we were doing."

By the time that return game at Portman Road came about, Brentford were in a very different place. They had responded to their festive setback with four wins out of five, including impressive victories on the road at Norwich, Leeds and Brighton. However, in the week following Alex Pritchard's winning goal at Elland Road in early February, Brentford fans, who had been dreaming the impossible for the past couple of months, saw those dreams come crashing down around their ears. The owner and manager were about to lock horns in a battle for supremacy over recruitment, and once again, landmark events would unfurl which would become instrumental in delivering the Brentford Revolution.

CHAPTER SIX

It was at the start of February 2015, slap bang between a home defeat by the only goal of the game to Middlesbrough, and a win by the same scoreline at Leeds, that rumours first broke, in the Spanish press, of Brentford's interest in Rayo Vallecano head coach Paco Jémez. Coming from respected Spanish journalist Antonio Fuentes, they weren't rumours that were easily dismissed, although the feeling amongst Brentford's fanbase at the time was that it could be put down to the club sounding out potential replacements should Warburton be poached by a bigger club. There would no doubt have been a growing list of club owners impressed by his record of taking a team, put together on a relatively small budget, into the Championship play-off places whilst playing a cavalier brand of attacking football and showing zero diffidence to so-called bigger clubs. Norwich City were rumoured to have made an approach, and although it has always been strenuously denied, it was suggested by some that Mark Warburton had held provisional talks with the Norfolk club.

A week later, with Leeds having been duly dispatched and a home game at Watford on the horizon, another story broke, this time in the English press, with Matt Smith of The Times claiming that Warburton would be 'sacked' at the end of the season wherever Brentford finished. Mark Warburton had asked Matthew Benham point blank about the Spanish story, so Benham decided it would be best if he was open about his summer plans for the club. The report went on to say that Benham was "determined to pursue a new direction". It would later become clear that Benham had 'crunched the numbers' and decided the club's best chance of maintaining their promotion push was with reinforcements to the squad, many of which he had already identified, thanks to the statistical modelling which had made his sports gambling business such a success.

In Benham's eyes, Brentford were outperforming the model and therefore 'lucky' – he wanted to bring in new players to take advantage of where we were, before we reverted to mean. In short, Brentford's chances of promotion would be boosted by more than 10 per cent with a sprinkling of new players in vital positions according to his end of season promotion analysis.

Warburton, by contrast, believed that a tight-knit dressing room had got the club that far, and that disrupting it at such a critical stage would do more harm than good – despite players clearly beginning to tire as the season wore on. The official statement the club put out didn't help matters, neither denying or confirming the rumours, but instead saying it plans for "various possible eventualities", and as a "progressive club", talked to people in the game to "learn about other ways of doing things" and "consider novel strategic approaches". A paragraph about football being "a village" was roundly mocked and, unfortunately, added fuel to the fire for those wishing to pour scorn on the more pertinent aspects of the statement. With that, the club closed ranks and braced itself for the somewhat inevitable backlash and ridicule.

As you would imagine, the Griffin Park Grapevine, the independent Brentford fans' message board, went into meltdown, with supporters trying xto make sense of what was unfolding. "If it is true (which is highly unlikely) then the only explanation would be that Warbs has agreed to go somewhere else in the summer" said Guildford Bee. GBems92 rightly observed; "I think you underestimate how much Mark Warburton enjoys doing what he's doing right now, he clearly has a passion for coaching and managing and I doubt he would want to step back into the director's box. He quit a well paid job to follow his passion and wouldn't have taken over the reins if that wasn't really where his passion is." All very valid points, with this last comment obviously written by a fortune teller (LP_Brentford). "As unlikely as it is! Nobody else worried that QPR is going to come swooping in for our Warbs?"

While Bees fans tried to make sense of how their dream start to life as a Championship club had suddenly turned from a joyous fairground magic carpet ride into a potential ghost train nightmare – pundits lined up to take shots at a club which no longer fitted their narrative of plucky underdogs sticking it to the big boys.

Who did they think they were, casting aside the man who had led them to promotion and the Championship play-off places from the dugout, in favour of these new-fangled ' ideas of stats-based 'Moneyball' football? Daniel Taylor's Guardian article, headed 'Silly Party candidates bidding for a majority in football's boardrooms', even compared Benham (saved club from financial oblivion, rescued and funded new ground plans, funded rise from nether regions of League Two) to Vincent Tan (caused outrage by changing both the club badge and colours at Cardiff City), Fawaz al-Hawasi (delayed wage payments, caused transfer embargo and accused of meddling in team affairs at Nottingham Forest) and Massimo Cellino (twice disqualified by the Football League, made insulting statements in the press about club staff, banned Sky Sports camera and fell out with fans and numerous managers at Leeds).

Taylor's Guardian article, which posed the question 'has there ever been a more bewildering bunch of owners across the country?' concluded; "Hopefully there's still time for the owner and manager to work it out and Benham will think again. He really ought to because – whether it is fair or not – he is opening himself to allegations of being another Silly candidate (Monty Python sketch) with more money than sense. He just has to look around the rest of the league to realise there are enough of them out there already."

The evening of the day of the Times story, Brentford hosted Watford in a surreal Griffin Park atmosphere. The players made their feelings known when, after Andre Gray gave the hosts a second half lead, the scorer and his team-mates all ran straight to the touchline to mob Warburton. Sadly, in keeping with the feeling of impending gloom, an Odion Ighalo brace, including a last-minute winner, saw the visitors take the points. The match referee, Keith Stroud's performance had also contributed to the defeat in many Bees fans' eyes. Four days later, a still shell-shocked Brentford side travelled across London and were hammered 3-0 by Charlton Athletic. Finally, three days after that defeat, there was some clarity as Brentford released another statement, confirming the departures of Warburton, David Weir and Frank McParland that summer and outlining changes which would be made to the management structure, "to ensure the long-term prosperity of the club". It revealed that discussions about the future direction of the club had been taking place before the press stories had broken.

Again, the press release sparked confusion and outrage in some quarters – all understandable emotions when so much uncertainty and mistrust are allowed to grow without clear explanation. However, some fans could see the bigger picture that was coming into play, and revisiting the Griffin Park Grapevine message board provides a perfect snap-shot in time. "I never thought I'd read 'sustainable Premier League football' and 'Brentford' in the same statement. I beelieve in Mr Benham! (But)Warbs will always be a Brentford hero" was Eieieio's thoughts after reading the latest club statement, while Nocoat felt that it was, "Very sad news, but the most important thing is Benham is still on board and has grand plans for the future. Good luck Warbs, but long live BFC." Indian Bee was another with mixed emotions; "Mathew Benham will always have my unreserved and total support. However, this is the worst outcome ever. I feel empty inside. At least we have some clarity on what our situation will be at the

Brentford players mob Warburton after Gray's goal against Watford

end of the season. We will not forget what Mark Warburton has brought to the club and given us the best football ever. It's a sad day for Brentford Football Club. I hope in years to come we do not regret the decision today. Onwards and upwards."

The press release went on to introduce a new management model, with a proposed head coach supported by a sporting director encapsulated within a new recruitment model, "using a mixture of traditional scouting and other tools including mathematical modelling" – with the head coach having an input but not an absolute veto. Warburton, Weir and McParland told the club they felt unable to work under the new structure, with McParland placed on immediate gardening leave. Benham recalls it as an "extremely hard decision", adding: "It is difficult to seek to implement change, particularly when things appear to be going so well, but I am single minded in my resolve that we can leave no stone unturned in our quest for sustainable Premier League Football. Innovation, not increased funding, can be the only route to success for clubs such as ours, and I fully accept that innovation is never without risk. We are continuing to build a strong base for the future. Everything has been perfectly amicable between all parties and we remain friends."

If ever there was a sentence that encapsulates Brentford's vision for a successful future, there you have it. It is probably worth re-reading in fact, "It is difficult to seek to implement change, particularly when things appear to be going so well, but I am single minded in my resolve that we can leave no stone unturned in our quest for sustainable Premier League Football. Innovation, not increased funding, can be the only route to success for clubs such as ours, and I fully accept that innovation is never without risk." That, in essence, is The Brentford Revolution's blueprint.

Club chairman Cliff Crown said in the statement: "Lots of clubs are criticised for short term thinking – we want to take a long-term view and put structures in place that both the board and the owner believe will be to the benefit of Brentford FC for years to come. The new structure is unusual in English football, although commonplace in other European countries and in other sports. We would have loved for Mark to stay, working within the new structure, but he feels that this is not right for him. We understand that decision completely and had to weigh up the benefits of the new structure against losing a fantastically successful manager before taking this decision."

Warburton himself added in the statement: "While I am disappointed that we have been unable to reconcile some key philosophical differences, I'm relieved we now have clarity. In my remaining time at the club, we shall move heaven and earth to get the promotion that the players, fans and Matthew deserve and, going forward, I wish the club every success in its ongoing adventure. I have enormous respect for Matthew and his investment in the club, and he has the absolute right to run the club in the manner he deems most appropriate and beneficial."

Despite releasing a more detailed statement, and outlining a better vision for the future, there was undoubtedly a wedge dividing fans with two distinct camps emerging – and it is no exaggeration to say that a toxic atmosphere continued over the issue for a significant time to come.

Not all fans had pressed the panic button, however, and one reply to a Beesotted website article looks particularly profound when afforded the benefit of time and hindsight. Stephen O'Brien countered the anti-Benham sentiment, and touches upon the binary fan divide, by saying: "Benham has pumped his hard earned/well placed bets/luckily gambled money (you choose) in to this club and done so without ever wanting the spotlight, never courting the press, never wanting to be interviewed and turning up in his green fur lined hooded Parka, with denim jeans and loafer slip ons, walking up to the gate shaking nervously anyone's hand who puts it out to him, although you get the feeling he'd rather just shuffle in and out without any fuss whatsoever, enjoy his game and then return to whence he came. But make no mistake about it, he will continue to walk to the ground, albeit maybe only from the directors car park in Brentford School for Girls but maybe just as likely having just jumped off the E2 or 65 bus and his head will be held high I'm sure.

"I have no doubt in my mind that there are some misguided (to be polite to them) fans, who will give him their tuppence worth, becasue

'I'm owed that as I pay the club's wages' and thereby completely ignoring the multitudes of pounds that Mr Benham has decided to invest in his hobby, giving us a new modern ground in a few years, trips to state of the art training camps in the USA, back room staff to be proud of, a training ground improving all the time, a luxury state of the art facility for youth development in Uxbridge and so much more. But will this man who quietly walks up to matches, enjoys the game and walks away, really want to be doing that when, or if, he is getting weekly abuse and vile chants at him? Answer is, I highly doubt that for one minute. He's in it for the long term, he's in it as maybe another chance to show how successful a man he is, but he has dangled a carrot in front of us fans when four or five years ago, we had nothing. Nothing of the sort, so let's give the man a chance, let's give him his due and let's give him some time to lead us to where his visionary outlook might do.

"Surely, as fans who were craving the holy land, the messiah, the promised land, of the all singing, all dancing, Premiership must, absolutely must, realise that if Brentford, tin pot Brentford, were to get there, there would be forced on us wholesale changes. It's part of the territory. I am not slightly bothered by the loss at Charlton, because I don't really want to go up. Not yet, not 'til we're ready and that's in the new stadium, in preparation, off the field, press, ticketing, professionalism, but most importantly, 'til us as supporters have got used to the idea. Yes, a carrot has been dangled in front of us by the ridiculously great football we've played this year, turning over team after team, week in week out and boy have we enjoyed it, every single, mouth watering minute of it but hold our horses. Wait just a second, we want it all and we want it right now. Why?" Some fans would need more time before they could visualise the Brentford Revolution with similar clarity and foresight.

Looking back on that time, Warburton said: "I've got the fullest respect for Matthew and that will never change. The simple fact is Matthew was massively influenced by his background and his knowledge of players, and he wanted to bring in a number of players – the likes of Djuricin and Gogia – and my point was don't bring them in in January, but Matthew wanted to. He worked the stats and said our chances of going up would be two per cent better if we had these players, and my point was the dressing room was strong and solid, and to bring non-English speaking players in at that stage – I said do it in pre-season, do it in the summer. At the end of the day, it's Matthew's club though. He writes the cheques, and I've always been clear about that.

"I was sitting in my office on a Sunday morning with David Weir. We had a good result on the Saturday, and I saw in the Mail on Sunday it said 'Rayo Vallecano coach turns down Brentford approach'. David's words to me were: 'I think that's a game-changer gaffer'. I phoned Matthew, and

Matthew can't lie. He said I need to speak to you. I said lunch on Monday? And that was it. He wanted to do that with the players, but I know I was right in terms of that dressing room. I had no problems with the players coming in the summer, but just not at that time. That was the problem, and that's why we fell out. I asked Matthew if he wanted me to carry on, and he said yes please. The only thing we fell out over, and to this day I tell him I don't even know who the bloke is, was an article by a bloke called Gabriel Marcotti. I don't know who he was – I do now – but it was nothing to do with me. Matthew was convinced I'd leaked it, but I can honestly say to this day it was nothing to do with me. That caused some ill feeling at the time, but I'm never going to lose respect for Matthew. I have nothing but admiration for the job he's done, and I hope we're on good terms now.

"At the time it was difficult, but we carried on. We played Watford, and you saw the reaction when Andre Gray scored. I had no idea they were going to do that, but it was a very proud moment. When Andre Gray and five others jump on my back, my legs were all over the place, but it showed the squad was together and the unity was strong. We were really good that night and we kicked on. To come fifth with a 21st place budget, the players did magnificently well. I knew that if we got to the Premier League I was still going to be removed, but Matthew was firm, and it's his prerogative. What that meant was I knew, and not in an arrogant way, that my stock was high, and I had various offers. I wouldn't have left in January because of the players, I had a great relationship with them. I asked Matthew if he wanted me to stay, he said he wanted me until the end of the season, and that was literally it.

"In Frank McParland, we had someone who has signed some of the best players going. He'd been at Liverpool for 20 years and had a fantastic eye for a player. We also had David Weir's playing career and my own knowledge. Matthew's got his data-driven side of it, and that was always at his control. As its impact grew, he was always going to want more data coming in, and obviously these are players he could see having the same impact for less money. It's not that his model hasn't been proven – there's been many right and many wrong, more right than wrong. But the fact is, at the time, I was trying to show things from a dressing room perspective. That's one of things with data – you can't measure unity, combativeness and togetherness. Matthew used to ask me for a figure on momentum (as he didn't believe it is a factor) – I'd talk about momentum, and he'd say can you measure it? I understood where he was coming from, and it was coming more and more into the data, but I knew I was right, then, to keep that unit together and strong.

"We knew the market, and we'd talk to Matthew all the time about players. I'd known who guys like Bidwell and Forshaw were since they were 15, the same as Pritchard, Saville and McEachran. Frank went to watch Jota play for about half an hour, then phoned me up and said 'sign him', it was that quick. Judgey I knew from Notts County, and we knew the impact he could have. We had good knowledge of players and it tied in with Matthew's support. Matthew was finding out the data and looking at the leagues. He's layers ahead of me in terms of grey matter, but I know I'm good at what I do, just as he's outstanding at what he does. We complimented each other really well, but unfortunately what happened, happened. It's part of learning, and we both learnt from it. Brentford eventually got their promotion, and I got promotion on my CV with Rangers, which all comes down to Matthew giving me a chance. Had we sat down and Matthew had said look, this is what I want, then yes, we could maybe have worked it out, but his mind was made up as he wanted the players in January, and I didn't think it was what we needed. I think Matthew would agree he didn't understand the dressing room side as well as I did, and I didn't understand the data as well as he did – nobody will really.

"Matthew was clear with what he wanted to do, and I didn't fit in with his approach at the time, but you have to respect the person who writes the cheques. Could we have resolved it? Yes, we probably could have at the time, but two competitive people wanted to push forward. It was obviously awkward, but it was about the team. It was a difficult one, because obviously the football world was going to get behind my side – because from the outside it looked bizarre that I was going anyway – that irritated Matthew, understandably so. I go back to that point that he thinks I released it, but I never would, I'm not that way made. It was never going to be a clean, happy respectful break because you've got two sides with different opinions, but I think we're in a good place now.

"It was the first disagreement we'd had in five years working together, and it was a big one, but it happened, and hopefully we all learned from it. It did move quite quickly towards his way of doing things, but when you're writing the cheques, you want to put your own fingerprint on the club. He has a clear vision and is such a clever individual. We had a saying, which is still relevant now, that data is a massive part of it, but only a piece of the pie. It was about knowing the character of the player and everything else. It didn't cost us promotion, the team remained driven. There were some tough games to get through, but the boys deserve enormous credit for the way they maintained focus and concentration."

Benham, himself, later reflected on the need to move away from what he saw as an outdated ownership model. Despite being largely vilified outside the club (and, at times, inside it), Benham stuck steadfastly to his belief that his methods and expertise would be the best way forward for Brentford. "We still had the traditional English model, where the manager is your Fergie or your Cloughie, a combination of head coach, director of football and owner, all knowing and all powerful," he said. "And basically, the actual owner, his job is to keep his mouth shut and write the cheques. Eventually at Brentford, we moved away from that model. It's a specific norm in English football, or it has been over the years.

"So, for example, when he was at Liverpool, Brendan Rodgers wanted full control of transfers. Instead, they introduced their infamous transfer committee, and the club got slammed by the media that it was absolutely wrong. In England, there has been this tradition that the manager is all-powerful. I've always been of the opinion that decisions are best made not by an all-powerful leader, but by consensus. Not by 'group-think', where everyone just agrees, but where you have a group in which everyone is allowed to have their own independent thoughts, where there's vigorous debate and decisions aren't weighted by the seniority of the person giving their opinions. I would say, for a long time, the media presented it as this binary option where either the owner just writes cheques and keeps his mouth shut, as he should, or he's interfering in absolutely everything and running down to the bench at half time. The fact that I didn't want to be in the former camp meant that there was lots of crap about me trying to dictate team selection and so on.

"I'm probably less involved than people think. Certainly in terms of the maths, that got really exaggerated. At the time of 'Villagegate', we were caught on the back foot. We felt we had to say something, so we made this point about mathematical models, but with hindsight, we should have just said absolutely nothing. The funny thing is that when we were talking over the press release, we said if we put this in, they're going to write 'oh so they're only using maths and not humans', so we're going to make it absolutely clear, as clear as possible, that there will still be traditional scouting. That made absolutely no difference. We still got slammed for dispensing with our traditional scouts.

"I'd say it was always exaggerated how much maths was going to be involved. But having said that, I would have anticipated that our models would have had more impact than they actually have. So, I'd say instead, the big change hasn't been so much that, but more that it's now a collaborative effort rather than the tradition that a manager says 'I want to sign this guy because he used to play for me and I trust him'. The other most common lines are 'I know him' or 'we share the same agent' or 'I saw him on TV the other night, and he had a really good game'. So I think the really big change is that it's a more collaborative effort. Lots of different people having input.

"I think we all got a bit caught up in it. The first few months after that there were press releases blathering on about analytics and all of that, and then we quickly realised 'shit, this is getting out of hand'. And ever since then, we've been trying to downplay all that sort of 'Moneyball' nonsense, but generally, it's much more qualitative than quantitative. Traditional scouting, albeit with a little bit more video scouting than live scouting. We do some live scouting, I get it that in the flesh you can see more, but if you're considering an overseas player, then for the time it takes to go over there and watch him, you could have watched ten matches on video, especially if you're just watching that player's actions."

Benham would also later set out his beliefs in an interview with Sporting Intelligence, saying that there was an element of fortune in Brentford's fifth-place standing at the time of the fall-out with Warburton, with his modelling showing the Bees were, at the time, only the 11th-best team in the Championship. "The table is notoriously inaccurate because there's just way more randomness than people understand," he said. "Usually, the way the fans, and especially the media, look at it, randomness is quite an unsatisfactory explanation, so they like to look for stories and a narrative. But very often, randomness is the main explanation. One lesson I've learned is if you go to a manager and say you've been unlucky and you actually deserve to be higher, that's actually quite an easy message to give naturally enough. But if you go to a manager and say you've been lucky, you deserve to be lower, that's an incredibly difficult message for the manager to swallow."

For Alan McCormack, it was a case of respecting both sides, and he denied rumours that Benham was made unwelcome at the training ground in the aftermath. He recalls; "I don't think they had a falling out, it was more to do with the way Matthew wanted to go, and Warbs didn't want to work that way. They still have massive respect for each other, but it seems the best thing was Matthew found a new manager and Warbs found a new club. The players were devastated, I remember the Watford game when Andre Gray scored and everyone was straight to Warbs. I don't think it was pre-planned, just an emotion that came out. It was strange to hear what was going to happen at the end of the season in January time, but the players always had massive respect for Warbs, he'd do anything for the team. After the news broke everyone was gutted. For us, it was out of the blue. Something started to feel not quite right a day or two before it broke, little whispers about Warbs wouldn't sign a new contract and the club was going to change things, but the players don't get involved in that. The captain and maybe one or two knew about it.

"Matthew is the owner, he saved the club and he supplies the funds, so you've got to respect his decisions. At the same time, we loved Warbs and didn't want to see him go. We understood it when he explained it to us, but we were gutted. Matthew wanted to do something outside the box, which is very much the Brentford way now. Sustainability is the biggest problem in football at the moment, so Matthew was already ahead of the game. He always said it would take a bit of time, but it would work.

Warbs thought differently and wanted to keep the dressing room spirit we all trusted, and Matthew trusted his way. Both decisions were massively respected by the players. Matthew came down to the training ground many times after that and was always greeted by the players. People may have put two and two together and thought because we celebrated with Warbs that evening we weren't with Matthew now, but no, players don't act that way. We respected both individuals, it wasn't the sort of club that makes divides."

For Richard Lee, it was a case of both owner and manager being in the right. He said: "It came out the blue really, and it's a shame because it could not have been more positive at that point. It did derail us slightly and was a bit of a disruption. A few conversations took place, but it seemed to die down. It was just for a small period of time, and then handled again once the season was over. But we did manage to get ourselves back on track pretty quickly, and that's where the culture was strong, we didn't take long to get back on a good footing.

"Ultimately, Matthew is very process-driven, and if you get the rewards, that's great. But it's knowing you will get the rewards at some point if you follow the process. Whether they happen instantly or over a period of time is irrelevant, they'll get there in the end. Naturally, from Warbs' point of view, with things going as well as they were, you can appreciate his stance – let's crack on and go for promotion and then figure it out. Both were within their own rights. Warbs has gone on to prove he is a good manager, and there's nothing negative you can say about Matthew – not many club owners can say they've done what he has."

Sam Saunders – who soon after Warburtongate broke would be sent out on loan to Wycombe for the rest of the campaign, but revive his Bees career the following season – looked back philosophically, seeing it as just one of those cycles that happens naturally within football. He said: "It was kept away from us as much as possible and we just tried to stay professional and keep winning games, as did Warbs. He knew he'd be going at the end of the season, but knew his best chance of getting another job was to keep winning games, so at no point did he show anything less than 100 per cent effort, and neither did the players. We had a dream of getting into the play-off places, and nothing was going to get in the way of that. The professionalism and the culture of the club got us into that position.

"You don't know (if a raft of January foreign signings would have disrupted the dressing room), but he was right in that it was the most tight-knit dressing room I had been in. The work ethic was good, and we all went out and enjoyed ourselves together. There was a really good mix of knowing when to work and when to relax. I'm still friendly with a lot of that squad, which speaks volumes as to how tight knit it was. As players, we were paid to play football and didn't get involved in off-the-pitch stuff.

Jota scores in the last minute of the 4-1 win over Fulham

Matthew Benham is a very clever guy, and you can't argue about his methods – they haven't done too badly, have they? I was sad to see Warbs go, and he has proved himself as a coach, but when you've been in football long enough you get dead to seeing people move on as it's part of the game. Football keeps moving forward and it's part of the journey. Football teams have a two or three-year cycle and then you move on and refresh, six or seven players come in and six or seven go out, that's just football."

On the pitch, Brentford did admirably to turn things around quickly in such circumstances. That defeat at Charlton was followed by two impressive home wins in quick succession, beating eventual champions Bournemouth 3-1 before a Jon Toral hat-trick helped sink troubled Blackpool 4-0, in a game that Brentford clocked up an increadible 43 shots at the visitor's goal. Other impressive performances over the remainder of the season saw Huddersfield Town and West London rivals Fulham both beaten 4-1 and a midweek 3-2 comeback win at Blackburn Rovers, while the Bees saw out the regular part of the campaign with wins over Reading and Wigan.

It wasn't entirely unthinkable that Warburton would depart his post with Brentford in the Premier League. However, the one side they would have wished to avoid in the play-offs was Middlesbrough, who were something of a bogey club during the Bees' early seasons in the Championship, and duly dispatched Warburton's men, somewhat comfortably, 5-1 on aggregate in the semi-finals.

Reflecting on the play-off games and his subsequent departure, Warburton said: "Middlesbrough was a painful time, a very sad time. I knew if

I'd stayed, we would have had to have mixed it up. You look at teams and how they play in that first season, and you have to adjust. I knew we'd have to make some changes and bring in some additions. It was just sad that we had a very good thing going and it was cut short, but that's life, and we all learnt from it. The next manager didn't work, but Brentford went on to maintain top ten places in the Championship and I went on to manage a global club like Glasgow Rangers. I got a lovely vase from Brentford and sincere thanks for all that we'd done. I've nothing but respect and admiration for Matthew as he gave me my chance in management, and in football full stop, so I will always be thankful. I'm delighted that Matthew has done so well and I hope my five years there were a big part of the journey for Brentford.

"Later, when I was at QPR, we had a game against West Brom on the last day of the 2019-20 season and everyone thought we'd be steamrolled. We drew 2-2 and could have won it, which did Brentford a massive favour – Matthew sent a nice text about our commitment and professionalism. When they went up, I sent a very genuine well done to him because it's a fantastic achievement. For the club to be in such a good place, with the new stadium, is testament to his vision, which he had a long time ago when they were 18th in League One and he bought the club. It's been an enormous journey, and I know I played a big part in it because I know what Matthew wanted. We came across each other at the right time. I never have or will be derogatory about the club in any way, shape or form, I've never been anything but respectful. I will always be thankful, and that will never change. It was a privileged time, and there were some great nights, like 'Jota in the last minute'. Those sorts of scenes were special, and I hope they still are."

As Ankersen explained in the previous chapter, conversations had already started to take place about how to replicate Midtjylland's success at Brentford. "I just think it's a fascinating project to try to change an industry and try to explain the inefficiencies of an industry with a smaller budget than the competition," he'd stated. Whether or not Warburton could have been a part of the new system, if he'd agreed to give up having a veto over incoming players, is one of life's great unknowns, but that was never going to be likely, and so the club found itself looking for a new coaching team at the same time as introducing a new recruitment system. A summer of mayhem was on the way, but one which Brentford would, ultimately, learn some valuable lessons from.

Ankersen underlined that there would be no turning back: "As we had these conversations, it was obvious there was a fall out, and the decision to replace Mark was taken about that time. It was a weird situation as Mark was upset obviously, and leaving him in that role did not make for a healthy situation. Matthew was very frustrated with not being able to implement what he thought was obvious – things to do to increase the probability of winning. Matt is not a political guy, he's quite straight, but also someone who it's sometimes easy to take advantage of in a working environment. I don't think he was not welcome (at the training ground), but I don't think he enjoyed going there. A lot of that was him feeling he wasn't able to affect the environment the way he wanted to affect it.

"At the same time, we had to think about how to put things together after the summer, and we had to do it from a distance as me and Phil (Giles) couldn't go to the training ground. It hadn't been announced, at the time, that we would be co-directors of football, so it was really difficult to do what was required from a distance. There was not a nice environment, with all kinds of stories going around about the manager not selecting the team – that it was us and Matt doing it in the background – there was a big mistrust I think. At the same time, we wanted to drive a lot of change. The first conversation I had in my role was to tell Jonathan Douglas he was not part of the future, and that affected a lot of the other players as well – he was a big personality in the dressing room at the time."

Ankersen eventually settled into the co-director of football role with Phil Giles, a former quantitative analyst with Benham's Smartodds company, having also worked as a football trader for sports betting company Spreadex. The Bees had experimented with a director of football role through Warburton himself, but it was still something unusual to English football, as Benham admitted. "We did have what I'd call a 'director of football lite' from the summer of 2011, but English football and English media have hated the concept of a director of football, and if they've tolerated it at all, it's director of football lite, which is that he is subordinate to the manager – reporting to the manager rather the other way round – he sees himself more as the manager's recruitment assistant.

"I tried to say at the time it wasn't that controversial, because if you look at professional team sports anywhere else in the world, apart from football in Britain, this is the model you had. Whether you call it a general manager, sporting director, director of football, you had someone at the head and then all the departments report to them. The head coach is chosen because he's an excellent coach. I should also add, even though I myself had cynicism about a manager saying 'oh, I like him because he's played with me before', obviously with Dean Smith we bought in Rico Henry and Romaine Sawyers. Then with Thomas Frank we bought in a million Danes, so maybe I'm not as anti that concept as I was. Having said that, pretty much all of those players we would have gone for anyway."

An interesting perspective on the fall out between Benham and Warburton is provided by Ted Knuston, a University of Oklahoma graduate, who had spent seven years working in new products, analysis tools and metrics for Pinnacle Sport, an 'alternative bookmaker', before being hired by Benham's SmartOdds in the summer of 2014. Knutson would become responsible for player analytics at both Brentford and Midtjylland, but at the time of his arrival, recruitment was done purely by what he calls Warburton and Frank McParland's 'group', with Knutson initially brought in to work with them.

"Mark and Frank's group brought in some good players and they were having some success, but also knew they were a little thin up front, and I was asked to give a couple of names that looked interesting to bring in as a forward," Knutson told the StatsBomb podcast in June 2021. "Andre (Gray) had played a lot of minutes, and we wanted to make sure we were fresh. The only other forwards we had were Tommy Smith, who was not young, and Chris Long, who was 19. The two names we quite liked were Jonathan Kodija, who ended up at Bristol City and Aston Villa, and Florian Niederlechner, who ended up having a very good career in the Bundesliga, but was totally unfancied and almost completely unknown at the time. These guys were £2m-£2.5m, but they ended up not getting brought in and we got knocked out in the play-offs.

"The next summer was one of huge transitions – the stuff between Matthew and Warbs had gone down in February, and there was big unhappiness about who controlled what. One of the elements of this was Matthew had offered to bring in Gianni Vio to help out with set pieces as he knew that was a weakness we'd had before, but Warbs and his group had no interest in it. Alongside this, Midtylland were winning the Danish league for the first time in their history on the back of scoring three goals in every four games from set pieces. Going into the 2015 summer, we're overseeing the club and there's a lot of ignorance. We're not very seasoned and have to pick everything up from scratch, we have no scouting network or anything. This was wild – never do this – but we had to because of the turnover of the club.

"We had to build a whole infrastructure, but it took us months to get a data deal agreed with Opta, so we were scouring in-stat data to find guys that were interesting to scout.

"We had to bring in 11 people because there were so many likely outbounds and others we needed to replace. We also had two centre backs out on loan who we had no information on when they came back. Nobody in the Warbs/McPartland group was keeping any record of them in any written format, and they left no information. Alfie Mawson and Jack O'Connell's agents wanted to know what we were going to do with them, but we had no information on either – which goes to show the chaos."

Chaos was certainly one word for it that close season with changes coming thick and fast. Warburton's replacement would unfortunately not be Jürgen Norbert Klopp, as one bookmaker had given short on it being, but the 43-year-old Dutchman, Marinus Dijkhuizen, who'd led VV

Marinus Dijkhuizen and his assistant Roy Hendriksen were certainly a left-field choice to kick-start the post-Warburton era

Montfoort to successive promotions, in 2009-10 and 2010-11, and took the unheralded SBV Exclesior into the Dutch top flight in 2013 14, before keeping them there the following season. Interestingly, he was credited with introducing a more attacking style of football to get Excelsior promoted, and then, having discovered playing the same way at a higher level would 'kill' his side, adopted a more defensive side of the game to ensure Eridivisie survival.

"They came to me based on statistics," Dijkhuizen would say. Indeed, Excelsior's performances under the Dutchman came out well in Benham's modelling – performing exceptionally well with a tiny budget – and according to their data, it was down to the head coach. He was, said Ankersen, an open-minded coach who had shown he could achieve results by thinking differently. He set his team up differently to most of the bigger and richer Eridivisie clubs, sitting back and patiently waiting for opponents to make a mistake before countering, which Ankersen believed showed that Dijkhuizen was open to innovation.

According to a De Correspondent article from the time, Dijkhuizen impressed with a power point presentation in which he talked about leadership, tactics and giving players clarity regarding his decisions, saying "as a player, I often only heard I was not allowed to play, without further explanation from the trainer". He also spoke of his willingness to learn, regularly bouncing ideas around with coach Berry Koeleman, and it went down especially well that he spoke of learning from other sports, not least from water polo and an Olympic-winning coach in the sport, Robin van Galen.

Dijkhuizen was immediately impressed with his roster of 25 employees - "just imagine, I now have three video analysts" - including a mental well-being coach, a free kick coach and a throw-ins coach. He signed an eight-rule cultural manifesto, saying his favourite line was: "'No idea of anyone can be brushed aside without arguments. I can't just say I'm the trainer, that's how we do it. I like that, that's how I actually worked at Excelsior."

Indeed, no stone was being left unturned as Brentford sought to gain an advantage over bigger rivals with equally bigger pockets. As stated, the club saw set pieces as a major area of inefficiency, and so regular meetings between the directors of football, players, coaches and outside consultants were set up to discuss them. Midtjylland had scored nearly a goal a game from set pieces during the 2014-15 Superliga season, and as well as players capable of delivering them, the club wanted a coaching staff willing to improve that aspect of the game.

Dijkhuizen went on to explain how he fitted into Brentford's new model, whereby randomness and chance were given due consideration, and league tables were not the benchmark for how success was judged. "My job is coaching and tactics, that's what I can do, and if that goes well, the model will show that," he said. "Then we have a good opportunity ratio. For example, if you're eighth, but your odds are fifth, you'll end up higher than eighth in the long run. But not always, they explained to me. A competition only lasts for a relatively short time. I am judged on the result minus chance. Fair enough!" If there was to be a 'long run' of course.

Dijkhuizen would ultimately be judged on the ideas he brought to the club. He was also to be Brentford's first head coach, the man chosen to break away from that aforementioned, traditional, all-powerful role of manager, which Benham confidently felt to be so inefficient and counter-productive... but eyebrows were certainly raised once more when the Dutchman was unveiled.

Saying that, Brentford certainly weren't total trailblazers in adopting such a model as, two years previously, Southampton's Romanian owner, Nicola Cortese, said of manager Mauricio Pochettino: "We came up with some plans that were not traditional in English football, of how we want to structure the club. We wanted a more continental approach in terms of the company structure. In terms of the manager, he has an important role, but basically is just a department head like others." Benham's belief was similar: "There should be no one who is the all-powerful dictator. The idea is simply to involve many, many smart people in the club, to have a lot of debates and interaction, and always look at how we can get better."

Reflecting on the stick he took for introducing such a way of thinking, Benham said: "English football is just dominated by this idea that we have to do what everyone else does... as if it's a law. Because everyone says it's the way to do it, doesn't mean it is the way to do it."

Excelsior's fans were certainly sorry to see Dijkhuizen leave, as they told a Beesotted podcast in the summer of 2015. "He is a trainer who can make broken players better, and who is willing to take star players out," said one. "Inexperience is his only weakness, but he learned from the trainers at Ajax and Feyenoord and really invested in himself. He is really open minded about new things, we're going to really miss him." Another said: "He's a good guy, down to earth, really straightforward, and what you see is what you get. He has good organisation, starting at the back and building from there, everyone knows exactly what they need to do. We're five seasons in the top flight now on pretty much the same budget of €4m for everything at the club, not just players. He completed us and made all the players better."

On paper, it sounded like a decent match, but the footballing world would be watching to see how Brentford's new philosophy would pan out. Benham knew this all too well at the time, and knew the knives would be out as soon as there were any signs of the project faltering. "Obviously, over the next couple of years, we'll find out if we're right or not," he said at the time. "I think there are a lot of people who are going to watch the project – a lot of people will hope we'll succeed, and a lot of people will hope we'll fail. So it'll be pretty interesting."

Unfortunately, signs that it would fail under Marinus started to show fairly quickly as far as the club were concerned – in truth things were probably stacked against Dijkhuizen's Brentford from the start as he had pretty big boots to fill and expectations were super-high – but it wasn't all his fault. During a 4-0 home humbling by League Two Oxford United in the League Cup, Brentford's marquee signing, Danish international centre-back Andreas Bjelland, suffered a season-ending knee injury that was more than likely caused by a calamitous pitch relay during the closed season.

Of the other summer arrivals, only Lasse Vibe and Maxime Colin could be considered successes – Akaki Gogia and Philipp Hoffman flopped spectacularly, and while Konstantin Kerschbaumer would later enjoy a brief purple patch as Scott Hogan's provider-in-chief, it would not be enough to be considered his time at Brentford as a hit.

Equally, Josh McEachran, who'd arrived with a fanfare from Chelsea, was unlucky with injuries, but he flattered to deceive when he did play, and while Yoann Barbet later looked decent in a back three and showed a neat line in defence-breaking cross-field balls, the Frenchman struggled in a back four and when deployed at left-back. Most bizarre of the lot was Ryan Williams, a free transfer from Morecambe, whose only appearance came during that League Cup humiliation. It was later revealed that Williams, who went on to play lower league football in Scotland, Canada,

Brazil and Sweden, had been brought in as a "low risk" signing with "development potential", but had ended up being more of a training ground set-piece expert and seen as a mystery figure by supporters on a par with a certain Javi Venta, who had arrived from Villarreal under a cloud of secrecy in July 2013, then had disappeared without a trace within a month.

At Midtjylland, using a quantitative approach to recruitment had helped them land the likes of Tim Sparv, the previously unheralded Finland international midfielder who Benham's Danish side had plucked from the German second tier, then played a key part in landing their debut Superliga title. Called the "no-stats all-star" by Ankersen, Midtjylland's modelling ignored the fact that his duels won and balls recovered stats were unimpressive, as his positioning and ability to see problems before they unfolded meant he didn't need to tackle and run as much. The defensive midfielder appeared on Midtjylland's radar as the club's model, which ranks all European clubs as if in one big league to allow for easier cross-referencing, identified Sparv's club, Greuther Fürth, as having been good enough to play in the English Premier League the previous season.

The model pretty much led to almost instant success at Midtjylland, but back in TW8, Brentford would have to endure their share of Gogias and Hoffmans before patiently unearthing the likes of Maupay and Benrahma in the years to come. Ankersen later admitted that too many changes were made too quickly in that summer of 2015, but even then, he appreciated that piling in with everything at once would be a mistake, saying: "It's important not to make the shock too sharp, you eat an elephant one bite at a time. We will make mistakes, no model is perfect, but we trust that ours is very good."

As well as that host of new arrivals, using the new methods, there were also key departures over the summer, with important members of Warburton's squad – Jonathan Douglas, Stuart Dallas, Andre Gray and Moses Odubajo – all leaving. Brentford's biggest problem, however, was that Dijkhuizen just didn't seem cut out for the English game. His relaxed approach to training would see fitness levels build up over the course of the season, which is apparently a common approach in the Netherlands, but something alien to English players. Rumours circulated that players pleaded with him to up the intensity levels during training. Alan McCormack concurred: "It was very much the Dutch way of playing, with everything at a slower tempo. Pre-season wasn't particularly hard, they were pretty easy-going. I've got to be honest, we were used to the hard and fast English way with lots of fitness work. It took us a bit to get used to, but by the time the season came around we weren't fit enough for the level we were in, and you could tell by the results in the first six or seven games."

Dijkhuizen's reign lasted just eight games, in fact, five of which ended in defeat. Although unbeaten in his opening two matches, the warning signs were there. It took two injury time strikes to scrape a home draw with Ipswich, and the Bees had to come back from two goals down to win 4-2 at Bristol City. The only respite in a run of defeats – to Burnley, Reading and Middlesbrough – was a decent 1-1 draw away to Uwe Rösler's Leeds United in which Marco Djuricin, one of the players Benham had wanted to sign the previous January, scored a debut goal, the first time the Bees had opened the scoring that season. But after the Bees again came from behind to beat Preston 2-1 at Griffin Park, a 2-1 home defeat to Sheffield Wednesday in the following game proved to be the last straw, and Dijkhuizen, along with his assistant, Roy Hendriksen, was dismissed. His replacement, on a temporary basis at least, would be the Bees' development squad manager Lee Carsley.

McCormack said: "There was a lot of turnover and a lot of new bodies with not much experience of the English game, and it just really didn't take, but it was a learning curve for everyone – for Matthew, the sporting directors, recruitment – everybody. They quickly made the decision that it wasn't working and had to restructure it. Nobody wanted to see Marinus sacked, the players really liked him and he wanted to play football, but he just wasn't suited to the English game, which was a shame.

"We were struggling possession-wise on the pitch and with fitness, with getting close to people. We were a hard-pressing team but weren't able to do what we did best. When Matthew and Ras and Phil look back, they will probably agree that with all those new players and a new manager, there were a lot of changes, and it takes a lot to get used to everybody. The players coming in had to get used to the English game, the English way of life and living in London. All these little aspects were going to take a long time, but it happened too fast, but they realised it quickly and steadied the ship with Lee Carsley."

Sam Saunders added: "It was a case of too many foreign players at once, and a foreign manager who didn't understand Championship football and the stresses and strains that go with it. Training wasn't hard enough, and players were asking for more as we felt it wasn't to the standard we were expecting. But then, the club has always admitted it tries to do things differently, and you won't get it right every time. But what they do is move forward, and if something doesn't work, they try something else. That's what happened with Marinus."

Phil Giles would later admit that part of the problem was bringing in a whole new behind-the-scenes team at the same time as a new management team and players, and that they were based away from hub of the operations at the training ground: "It was always going to be a challenge to make that work effectively at the first time of asking." Of the situation the players found themselves in, he added: "It was always the case that they'd need time to bed in. The mistake we made wasn't so much buying players and not giving them time to bed in, it was so many at the same time – it was unfair to expect them to hit the ground running.

"Coupled with injuries, so they had to play – they had to adapt in the job, so to speak, rather than being given time. Yoann Barbet was given more time, because we had Harlee Dean and James Tarkowski, so he played in development squad games. He had more time to adjust, whereas other players had to come in and do it straight away. We always said it would take time for players to adapt. It takes time and it always will."

Rasmus Ankersen agreed. Speaking a couple of months after Dijkuizen was sacked, he said: "Sometimes it was like throwing darts in the dark because we were not there (at the training ground), we were rebuilding the club from a distance. It was never going to be easy for Marinus. If he had come in now (two months on), he would have had a better chance of being successful. Four months into the season we have a much more precise idea about what's good, what challenges we will face and how to overcome them."

Looking back seven years later, Ankersen speaks of a power vacuum following Warburton's departure, which was precisely the wrong sort of environment for someone of Dijkhuizen's nature to come into. The recruitment was still messy at that stage, with a lot of key players leaving and a lot of unknown quantities coming in, and those players left behind were unsettled. The Dutchman's record in his home country was impressive, but it would have required a different sort of head coach entirely to have picked his way through all the problems the club was facing at that time and still been a success on the pitch.

"We made the wrong choice with Marinus, but it was also very difficult for him to arrive," Ankerson admitted. "Warburton was a strong leader that everyone looked up to – him leaving created a bit of a power vacuum. Everyone tries to grab that power, and if you don't have a strong leader to come in and grab it, then it can easily lead to a lot of confusion, and I think that's what happened.

"If you looked at the ratings he drove at Excelsior, they're quite impressive, but you can easily misread success – you don't know if it's the manager that's driven it, the recruitment – what was the cause-and-effect process there? But he did very well in the interview process, came across well, and we could see some potential in him. What we underestimated a bit is, if you are coach at Excelsior, you have to lead an assistant coach, a group of players and maybe an analyst, whereas we had about 25 staff he had to lead, on top of the players. That's a big ask – and then it's a new culture, a new language, a dressing room with unsettled players – lots of factors. The situation probably needed a much stronger leadership than we originally anticipated.

"At the training camp in Portugal, we had some doubts over what we saw and the leadership. I remember when we decided to replace him, I was pushing it quite hard with the board because I felt like we had to act if this was ever going to work rather than try to go another five or ten games. It wasn't so much the results, but the underlying processes. It was the right decision – when you know something is not going to work, you have to cut your losses. Phil and I had already spoken about the fact this was going to set us 12 months back, which was a shame really.

"That's probably the biggest lesson we learnt, that we were trying to change too much too quickly. If you want to invest wisely you have to invest in a structure that you know works and is stable, rather than putting a lot of money into a structure that is unstable. The structure had to be fixed first, and I think that's where we tried to do too much too quickly. A football club is the ultimate people product – 11 people out on the pitch and your backroom staff – and there were too many relationships. There's a lot of relationships that could go wrong at a football club and disrupt things, and there were too many new relationships that had to be built."

Right man at the wrong time for head coach perhaps, but the recruitment side of things was also going to need more than fine-tuning, the volume needed to be cranked up significantly for the new structure to push on to the next level. Although the summer of 2015 transfer window is widely seen as a disaster by Bees fans, Knutson, having earlier described the chaotic conditions of the early days under a whole new recruitment model, is keen to paint a different picture of some of those signings. Ryan Woods can indeed be placed in the "success" category, but he came in at the very end of the window and didn't feature properly, aside from a few late cameos as a substitute, until Lee Carsley took over.

"On the buying side, we were quite excited by Maxime Colin, but he was our ninth (choice) right-back," said Knutson. "Phil Hoffman, we paid £2m for and he didn't work out. He was a German under-21 international, but I don't think he liked football as much as he should and didn't have the aerial skills you'd hope for being nearly two metres tall. But we had to sign him as we'd gone through 10-15 forwards on our list without getting anything over the line, we knew Andre was going and we didn't have any other forwards. Marinus Dijkhuizen had been playing up front in training, so it was a huge problem.

"Ryan Woods, we bought for £1m and sold for about £6m, and Yoann Barbet was very under-rated and a solid contributor. Lasse Vibe worked out very well for us despite being above our normal age profile. Kerschbaumer we saw as a pressing number ten who didn't get the playing time or respect his skills deserved, but his output when he was on the pitch was outstanding. Gogia went on to contribute in Bundesliga 2, and both were sold for profit. Andreas Bjelland and Josh McEachran we were really excited by, but both had long-term injuries before they played a game for us. There's a lot of good stuff in there and a lot of stuff that was noisy and

Lee Carsley and Paul Williams were another short-lived partnership

messy. The majority of them turned significant profits. I think we made a bunch of mistakes though.

"We had a £2m cap, which was tiny at the time compared to now, and £8,000 a week plus bonuses on salary, which was less than half the division's average so you're dealing with real constraints – trying to find guys who you think are quite good and can spike into big sales, but also guys who can contribute straight away. We were having to do twice the recruitment work as we were looking for Premier League level players we could afford on our budget, and for Championship players at the same time. We had some high-end targets who ended up being successful in Germany. Pascal Gross was our number one midfield target but we couldn't afford him. We had two centre backs we loved, Willi Orban and Dominique Heinz, and one ended up playing in the Champions League."

In amongst all the failed signings of the summer 2015 transfer window, one which went under the radar at first, but proved to be a success later, was Sergi Canos. Although it would take a second spell following a permanent signing for him to become a true Brentford great, Canos initially arrived on a short-term loan from Liverpool on the final day of the window, in a deal which was soon extended until the end of the season. The much-loved Spaniard, who Liverpool had plucked from Barcelona's youth system aged 16, described how quickly the chaos he arrived into under Dijkhuizen turned into relative stability under Carsley.

"It was a strange atmosphere," Canos said of his arrival at the club. "It was strange, but nice, because it was my first time in a first team environment, it wasn't crazy bad. I had Marcus Tebar and Jota with me and that was a huge support, coming at 18 years old to somewhere where everything was new. After a few weeks, Marinus left and it was all very strange. But Lee was the best thing to have happened to Brentford at that time and he was outstanding in everything he did, the way he managed the big players and everything that was going on. We came back to proper training and had everyone on board. They did really well and we started winning games, and when you're winning everything is easier."

Indeed, after losing his first two games, Carsley steadied the ship with four wins in a row, including impressive away victories at Wolves and Charlton, then a first set of derby bragging rights over West London rivals QPR in 50 years. Marco Djuricin, then on loan from Red Bull Salzburg, faded after initially impressing for Brentford, but will always live long in the memory of Bees fans for scoring the only goal of the game against the Shepherds Bush outfit on a noisy Friday night at Griffin Park. Beating Rangers would soon become routine, but doing it for the first time in five decades was something special and the win was celebrated in the famous four-corner pubs that surrounded Griffin Park long into the night. However, even that vibe could not persuade Carsley. Despite being a popular choice both with fans and players from the outset – and the club hoping he would take the job until the end of the season – Carsley made it clear that he did not want the job full time.

The former Republic of Ireland international midfielder had always maintained that he was more interested in youth football development than being a first team club manager, and since departing Brentford in December 2015, he has been good to his word. Aside from a short spell as Birmingham's caretaker manager in 2017, Carsley has built a first class reputation working with Manchester City's U18s, Birmingham's U23s, and England's U20s and U21s.

Ankersen said: "Lee Carsley came in and did a good job, but he was also so hard to manage as he only wanted to do it temporarily, and was telling us after every game he wasn't going to take the next one. We'd originally had an agreement with him that he was going to do the whole season, and then extend to being assistant coach for the next head coach coming in – that's what we agreed and put that in a press release. But the day after his first game, he woke me up at 7am handing in his notice. He even said in the post-match press conference that he didn't want the job. That never really came out fully, but suddenly there was a lot of pressure to find a permanent replacement."

Brentford were once again on the managerial trail, and this time turned to someone a whole lot closer to home and altogether less 'exotic' than their previous appointment.

CHAPTER SEVEN

Before settling for Dean Smith, Brentford also courted Swansea City assistant manager Pep Clotet, who prior to becoming Garry Monk's second in command two years earlier, had enjoyed a long coaching career in Spain, Sweden and Norway with the likes of Espanyol, Malmo, Halmstad, Viking and Malaga B. Clotet had, in fact, looked the favourite at one stage, but turned down the advances to stay at Swansea.

In the event, Clotet left the Swans two months later following Monk's sacking and would go on to assist him at Leeds and Birmingham, as well as having unsuccessful spells as number one with the latter and with Oxford United in English football, then at Brescia and SPAL in Italy. Rasmus Ankerson recalled: "We met both several times and negotiated with both. Pep was a good candidate, but we felt a bit more of a risky one. In a way, he had more of a football mindset and the coaching and tactical skill we were looking for, but Dean was a safer bet for managing the environment. He was very strong emotionally, which is very important in football."

Dean Smith became Brentford's number one candidate before being officially appointed on 30 November 2015 after sitting in the stands to watch a 1-1 draw with Bolton. A week later, he oversaw a 2-0 win over MK Dons in his first game in charge. The former centre back – who as a player had scored against the Bees in a controversial 2-1 defeat at Leyton Orient in in 1998, and a last-minute equaliser for Sheffield Wednesday at Hillsborough in 2004 – had earnt a decent pedigree, first in youth football at Orient, then at Walsall.

In his four years as Walsall manager, Smith carved out a reputation for producing results by playing exciting football on a small budget, as well as developing young players. Initially saving them from relegation to League Two after taking over midway through the 2010-11 season, he also kept them up the following year before flirting with the play-offs in the next two seasons and reaching the Football League Trophy final. Smith had been handed the nickname 'Ginger Mourinho' from Walsall fans – is that a compliment or an insult?

Rico Henry, who came through the ranks under Smith at Walsall, and would ten months later join him at Brentford, gave an insight into Smith's character, saying: "He knows what he wants and is straight to the point. He likes hard work and players that are willing to improve, and he definitely improved me. He wouldn't stop training sessions but would let them carry on, let people work things out for themselves, and I think that helped. He wouldn't be afraid to tell you how it is though."

The players didn't necessarily take to Smith's methods at first, according to Sergi Canos, especially the more senior ones. "In my opinion, it took the big players at that time a bit of time to understand Dean," he said. " I think Dean and Richard (O'Kelly) came in and did really well, the way they approached the team and tried to manage was great, but it took a bit of time for the big players to get on board. What they wanted to do was long-term, and in the long-term it was going to work. But short-term, what they tried was to get everyone working together and for each other, as at the time, I don't think we were a team."

While Brentford had struggled under Dijkhuizen at the start of the 2015-16 season, Smith had led the Saddlers to the top of the table by the end of the opening month, earning himself the League One Manager of the Month award for August. An approach by Rotherham couldn't tempt him away, instead he signed a new 12-month rolling contract to stay at the Bescot Stadium. However, just six weeks later, Smith was named the new number one at Brentford, leaving Walsall fourth in the table.

Walsall fans, many of whom did not take kindly to his departure, warned that it would be feast or famine under Smith, with both long winning streaks and long spells without a victory commonplace. To an extent, they were right. But if ever there was a club that valued the style of the performances over a result by any means possible, and judged their head coach as such, it was Brentford. At this point, it's useful to quote Rico Henry again: "You always go through winning and losing streaks in football, but he always stuck to what he believed, and I think that helped. Sometimes if you change things too quickly it can go belly-up, so it helped us in the long run." What the Bees were looking for at that moment, after a very difficult calendar year, was some stability while they refocused – and stability was something the club felt Smith would be able to provide in bucketloads.

At the time, Ankersen said: "We were really impressed with Dean's leadership skills. He is a man of integrity and a good people-person, which takes emotional intelligence. The style of play he introduced at

Walsall really impressed us as well. We were never going to pick someone who is parking the bus." His co-director of football, Phil Giles, added: "Dean is a hugely likeable man with strong leadership skills and the ability to immediately manage and command the respect of the players and support staff. He wants to play football in a bright and attractive way – the way that Brentford fans have become accustomed to over recent seasons. Dean has a track record of developing young players and can help our relatively young squad to reach their full potential."

Looking back, Ankersen said: "At the same time, we were having to do a review of the academy, which we eventually decided to close, so there were huge decisions we were having to make – and not having that stability around the first team was a big risk. So I think the biggest job Dean did with us was providing that stability, which allowed myself and Phil to work on other areas of the club to try to get them right. He was a good, strong, clear leader, a good person. One of Dean's biggest strengths is that he is emotionally stable. He never goes too high when you win and never goes too low when you lose. That was the emotional stability we needed, and I think we felt that's what he could provide – someone to come in and just calm the environment down. We still had these stories flying around the dressing room that it was not the coaches picking the team, that it was us, which was rubbish, but the perception easily becomes reality.

"For example, we also decided to replace the strength and conditioning coach, as one of the issues was, under Mark Warburton, they were reporting to the head of medical, and that's a problem because the head of medical is always of a mindset of trying to avoid injuries. And how do you avoid injuries? By not training. We wanted to separate the strength and conditioning from the medical, so it became two equal departments. I remember our new set piece coach coming in, and, after two weeks, saying; "Ras, is this Brentford Hospital?" There was so much emphasis on not training, and that was an issue, so Phil and I decided to bring in a head of performance instead, which became Chris Haslam. Phil and I executed that decision but made it look like Dean did it – we wanted to build his authority in the dressing room. We needed the perception that he was controlled by us to change."

Smith, himself, said at the time: "It's nice to be at the football club where people want to get better – that's half the battle. We want to play at an intensity and play what we feel is the right way. We won't be changing too much, we'll drip feed a few of our ideas, but they're good footballers who know how to play. We want to play a certain way and the lads buy into that. It only needs minor alterations, just little bits and bobs really."

Things started well enough for Smith in West London. Following that initial win over MK Dons, his Bees side went to West London rivals

Dean Smith, Richard O'Kelly and Simon Royce form the new coaching team

Fulham and twice took the lead before twice being pegged back to draw 2-2, and having a 'winner' from Jota incorrectly ruled out for offside. Then followed two wins and a draw over the festive period, before the Bees began 2016 with four straight defeats, including an FA Cup exit at home to his former club Walsall, in which Smith was heckled mercilessly by the visiting fans who had even made flags to taunt their former manager and had caused trouble before and after the match around the streets of Brentford. Were there signs of feast or famine already? Smith wasn't helped by the controversy surrounding James Tarkowski's refusal to play against Burnley, who were 'openly' looking to tempt him to Lancashire ahead of a televised TV match between the two sides, or the transfer window departures of Jota, Toumani Diagouraga and, ultimately, Tarkowski too.

Smith said at the time: "The football club has come a long way in such a short space of time and time catches up a little bit. I think the players have been in the Championship for a long time now, or at least some of them, and some of them are just starting to know it. They know what it is about, there are some physical challenges you have to meet." With a nod to the difficulties under Dijkhuizen, he added: "Speaking with Lee Carsley before I came here, the intensity in training is very important, and if you can get that, then it matches what you're going to do on a Saturday, and you get that week in week out."

More problems were on the horizon, however, as February and March brought a run of seven defeats in eight games. These included a 4-0 thrashing at Sheffield Wednesday; losses to relegation-threatened Charlton and Rotherham; and a 3-0 drubbing at local rivals QPR, in which Brentford failed to field a recognised striker. Attacking midfielder Alan Judge played as an isolated frontman while strikers Lasse Vibe and Marco Djuricin sat on the bench with Brentford fans left wondering whether the club had made the right choice in their new head coach after all. The mood following the final whistle in the away end at Loftus Road was as dark as at any stage since the club had been promoted to the Championship.

A defiant Smith pointed to his somewhat inexperienced side, saying: "Some of them are still learning the game. It's a tough league to be learning the game in – there's some big strong teams in there and you have to learn fast, and unfortunately some of ours are finding it tough at times. It's a tough period that the lads and myself need to come through, but I went into Walsall when they were nine points adrift and stayed up. We had to build a structure and a team there. The team that got to the play-offs here last year has been very much stripped down – it's a young squad and the Championship is a tough league."

In the event, famine indeed turned to feast, and a magnificent 3-0 win at Nottingham Forest signalled a turnaround which saw the Bees end the season with seven wins from nine games – putting four goals past MK Dons and five past Huddersfield on the road – but most pleasingly, seeing off local rivals Fulham 3-0 at Griffin Park. A ninth-place finish was impressive after such a difficult season, and Smith reflected: "I've never feared for my job, Matthew said in March that he was happy with how things were going. We needed a change in fortunes and got that against Nottingham Forest."

Smith went on to say the unsuccessful training methods under Dijkhuizen actually helped Brentford in the final stages of the campaign, claiming: "Towards the end of the season, they should be getting fitter. Historically, teams start to flag, but it gives us the opportunity to outrun opposition teams." Keeper David Button added that Smith should take his fair share of the praise, saying: "It's been a great turnaround, and all credit to the gaffer for the big part he's played in that, we've come through the difficult phase as a team." It should, of course, be noted that the improvment in results came after the return from long term injury of Scott Hogan who scored seven in seven, aided and abetted by a resurgent Kershbaumer.

Phil Giles, at the time, pointed to an 'unprecedented' level of difficulties Brentford had been forced to navigate that season, more so than a single club could expect to face in such a short space of time. "You might expect one season with a lot of injuries, or a season when one player goes on strike, or a season where the pitch isn't what it should be, or one where you have three managers," he said. "For all of that to happen in one season is unprecedented. There's been so much happening this season – it can't happen every season, surely? Hopefully next season we'll be able to start to build a stable squad as opposed to the transition this season.

"But I wouldn't say we were concerned. There were never any concerns in terms of the quality of people at the club – all Ras and I could do was encourage and support them and say it'll all be good, and it was. We've got stability with the coaching staff and we've got a foundation to build on, compared to last summer."

Ankersen added at the time: "There's been a lot of ups and downs. It's a long-term project, and I think we've made some important decisions to take the club forward. We're still a club in transition, we're working on creating a foundation we can build on for the future, and we've taken important steps in the last 12 months. Some will like it, some will not like it. Some decisions will be successful, some will fail. We feel we've learned a lot and we'll learn for next season."

Looking back, Ankerson said there was never the remotest threat to Smith's future during that difficult run, and highlighted the fact that Brentford had also slashed the wage budget that season from the one which had led to a Championship play-off place the season before. He said: "You have to evaluate the process first and foremost, because randomness can play a part, which is sometimes difficult for people to understand. Football thrives on narratives, but sometimes there is no narrative, just random events. It was not a massive surprise we were not performing well given where we were in the rebuild phase, but it would have been crazy to throw out Dean."

"You also have to understand, that season we cut the salary budget a lot too. In the season Brentford finished fifth, they had the eighth/ninth highest salary budget, so we cut the budget almost in half. There was also a £5m pay out in bonuses when we reached the play-offs, but the club doesn't make any money from that – it makes money from being promoted – so we changed the bonus scheme to being promotion-based. We had to take one or two steps back to be able to take three steps forwards. We knew it would take some years to get to where we wanted to be, and we had to build it up bit by bit on a much lower budget."

Brentford's recruitment that summer took something of a 180 degree turn. In 2015, the data had led them to undervalued players with potential development and resale value from Europe's less celebrated leagues, and whereas the likes of Maxime Colin, Lasse Vibe and Yoann Barbet would eventually prove to be hits, the same could not be said of Philipp Hofmann, Akaki Gogia, Konstantin Kerschbaumer and Marco

Djuricin – although the Austrian striker's winner against QPR in October 2015, under the Griffin Park lights, will always be fondly remembered by the Bees' faithful.

Now, they would turn to young talent from the English lower leagues, with keeper Dan Bentley arriving from Southend United, centre back John Egan from Gillingham and left-back Rico Henry and Romaine Sawyers from Smith's former club, Walsall. However, Brentford would also return to the lower leagues of Europe with spectacular success in the years to come, with the likes of Said Benrahma, Neal Maupay and Henrik Dalsgaard, but for now, the system needed adjustment. It wasn't broken, but required a bit of fine tuning having moved so far, so soon.

"Our overseas talent hadn't really worked out, so we thought going for English players in the lower divisions would put us in a position where we wouldn't have to take an enormous amount of risk, and we thought there was a lot of value in the lower divisions," said Ankersen, looking back to that phase. "The difference between a top League One side and a bottom Premier League side is much less than people think. There were some good players with their contracts coming to an end like Romaine Sawyers, Dan Bentley and John Egan, so that is what we ended up doing.

Ankerson's comments regarding the 'similarity in quality' between some top League One sides, and struggling Premier League clubs, is based upon the 'Justice League' concept – a table that uses a set of football statistics which pits the position of each team in the English leagues, and leagues around the world, based on the quality of chances created (xG) as opposed to actual goals scored – it is a totally fluid table, not separated by traditional divisional markers. When viewed that way, and many pundits and critics have been quick to poo-poo the system, a team's key metrics (and therefore the players within that team) can be better equated and, just as importantly, forecast. There are many different versions of these justice tables based on slightly different information, but they broadly measure the same outcomes – with Brentford having their own bespoke system run by Mathew Benham's Smartodds analysts. For the last few pre-seasons, Brentford's pre-season friendlies have been arranged against European clubs who are positioned close to the Bees in that justice league. It is clearly no coincidence and helps to form an accurate barometer.

Ankerson continues: "We'd had an analytics team sitting in Smartodds making a lot of recommendations, so it became much more data-led – signing players like Hoffman and Kerschbaumer – we made a mistake in perhaps going too far down that route. There were too many chefs in the kitchen as well. Eventually, we decided to basically fire the whole analytics team at SmartOdds and build a new recruitment structure, and that's when we brought Andy Scott back in. It wasn't working, there was a mixture of personalities that didn't blend well together. Matthew had really wanted to have a go that season – he wanted to spend a lot of money buying players, but we put them into an environment that was unstable and dysfunctional. In hindsight, we should have fixed that first before making that investment."

As alluded to by Ankersen, one of the key figures in Brentford's new recruitment structure was Andy Scott. Yes, the same Andy Scott last seen leaving Griffin Park under a cloud four years earlier after his sacking as manager. Scott had tried his hand at management elsewhere – at both Rotherham and Aldershot – but failed to replicate the success of his early seasons with Brentford. After leaving Aldershot in 2015, Scott decided his future lay in recruitment rather than management and began scouting, back under Benham's wing, at Smartodds. Having come back into the fold, the summer of 2016 saw Scott officially take on the role of chief scout, where he set about forming a new recruitment department, of which he was later named head.

Looking back to that time, and reflecting on if he had decided management wasn't for him by that stage, Scott said: "After Aldershot, 100 per cent. It was chaos there, with no investment and it felt like I was babysitting players who weren't good enough. My whole reason for being a manager was to find players, work with them and mould them into a side I wanted. I didn't feel like I had the energy for it, and I had a legal dispute with Aldershot lasting 18 months, which took a lot out of me. It drained a lot of my love for the game and made me think about what I wanted to do next. So I went to see Matthew and said I'm not going to be a manager any more, have you got anything for me? You know how good I am at recruitment and finding players. Fortunately, we had kept in touch and had a good relationship.

"He wanted me to come and work for SmartOdds, in the data side of it, and that developed very quickly into chief scout part time, then head of recruitment full time, nine months later. I was very grateful to Matthew, and I still am to this day, because I was lost. I've always seen Brentford as a club which helps one another out and sticks together, it's still a family club mentality at heart. Once you're an ex-manager you can't go back into coaching because people think you're after their job, but all I knew was football."

Only four years may have passed since Scott's exit as Bees' manager, but the club had already taken a huge stride forward. Back in 2011, Benham had been in the background for a while, gradually increasing his financial commitment while also starting to influence the future direction of the club's culture. He was still a year away from taking it over completely at that stage, but by the time Scott returned in 2015, things were changing at a rapid pace. What was missing from the big data picture, however, was the human touch – judging a players' character as well as their stats – and that was where Scott came in. Indeed, trying to ensure Brentford signings were high quality both on the pitch and in their personal lives would later be defined by Thomas Frank as having a 'no dickhead' policy.

"In my last season at Brentford as manager, we were more involved with Matthew, and myself and Terry Bullivant went to SmartOdds a number of times," he said. "It was incredible, the information they had. We were fascinated by the people behind the scenes and how they did things. We were starting to use more of that, and we knew data would be more of an aspect of what we were doing. How strong a part of recruitment it would be was still up in the air. The year I came back, they were going through a spell where they didn't know if they were going to go fully with the data in terms of scouting or commit to the two. Ted Knutson was there and had a strong influence and built a magnificent data hub. It was about how we used it to recruit players, and that was a key point for me. I had some really good discussions and arguments with Ted, and Rob Rowan was brilliant as he really understood it all.

"It was like going back to school, it was intense and mind-blowing at times. But it was about translating that into what you saw on the pitch and in trying to bring a player in. I was fortunate that I went in at the right time for that and we helped balance it off. From then on, I was really keen on data, but using it in the right way and balancing it with the human element of bringing a player in and the environment they come into. It's all got to be considered when you sign a player. Numbers and figures don't matter at times when you're looking at a player having the right character and personality. All those things combine.

"My experience of being a player, coach and manager, along with a fantastic amount of data, worked really well at that time. My first remit really was to tailor a reporting tool for the watchers, showing what they need to look at rather than just the data – looking at the physical, technical and tactical aspect, different character and personality traits, the key factors. That developed into being one of those people watching players live, or on video, to see if they were the players the data was telling us they would be, then discussing why they weren't that player, critiquing it. We had a young lad from Morecambe come in (Ryan Williams, as mentioned previously) – the data said he was unbelievable, but he was very small and couldn't get around the pitch. Technically, very good, but never going to have an impact at the top end of League One. If it was like American Football, where you could just come on for set plays, he would have been brilliant. That was the sort of human element I tried to help with really.

"As chief scout, I was just watching games really. The watchers at Smartodds were brilliant and had so much knowledge about players, but we didn't have a scouting team, so I brought a few in. As head of recruitment, I was more involved with the agents, helping Phil with negotiations, a natural progression really. Matthew offered me the scouting job in the first place as he recognised it was something I could do. I'm not sure if he had identified it as something he needed or just wanted to see what I could bring. But Matthew, as everyone knows, is incredibly intelligent and forward thinking and wouldn't have just given me the job out the kindness of his heart."

Preceding Scott's appointment as chief scout by a few months was Ted Knutson's departure – leaving in March 2016 to co-found football data and analytics company StatsBomb. Although Knutson has often been accused of overstating the impact of some of the players signed in that transformative summer of 2015 – there were indeed some successes among the failures – the main factor was that Brentford learnt from it and adapted. It was certainly a more settled squad and playing environment under Smith, even if results and performances fluctuated. Off the pitch, Scott's return saw recruitment evolving towards the future transfer market successes Brentford would become renowned for.

"Ted did a good job for us – when I look back at some of the players he recommended at the time and where they ended up, he was spot on with a lot of things," said Ankersen. "But sometimes what the analytics guys forget is strategy. Picking the right players is one thing, but you have to implement all the ideas, because it was not just about the analytics and recruitment, it was also about trying to find more efficient team strategies.

"But a football club is a people business, and if you don't have emotional intelligence when you go in and try to implement things it's going to backfire massively on you. Sometimes the analytics guys would say 'why don't you just go and do it?' But we have to get people to buy into it and feel it's their idea sometimes, and there was maybe a lack of understanding in that department. But I didn't expect that from them, I just think we were trying to do too much at the same time and really stripping it down to a clean operation, which was another reason we got rid of the academy. We wanted to have something simple to get right and build it from there."

As Ankersen rightly mentions, another big change in the summer of 2016 was the controversial decision to scrap Brentford's academy in favour of a B team model aimed at introducing a new pathway – with closer ties to the first team – for players aged between 17-21. Brentford would no longer recruit or develop players below that age bracket. Ankersen and Giles had reviewed the whole system after becoming frustrated, not only at inefficiencies within it, but also in the fact that the Elite Player Performance Plan allowed top flight clubs to poach the club's best young talents 'for peanuts' after Brentford had spent time and money developing them. Ian Carlos Poveda, who went to Manchester City, and Josh Bohui, who was snapped up by Manchester United, were two prime examples. Both were clearly very promising young players and were in the England U17 set up, but were lost for a tiny sum of compensation (thought to be £30,000 each) before they could even turn professional with the Bees.

The EPPP had been introduced by the Premier League in 2011 with the intention of improving the quality of home-grown players produced by England's elite clubs, replacing the former academy system, and introducing the Professional Development League over the old Youth League system. The new set-up had been greeted with scepticism further down the Football League, with Gillingham chairman Paul Scally making the same accusation Brentford would in years to come. He said: "They can take our kids without paying what we regard as fair compensation. The Premier League can come into our youth systems and take which players they like and we get compensation through a ridiculous structure that has been developed by the Premier League. To me, it feels very much like the Premier League forcing the Football League into submission. There were very strong threats that if the League didn't agree to Premier League plans, they would hold back the funding that is very much the lifeblood for a number of Football League clubs."

Brentford were far from being the first to scrap their academy – Wycombe, Yeovil and Hereford had already done so after citing the cost of implementing the EPPP – but the Bees were the biggest club to have done so. Others later followed, including Bolton and Salford City, while in December 2020, then Championship rivals Birmingham City announced it would be replacing its development squad with a B team and its academy with a C team.

The statement Brentford Football Club released had echoes of similar press releases made by the club around that time – talking of "finding ways to do things differently to our rivals in order to progress", and due to not being able to compete financially with their competitors, not shying away "from taking the kind of decision that can give us a competitive edge". Indeed, it was a controversial decision at the time and provoked some uproar – mainly from those working in the academy or with children in it. In the main, supporters accepted that the return on investment just didn't make business sense for what the club were getting from the academy – and that the millions it cost to run could be better used elsewhere. Indeed, Ankersen said at the time that "development of young players must make sense from a business perspective", and in a system where Premier League clubs could pinch the best young players before they can graduate through at the academy, "the challenge of developing value through that system is difficult".

Looking back at the decision, Ankersen provides some further perspective. He said: "The academy was a pretty big investment for Matthew, which wasn't getting any return in investment. First of all, we didn't have a pathway to the first team, which was about culture. It's a misalignment between the manager and the rest of the club. Managers are in place for an average of 14-16 months, yet traditionally, they make all the important decisions. But if you're only there for 14-16 months, how long are you going to think ahead? You think about how you're going to win on Saturday, and that's it. So you're not going to give a young player a chance who may fail, so we didn't have that culture.

"The other thing was that the way the system worked, a player was free when he finished his scholarship – out of the traps. You spend all that money developing players and 95 per cent are never going to be good enough. But the 5 per cent who are, you want to properly capitalise on them, as they have to pay for everyone else. But if someone comes in, like Man City did with Ian Poveda and pays the player, family or agent much more than us, and we lose them for a ridiculous amount of compensation, then the business model simply doesn't make sense. That was the reason for going to a B team model. It's not for all clubs, but for us, at that time, it was definitely the right decision to invest in a different way."

Rob Rowan also played an integral part in Brentford's decision to close its academy and successfully implement a B team model. Rowan, who had started his career as a scout for Celtic, had been with Brentford since late 2014 and was appointed as the head of football operations in the summer of 2015, before a promotion to technical director in 2018. He explained the new set by saying: "A lot of football clubs have a hierarchy of first team and academy. I disagree with that and believe that, like in business, to maximise the potential in your assets you need to give them the best resources. We sign players on two or three-year contracts in that elite age group, from 17 to 21, where there aren't so many variables or influential factors. We're looking at players who have fallen out of the system from Chelsea, Arsenal, Tottenham, Manchester United, Man City, because it's inevitable they will make a few mistakes, that's the difficulty of recruitment – it's very hard to predict development. If you want to be a successful business or football club, you need to build it your own way, after considering what is sustainable, worthwhile and achievable within your environment."

The first few months of the 2016-17 season saw an inconsistent Brentford struggle to string a sequence together, despite a few decent results, as the new signings bedded in. With club record signing Andreas Bjelland still sidelined, the Bees looked to be lacking a natural leader, although John Egan and Harlee Dean had started to build a good understanding at the back. Egan proved to be equally useful at the other end of the pitch at first too, bagging a brace in a 2-0 win over Ipswich in Brentford's opening home game, before netting a dramatic late equaliser at Aston Villa a month later. Scott Hogan, scorer of seven goals in four games at the tail end of the previous season, didn't quite pick up where he'd left off but was still a danger, as he showed with a hat-trick in a 5-0 hammering of Preston in September – having also bagged both in a 2-0 win over Brighton and scored the only of the game at home to Nottingham Forest. Behind him, however, a midfield featuring the likes of Josh McEachran, Konstantin Kerschbaumer, Lewis McLeod, Nico Yennaris and Romaine Sawyers, while lacking nothing in skill, was certainly missing something in terms of steel.

Sawyers is an interesting case. Still one of the most skilful players to have pulled on a Brentford shirt, it took a long time after his arrival from Walsall in the summer of 2016 for him to be truly appreciated. Seen by certain supporters as lacking in desire for a seeming reluctance to put his foot in, Sawyers was booed off the pitch by some of his own fans after being subbed during a 2-0 home defeat to Barnsley in October of that year. It was a fourth game without a win for the Bees that month, having ended the previous one with an impressive 4-1 hammering of Reading, so the disappointment in the stands was understandable, although perhaps wrongly focused on a single player. Sawyers responded in the best way possible in the following game – scoring a spectacular goal at Loftus Road to seal a 2-0 win for the Bees at the home of West London rivals QPR. As time went on, it became more evident what Sawyers brought to the side, and as the quality of players around him improved, he was able to display his full, and at times breathtaking, range of passing skills – even adding a little bite to his game too.

Alan McCormack was probably viewed by many as the antithesis of Sawyers – a midfield general who would go in where it hurt and snarl at the opposition – but he could not speak more highly of his fellow midfielder. "One of the best signings we made was Romaine Sawyers – one of the most intelligent footballers I have played with," McCormack said. "Not just in terms of technical skill, but his understanding, reading and organisation of a game. He could figure out the opposition within seven or eight minutes of the game, and how to stop them.

"Romaine was very good at decision-making, and that was down to the way he was coached at Walsall. He'd worked with Dean previously, so he knew how Dean worked, learning how to read the game, understanding tactics, solving problems as a player and a team. That was a massive thing for Dean and he was very good at delivering it. Some got it straight away, but it took me and a few others a little bit longer – we eventually did get it."

Romaine Sawyers and Lasse Vibe were both technically gifted players in a Brentford side that struggled with consistency under Smith

In fact, for McCormack, Smith's approach of encouraging players to think for themselves in training rather than constantly 'coaching' them took some getting used to, but paid dividends for the club in the long run. He said: "It probably took us a little bit longer to get used to Dean and his way of coaching. It was very much questions and answers and problem solving. Training sessions would always have a problem – you might have an eight versus eight or you might have a nine versus seven – and the seven had to work out how to beat the nine. It took a bit longer to get used to that, especially the home-grown players, but it was all about you making those decisions on the pitch.

"The manager can't make these decisions on the pitch, so why should he be in training? That brought massive changes into the club in terms of the culture and style of play. We just seemed to grow from that, as when the penny dropped, we slowly kicked on as a team and started attracting Championship players. You could sense the club was growing and going places and was going to achieve something, but was just missing one or two pieces of the jigsaw. But you need to pay a lot for those final pieces."

As the winter of 2016 started to bite, however, that proverbial jigsaw remained spread across the table and only partially put together, with the missing pieces still stuck out of sight, under the sofa. Four straight defeats through November and early December, culminating in an embarrassing 5-0 drubbing at Norwich, had some supporters questioning Smith's position again – perhaps not how he expected to be celebrating a year in the job.

Looking back on his first year in charge, Smith said: "It's been a learning curve, we've been through a lot in a short space of time. I think there has been progress, and the feel around the place is better than when I arrived. We've got a better squad of players, a hungrier squad of players and a younger squad of players. I think it's an environment and culture that works well, and a place where people want to come and get better, and if they do, we'll progress as a club or they'll progress to a higher league.

"When I came in, there'd been a lot of changes at the club. The manager who had brought them into the league had gone, a new manager had gone, and then Lee Carsley. There'd been a lot of change, and they needed stability. A few people had seen too much change and wondered if it'd be the stable environment they wanted, but I think we've been able to give it more of a stable environment."

There was a lot of truth in what Smith was saying, but that didn't make the humiliation at Carrow Road any easier to swallow. There was even another dressing room inquest, similar to the one at Stevenage three years earlier, which had kick-started Uwe Rösler's reign and set Brentford on a course for the Championship. The turnaround wasn't quite so dramatic this time, but a run of two wins, two draws and a defeat in December – including a goalless draw in the return match against the Canaries – stopped the rot. It's interesting to look back, however, and see what was being said in the aftermath of that Norwich defeat.

"It wasn't a crisis meeting by any means – it was a discussion with the players of what I thought about them and what they need to do better and where they need to get to," said Smith.

"It was an honest, open and frank discussion. Nothing was left behind. The players know where I'm at and what I feel we need to do, and that wasn't acceptable."

Keeper Dan Bentley said: "If there's stuff that people aren't saying on a daily basis, then there needs to come a time where it has to be said. It was probably overdue after some of the recent results. It's not a matter of people falling out. It's a matter of people sharing their opinion." Utility man Josh Clarke added: "It was honest and heated. It was just a discussion of what's going on and what we're doing wrong at the moment."

Striker Scott Hogan spoke up for Smith and insisted the manager still had the backing of his players, adding: "To say we're not playing for the manager is incredible. It's incredible because it's incredibly stupid. For anyone to question the manager, or what we're doing for the manager, is stupid. A lot of home truths were said, a few people voiced their opinion, and I said my opinion.

Hogan continued: "There was a lack of quality, experience, and knowing what to do. We were lacking in every area, and it's had an effect. He (Smith) said it wasn't good enough and not what he's taught us. It's not what he sets up to do, it's entirely on us what's happened. He sets us up in a way that he thinks he's going to win the game and we didn't do it. We have a lot of respect for the gaffer. I have full admiration of his ability to turn up on Monday as if nothing has happened – that's one of his best skills. We let him down and we let the club down, and it's on us to turn it around. We're far from worried – we're having a bad run and it'll end soon."

Chief executive Mark Devlin added his weight to the support for Smith, saying: "I don't want to go around saying dreaded vote of support. As far as we're concerned, it's business as usual. I've every faith in the players, squad and manager that they'll put it right." Harlee Dean added: "I think it was similar to Stevenage. It was in the same manner, and the same things were said. You need to have them now and again to clear the air. It's like having a row with the missus. It was the right time to do it."

Once again, Benham showed that patience and belief in the process are among his main virtues – he stuck with his man. The Brentford owner did, however, make one significant change. In the week following the defeat at Norwich, a new face arrived at Griffin Park. With Flemming Pedersen's departure as B team head coach a few months earlier, Brentford's backroom team was a man short. So in walks, stage left, Thomas Frank, another Dane, and one with the brief of assisting the first team coaches. It is fair to say that little was known about the former Brondby head coach at the time, or importantly how Dean Smith and his assistant Richard O'Kelly would react to the appointment, but all that would be revealed and Frank's impact at the club would become the stuff of legend.

Greville Waterman, a Brentford historian and author of 'We're Just A Bus Stop In Hounslow', which chronicles the Bees first season in the top flight, feels there was another key appointment around this time, obseving, "Brentford were also pathfinders in continually looking for small gains and advantages off the pitch as evidenced by the use of specialist coaches in often ignored areas such as sleep and set pieces."

Waterman goes on to say, "A key hiring at this time was that of renowned sports psychologist Michael Caulfield, who had previously worked with Gareth Southgate at Middlesbrough. He had a baptism of fire as his first morning was on the Monday after the 5-0 thrashing at Norwich but he quickly gained the trust of the players and remains a key influence on the squad. His trademark is taking players for quiet walks around the Jersey Road perimeter generally accompanied by his beloved dogs, firstly Shankly and now Paisley, listening, reflecting back or even remaining silent as necessary, always available to offer sage advice on a plethora of on and off the field issues. Caulfield has been quick to praise the quality of the players at the club: "Take Ollie Watkins, for example, you could not meet a finer individual. If you go anywhere in life, you will not meet a better young man. If you come to Brentford now, there are members of this squad who are among the finest young men I've ever met in my life. Ethan Pinnock, Josh Dasilva and Christian Norgaard are just three examples. They are some of the kindest, sharpest high-achieving and decent people you could wish to meet." High praise indeed."

Off the pitch, Brentford unveiled a significant redesign of the club badge in November 2016, and although fans were unsure of the simplified, circular rebrand, or some of the marketing speak that accompanied its launch, looking back, the new badge can be seen as another successful landmark – even an essential part of the club's elevation. It can be argued that the badge on the players' shirts, and the replicas that generate so much turnover in the club shop, is largely irrelevant and, in Brentford's case, it had changed so often down the years that few fans were wedded to any particular version. But, for one supporter in particular, Tom Lonnen, despite actually liking the new badge, there were far bigger concerns surrounding the redesign as his comment on the Beesotted website explains; "It's a vast improvement on what we had before. Simplified yet bold. I much prefer the circle to the crest too. My only real issue is that last Thursday I had the Bees from the current crest tattooed on my left bicep... I've Tweeted the club to ask if they'll pay for my laser surgery!"

CHAPTER EIGHT

A few years later, he would become one of the most well known and most talked about head coaches in English football. But in December 2016, when he arrived in TW8 to assist Dean Smith alongside Richard O'Kelly, little was known about Thomas Frank.

After a short amateur playing career in his native Denmark, Frank began his career off the pitch as a youth coach with Danish sides Frederiksværk BK, Hvidovre IF, Boldklubben and Lyngby, while studying for a Bachelor of Sport degree at the Department of Sport in Copenhagen. He was then snapped up by the Danish FA, and was appointed manager of the Denmark U16 and U17 national teams in 2008.

Working with the likes of Viktor Fischer, Kenneth Zohre and future Bees icon Christian Eriksen, he led the U17s to the semi-finals of the 2011 European Championships and their first-ever U17 World Cup, before moving on for a year in charge of the U19s. He also served briefly as temporary manager for the U18s and U20s, and was assistant manager for the U18, U17 and U16 teams, as well as the women's U17s. Pretty much every up and coming player who came through the Danish international youth ranks for a five year period would have worked with Frank at some stage, which is a massively impressive list of talent in anyone's book.

Moving back to club football in the summer of 2013, Frank landed his first senior role when he took over as manager at Danish Superliga side Brondby, achieving fourth and third-place finishes in 2014 and 2015 respectively – the latter being their joint-best finish in a decade. Brondby qualified for the Europa League both times, but failed to make it out of the qualification stages. He left in March 2016 after an apparent fall-out with chairman Jan Bech Andersen, who had allegedly criticised Frank under an assumed name on an online fans' forum.

Frank then took nine months out of football, during which time Brentford were still coming to terms with life under a new management team. Serendipity, eh? As we have discovered in previous chapters, after a decent initial first month or so under Smith, the Bees had endured a run of ten defeats in 13, which would have seen some head coaches sent packing. The club's patience was rewarded with a strong finish to the season, with seven wins from the last nine. After a mixed start to the following campaign, that patience was tested once more with a run of six defeats from eight, culminating in that humiliation at Norwich. But as Ankersen points out, looking back at the decision to hire Frank to help rather than throw the baby out with the bathwater, it was typical of Benham.

"Matthew is very dispassionate, which is a very strong skill to have in football as an owner," he said. "I always felt one of our biggest advantages was that we would always have very open and calm conversations about things. It's very difficult not to let emotion come into it, but because he was calm, we could be calm and project the right message to the head coach – and that makes for a very stable environment. At that time, we clearly had some issues with performances and how to structure the team. It wasn't that we thought 'oh he'll be fine', but we are always critical of the underlying process and underlying performance, rather than the outcome.

"We had some tough discussions about things that had to improve, and that was also the reason we brought in Thomas. We felt that to execute the vision we had, we needed someone who would raise the level in training and add more tactical detail to our style. We agreed this was the type of profile we wanted to add to the coaching staff, and we interviewed various people. It was a risky operation, because we were not performing well or getting the results we wanted. Thomas hadn't been a head coach, apart from at Brondby, therefore you can see the narrative around how the appointment could be interpreted. So, what we did was extend Dean's and Richard's contracts at the same time, to make it clear we weren't replacing them, but adding to them. That was a strong signal, but in a paranoid football world, it was a risky operation.

"Flemming had a really tactical mind – style of play and things like that. The way he slightly failed is that you need to put the relationship first and then tell people what they need to do differently. If you do it the other way round, it's likely to backfire. When Thomas came in, I said make sure you build the relationship with Dean and Richard, and then you can go in with the tactical instructions and drive the change. His social skills are very good, and he actually lived with Dean and Richard for the first few months, so that's one of the reasons why he was more successful than Flemming (Pedersen) in that respect."

Dean Smith are Richard O'Kelly are joined by new boy Thomas Frank

Smith admitted the plan all along had been to bring in an additional member of the coaching team, as it had been what Pedersen was doing before taking on U21s and B team duties. Calling Thomas Frank "a great fit for the role" who would add to the skill set of the staff already in place, the Bees' head coach praised Frank's development of young players and described his tactical knowledge as "excellent". Smith went on to say: "He's a really good bloke. He's been living with me and Richard (O'Kelly) for the last couple of nights, so you can imagine the salt and pepper pots moving around the table quite a lot. I spoke about a different skill set – well he's been coaching at a different level in a different league, so if we can swap ideas and get the best out of it that way, we certainly will."

Frank's arrival coincided with a brief upturn in results as the Bees took three points off both Burton Albion and Bristol City before being brought back down to earth with a last-gasp defeat at Elland Road to Garry Monk's Leeds United – a place where the Dane's name would be taken in vain in a few years' time when Frank upset the home fans with some pre-match comments as Brentford and Leeds vied for promotion. A mixed festive season saw stalemates with Cardiff and Norwich – just four weeks after the Canaries put five past them – before 2017 started with a pleasing win at a Birmingham City side struggling under newly-appointed manager Gianfranco Zola. The Blues, who were about to embark on a game of managerial merry-go-round having 'infamously' sacked Gary Rowett and his backroom staff while sitting seventh in the Championship, were certainly not on the same page as Benham when it came to showing belief in the club manager. BirminghamLive football editor, Mat Kendrick, summed up the contrasting mindset at St. Andrews when he reported: "Blues have lurched from one crisis to another since triggering a shitstorm of their own making by trying to solve a problem that didn't need solving."

With the next transfer window now open, Smith looked back on the previous January, hoping for a somewhat quieter month than he'd had 12 months before, when Toumani Diagouraga left, James Tarkowski went on strike before leaving, and Alan Judge was linked constantly with a big money move away. "We're more pragmatic about it, our planning will be better this year," he said. "I came in at the start of December last year, so it was hard to plan for January. A number of things made it more of a window than it should have been. We had all the rumours about Judgey, and we had Toums and Tarkowski going on in the background. But the planning which went into the close season and into this window means we should be better prepared."

The club certainly added to its firepower during that month, bringing in Florian Jozefzoon from PSV Eindhoven – a former Dutch U19 and U21 international whose career had been stalled by anterior cruciate ligament problems – and Sergi Canos, who had previously enjoyed a successful loan spell from Liverpool but was this time signing permanently after enduring a frustrating few months with Norwich. Jozefzoon went on to make some useful contributions in a Bees shirt, as well as turning a tidy profit when he was later sold to Derby County, while Canos wrote his name in Brentford folklore as not only was he a central part of the team which won promotion to the Premier League, but he scored the Bees' first goal back in the top flight.

Good business on the incoming front then, but if Smith was hoping for a quieter month in terms of outgoings, he was to be sorely disappointed. Scott Hogan's run of seven goals in four games at the tail end of the previous season, having returned from a nightmare (almost) two-year spell out injured, had made other clubs sit up and take notice. A further 14 goals going into the New Year during 2016/17 meant the striker was hot property as the January transfer window opened, with West Ham and Aston Villa both battling it out for his signature.

What really frustrated the club in the run up to Hogan's eventual deadline day move to Villa was the conduct of those advising him. After scoring his last goal for the Bees in that win at Birmingham, Hogan was benched for the next league game, a home defeat to Newcastle, and was left out of the squad altogether for the following week's defeat at Wigan, as speculation surrounding his future intensified.

Phil Giles seemed uncharacteristically angry. Letting off steam to GetWestLondon, he said: "Agents are making the calls telling him you're going to get a big move, it's your big chance. Of course, he's going to get distracted by that, no criticism of him whatsoever. The whole system is completely crazy. He was meant to be involved today (against Wigan) and then he gets a phone call, it changes our plans completely. The whole thing is ridiculous. We're looking ahead to next week – what are we going to do then? We want to pick our best players. What can you do about it? A more constructive process to look at the system and the January transfer window. It (not having a window) was a far better system. You never saw players dropping out, and it reduced the power of agents and outside influences that affected the market."

The inflated market in January is indeed something Brentford have always held strong views about under Benham, with the club eager to avoid doing too much business at a time when clubs are panicking, or throwing money around in desperation, which they feel leads to artificially excessive prices. Smith said at the time: "The January window, for me, has no value. People are paying crazy money. We're not a club like Aston Villa or Sheffield Wednesday, so we have to be more astute in the market. The value is the important thing."

Ironically, 'big spending' Sheffield Wednesday would later be deducted 12 points (and handed a transfer embargo) by an independent disciplinary panel for breaking spending rules, linked to the financial reporting of its stadium sale. Although the deduction was later reduced to six points, and transfer sanctions lifted, the Owls were relegated to League One at the end of the 2021/21 season, as Brentford were promoted to the Premier League. Villa, meanwhile, gambled everything on the 2018-19 season, which ended in promotion via the play-offs following a 2-1 win over Derby in the final. It has since been billed as the most expensive football match ever, as Villa would have been in serious financial trouble had they lost, while since losing, Derby have lurched from one financial crisis to another.

Of the Hogan situation, Smith added: "As soon as a team like West Ham makes a bid, that player's head is turned – we had it with Toumani Diagouraga (Leeds) and James Tarkowski (Burnley) last season. Scott hasn't been disruptive, but he's not trained to the level he was at, and that's understandable. It's the effect representatives and agents have on players – but that shouldn't affect the teams you pick."

In an interesting turn of events on January 31, 2017, Hogan finalised his deadline day move to Aston Villa and was a flummoxed observer as his new side were handed a 3-0 thumping by his old club in a memorable match played at Griffin Park the same evening. If Bees fans had any fears about what life would be like without their top scorer, the boys in red and white stripes answered them in style, with Lasse Vibe scoring twice (Nico Yennaris got the other) to demonstrate he was more than ready to step into Hogan's shoes. Although Hogan had stolen the headlines, it should be noted that Vibe had also finished the previous season in hot form, with seven goals in as many games. He then netted just two in the first half of the 2016/17 season, but Hogan's departure was the making of the Dane as he finished the campaign with an impressive 16 goal haul.

Even before he had fired down Villa in spectacular style, Vibe had returned to the goal trail after ten games without netting with a strike in a 5-2 FA Cup win over Eastleigh, which brought an interesting clash of styles to Griffin Park as it saw the return of Martin Allen, who was now managing the non-leaguers. Allen had been a popular figure throughout his two year tenure as Brentford manager, during which he had saved them from almost certain relegation to League Two, then guided his side to the League One play-offs twice in successive seasons.

It was never a dull moment under Allen, whose touchline antics and whipping up of the crowd had become legendary. It was an interesting contrast with Dean Smith, who had been perhaps unfairly criticised for his somewhat quieter and more reserved touchline demeanour. But what some supporters mistook for a lack of passion was, in fact, the calm and measured approach the club had been looking for when appointing him – aligning with the owner's desire to take emotion out of the decision-making process.

In the run up to the game, and reflecting on Allen's madcap antics, which included taking a dip in the Solent to make a point to his players, Smith said: "I know Martin well, he's a good guy and very passionate. He did very well here and will get the reception he deserves for what he did, but the only swimming I'll be doing is in my bath!

"My character is my character, it's each to their own, but even Martin has said he is calming down a hell of a lot. That was his character, and I am who I am. I think you have to go and be a head coach or manager as your character fits. Did we need a steady hand? The club certainly thought so, and that's why I was appointed. I feel the ship has been steadied and is moving in the right direction. We're an ambitious club and want to go places, but we also know you need to walk before you can run."

As we recalled, the January transfer window of 2017 saw Brentford improve their attacking options with the arrivals of Canos and Jozefzoon, but they were also boosted by the return of Jota after a year on loan at former club Eibar. The Spaniard had been one of the undoubted stars of Brentford's first season in the Championship, not least for his famous last-minute winner against rivals Fulham, as well as spectacular strikes against Cardiff and Blackburn.

The loss of Jota to an ankle ligament injury on the opening day of the 2015/16 season – inflicted by former Bee Jonathan Douglas no less – only added to the woes Brentford were experiencing at the time, and his return via a few substitute appearances over the 2015 festive period was only a precursor to him rejoining Eibar on loan, having asked to return to Spain for personal reasons. Most Bees fans had given up hope of seeing the mercurial Spaniard again, but in January 2017, he was recalled early from his 18-month loan deal.

Although never quite the same player the second time around, Jota did show glimpses of his old self on more than one occasion. Having made his return in that FA Cup win over Eastleigh, scoring his first goal back in Bees colours in a 2-1 defeat to Wigan, Jota truly announced his return with a spectacular run of form in February, with five goals in as many games, including his first Bees hat-trick – two of them in injury time – to earn a 4-2 win over Rotherham.

But for all their new attacking swagger, Brentford still looked vulnerable at the back – a frailty that would plague them for a few years to come. This frailty was perfectly encapsulated in a crazy game at Burton Albion in mid-March, where a shocking first half defensive display saw the Bees trail 3-1 at half time. After the break, Brentford were a different side and looked like scoring every time they attacked. Canos and Jota bagged a brace apiece as the Bees turned it around to win 5-3, but attacking brilliance hindered by defensive lapses would remain a hallmark of Smith's Brentford teams.

Smith said after the game: "It is the moral of our story at the moment. We seem to be making things really hard for ourselves, either at the end or in the first half, like Saturday. Midfielder Ryan Woods added: "I think there was anger given the way we were controlling the football, although we weren't hurting them. We were superb in the second half, that's how good we can be and we need to do it more often."

While Jota's return, ultimately, failed to live up to his first spell in Bees colours, Canos was certainly enjoying his return to Griffin Park a lot more. Having been snapped up for £2.5m by Championship rivals Norwich in the summer of 2016, Canos never really got a look in at Carrow Road, making just three league appearances in the first half of the season (starting just one of them), plus six cup appearances – half of them for Norwich's U23s side in the Football League Trophy. It was no surprise, therefore, that he jumped at the chance for another opportunity at Brentford, where he found, much like in his first spell, a team which could play some brilliant stuff at times, but was lacking in consistency. It was, however, a much improved atmosphere he returned to, especially compared to the one he was leaving behind in Norfolk.

"When I came back, it was a nice family atmosphere, with Dean and Richard trying to put smiles on people's faces, and that's what Brentford has now," he said. "Everyone you see around the club now has a smile on their face, and fair play to Dean and Richard as they started it. That's what Brentford tried to do through them. Norwich was really different, it was like two teams – players and staff. Some staff were really connected with the team, but it wasn't a good atmosphere, not because of the players, but what was going around the staff.

"Brentford at that time was a team that depended on results – when we won two, three, four games in a row everything was fantastic and we were one of the best teams in the league, but then if you lose two or three in a row then everything got really low. You were either in the sky or on the floor, and that's what has changed over the years. We are consistent now, but we were not at the time and we couldn't change that. Right now, what we have changed is that we are still brilliant going forwards, but defensively we have improved a lot, and that was one of the main things we had to get right."

Around the same time, Thomas Frank gave an insight into his first few months with the Bees in an interview with GetWestLondon. Although still 'just an assistant', Frank sounded like the perfect fit for Brentford and appeared genuinely intrigued by this new project. In fact, it's hard not to see his mindset aligning perfectly with that of the owner. "I knew Brentford because of Matthew and Mitjylland, and I'd heard about Smartodds and how they use the numbers, and I like it a lot," he said. "I'm a football man, but I like the statistical approach because there is something we can win. All clubs are looking for the extra per cent to get ahead of your opponents, and that could be one of them.

"I think it's a brilliant club in many aspects. They have a big history and think differently. They respect their history and try to be a bit more innovative. They try and do different things to stay in the Championship and develop the club. We're aiming for bigger dreams, and I like that a lot. I would like to manage again, but now I'm here and I really enjoy it. The main thing for me was to go out to a good club and a good project, and we're going into a bright future. I think we have a good side, and I think we have potential to progress and develop into a better team. On our day, we play some of the best football in the Championship, and that's one of our big advantages. It's one of the youngest sides in the league which shows the potential. We need to create that culture and do better every single day."

Following that roller-coaster of a game at Burton, Brentford saw out the season in decent form, with five wins and just two defeats from the last nine games. These included an impressive 4-0 hammering of Derby County and another local bragging rights win over QPR, in which Jota was in irresistible form. There was a pleasing moment off the pitch too when Kevin O'Connor was awarded the Sir Tom Finney Award, which recognises players who have had an outstanding career and made a valuable contribution to the English Football League. Having chalked up more than 500 appearances for the Bees, O'Connor had hung up his boots in 2015, immediately beginning a coaching role with the Brentford development squad under Lee Carsley. O'Connor would later become Thomas Frank's assistant first team head coach but at that time was B team head coach, having taken over the role from Flemming Pedersen.

On receiving the award, O'Connor looked back at the journey he had been on as a player with the Bees – starting in 1999 as a young forward, before filling almost every position on the pitch. He recognised that relegation to League Two in 2007 – painful as it was at the time – was the start of Brentford's journey. "The worst was relegation from League One," he said. "We had a tough season, all of us, including myself. Things weren't great off the pitch, but you have to have those periods to enjoy the good times. We used that to help get the club back up where it belongs. It feels like two different clubs. There were some dark days and tough moments, but the pleasing thing is to see where the club is going now. It's building slowly and surely, and I hope the club can continue on an upward curve for a long time."

Always one who preferred to be in the background and away from the limelight, O'Connor was nevertheless someone whose influence at the club would never go unappreciated – someone who had been there and seen it all on Brentford's journey and understood the club inside and out. Having previously praised the effect Lee Carsley had had on the side before he took over, Smith had this to say of O'Connor: "Every club has its own characteristics – and as someone who has been there through an awful lot, there is nobody better to pick the brains of to find out the characteristics – he's been very helpful to myself and Richard. His professionalism is second to none and he's developing into a very good coach."

One of O'Connor's former team-mates, who was becoming a regular face around the club once more, was Marcus Gayle. As a player, Gayle had enjoyed two spells with the Bees – winning promotion to Division One (second tier) under Phil Holder in 1991/92 before leaving for Wimbledon two years later, then returning in 2005/06 and narrowly failing to win a second promotion with the club, under Martin Allen. After retiring in 2008, Gayle had briefly tried his hand at management, with AFC Wimbledon reserves and at Staines Town, then after being inducted into the Brentford Hall of Fame in 2015, returned as a matchday commentator before being appointed club ambassador in 2020.

"The club has got a great potential," Gayle said, as the 2016/17 drew to a close. "It's still punching above its weight. I hope the club can stay at that level, get the new stadium underway, and then you take it from there. We saw (this season) a young sides' inconsistency, but I saw the team mature and make cute fouls or over-elaborate on contact. They're starting to influence the referee, and that takes time. Hopefully you can retain your best players and they can see Brentford is a team that, if everyone is consistent, they can be in the play-offs or even better. Once the new stadium is there, we'll be able to retain the top players we have. If the team is consistent, they can stay in the top ten from the start of the season and maybe cause an upset."

Around that same time, as the 2016/17 season reached its conclusion, Smith spoke of his relationship with the club owner, and how the sharing of ideas helped take the club forwards. He said: "I speak to Matthew once or twice a week, we speak openly and frankly about the club, our ideas and strategies going forward. He's interested in your ideas, and in what you're thinking, but he'll also give you his ideas for you to ponder as well. I think when you see the sums of money and the amount of time he's been here, he's an absolute godsend for the club. I've been very fortunate, and I can honestly say that at all three clubs I've worked at in my career, I've been able to build. You don't get immediate success unless you've got the money that Roman Abramovich has got. You've got to have time to build, and it's really rewarding at the moment."

For all the progress that had seemingly been made in stabilising the club and creating a calmer and more confident environment, one in which players could develop, the Bees had finished a place lower (10th), with a point less, than where they had at the end of the unsettled and uncertain 2015/16 season. In many ways, it had been a transitional season, and as Benham and his team have made clear on many occasions, league tables are far from being the only determining indicator of how well a squad is progressing. "The table is notoriously inaccurate because there's just way more randomness than people understand," is a common theme and is core to the Brentford mindset. "Usually, the way the fans, and especially the media, look at it, randomness is quite an unsatisfactory explanation, so they like to look for stories and a narrative. But very often randomness is the main explanation." Despite failing to make progress in terms of the league table, the club were indeed pleased enough with the direction Smith was taking the club.

Smith himself said at the time: "I think we have progressed as a team and as a club from the moment I came in, to where we are now, whether we pass the points tally or not. Our football is better, the style of play is getting there, the players are looking better and competing at a higher level in this league. Although we know there's been real progress made, people from the outside don't see the work that goes on, they see league standings and points. To progress for a lot of people, they'll need to see the tally overhauled, but we know there's been progress at the club.

"In terms of recruitment, we need to add quality as well as being more consistent. I think we will become more consistent as the players have now played a lot of football in this league, understand what it takes and what's involved in committing to this league. Looking at the players, their attitudes have changed, and I see a lot of players who want to get better. It is a young squad but they're getting better."

Although the summer of 2019 will go down as the transfer window which proved the true catalyst for Brentford's genuine Premier League readiness, the recruitment also took a huge step forward in the summer of 2017. Out went some of the misfits from that initial summer under the new model – players like Akaki Gogia, Philipp Hoffman and Konstantin Kerschbaumer who had already been sent out on loan deals – and in came replacements that proved integral to Brentford kicking on in the coming years.

Denmark international defender Henrik Dalsgaard arrived from Belgian side Zulte Waregem and would go on to become a true leader and a vital player in Brentford achieving top flight status. The Dane also became the first player to appear at the World Cup while contracted to Brentford, and became the Bees' most capped player while at the club. Sadly, after doing so much to help them get promoted, Dalsgaard left the club at the end of the 2020/21 season and wouldn't get to play in the Premier League for the Bees – instead returning home to link up with Brentford's sister club, FC Midtjylland.

Other pivotal arrivals included forwards Neal Maupay and Ollie Watkins – from St Etienne and Exeter City respectively – both with £1.8m price tags. When Brighton and Aston Villa subsequently paid a reported £16.5m and £33m for them, not only were both held up as shining examples of Brenford's ability to find and polish rough diamonds before turning them into huge transfer profit successes, it was their financial windfalls that helped underpin the club's next passage of evolution.

In truth, Maupay's first season proved to be something of a struggle, and despite a fairly decent return of 13 goals, he suffered long spells of nine to ten games without finding the net, and was roundly mocked after an astonishing miss against Cardiff City during a 2-0 defeat to Neil Warnock's Bluebirds.

But it was clear there was a talent there and the faith that was kept in him by Brentford was duly rewarded the following year when the young Frenchman took the Championship by storm by smashing in 28 goals.

Watkins also had a relatively slow start before developing into a useful winger with the ability to cut inside and contribute spectacular goals – the future England man hitting double figures in both of his first two seasons with the club. But it was the 2019/20 campaign which was the making of Ollie, when rather than replace Maupay, a twist of transfer market fate meant the club decided to push Watkins into a central striking role at the heart of what would become the legendary BMW front three. Watkins responded with 26 goals as the Bees just missed out on promotion. However, back in the summer of 2017, for the moment at least, the duo were simply just more new parts for a jigsaw puzzle that was tentatively starting to come together nicely.

Smith said of the recruitment that summer, and the culture being created at the club: "I feel our recruitment policy is as good as anyone's as we don't have to spend the amount other clubs do – we feel we can develop players into Premier League players. If it was all about money, we may as well pack it in now. It's about team spirit, quality and a group willing to fight for each other. I feel we're on an upward curve, and we want to continue that. We're thankful to an owner who has put in money out of his own pocket to make us the force we are, but we have to be a sustainable club. There's optimism throughout the football club – through the board, players and staff – because of the quality of the squad we've got."

On the training pitch, whereas two years previously the players had been urging Marinus Dijkhuizen to increase the intensity, they were now noticing that it had stepped up to a whole new level, as Smith introduced a new counter-pressing style. "It has probably been the toughest pre-season since I came here to be honest," said Harlee Dean. "We've had a lot of sessions with not a lot of days off, and this new counter-pressing system means that we have to be as fit as possible. The new lads haven't really had a chance to get away from us because we have been in every day, so you are going to get to know each other when you are with them 24/7. Everyone seems like the same sort of character and personality, and everyone seems driven to achieve the same thing."

Dean's determination to push on and improve what had been achieved in the two years since promotion was echoed by new keeper Luke Daniels and by the gaffer himself. Smith said: "It's a tough, intense period of training where you see a lot of that team spirit and driving people. The chat we had at the start was about getting better, pushing the limits and seeing what we can get from that." Daniels added: "We want to better what we've done so far in establishing ourselves as a top half team. You have to look at the setup. It's down to the players to go out and use what's been given to us to get off to a good start."

Unfortunately, despite those loftier ambitions, it was anything but a good start, as the Bees kicked off the new season by going eight straight league games without a win. The poor run included a 4-3 home defeat to Nottingham Forest in what was (then) Forest manager Mark Warburton's first return to Griffin Park since leaving under the Warbsgate cloud. It is fair to say that the former Bees boss received a mixed reception – booed by some supporters and cheered by others. Indeed, it should also be noted

Watkins scores his first goal for the Bees during a draw with Bristol City

there was still a sizable section of Brentford fans – not to mention those in the football world looking in from the outside – still to be convinced that the club had done the right thing in parting ways with their promotion winning manager. Although the club were happy with the steady progress being made on the pitch under Smith, and the development of the system off it, runs like this one did not help reassure those who believed the club had made a big mistake in letting Warbs head off to pastures new.

The only respite in the latest winless run was a 4-1 hammering of West London rivals QPR in the League Cup at the end of August. QPR boss Ian Holloway, a former Bees player back in the Eighties, had 'enjoyed' a mixed relationship with Brentford fans over the years – but he stuck up for his former club and its head coach both before and after the game. He said; "A lot of our fans won't like that, but Brentford have probably earned respect over the last few years, with getting into the play-offs and nearly getting there again. It's a credit to the club behind the scenes, and it's a credit to the new management, who have picked up a team that was already doing well and carried it on.

"It's a wonderful thing for Dean Smith to have achieved, and he deserves it because he was in the lower leagues for a while, and he's a very accomplished manager. He is a very good man as well and he deserves a lot of credit. The way they go about their business has been impressive. They have created lots of good players, which other people have bought off them, but Brentford have continued to play very good football."

Holloway could certainly see the bigger picture, but despite those plaudits, Brentford couldn't buy a win in the league and were propping up the Championship table going into September. After three defeats out of four at the start of the campaign, the Bees had stabilised slightly thanks to draws against two of the division's big guns, Aston Villa and Wolves, but the first three weeks of September went by with still no ticks in the win column.

Smith was not only frustrated, but also confused at his side's failure to get off the mark for the season, when performances hadn't actually been that bad: "It's hard to put your finger on it," he said. "We've probably not scored enough when we've been on top, and defensively, we've been really good. We've conceded less chances this season and would be in the top five in least chances against us. We feel we've got better defensively as a team, and the quality of our play has been the same – we just haven't taken our chances. I'm sure it will improve, the players are very confident in what we do."

The players agreed, with keeper Dan Bentley saying the performances hadn't got the results they deserved, but in keeping with the club's philosophy, there was no panicking yet. "If we knew what was wrong, we'd be here with maximum points – a little bit of luck is probably needed," said the agile shot-stopper. "If you look at the scale of the performances across the season so far, I think they have been good, but the results have not matched the performances. It's not so much stuff going wrong, more that things aren't going as right as they could. We're not at panic stations by any stretch though. There's a belief in how we play and a belief in each other as players. There's a belief in the manager and staff – he believes in us, and we believe in him. The results have not been what we wanted but he appreciates the way we've been playing – it's not like it's been horrific and we've been slaughtered every week. The performances have been good, we just need that rub of the green."

Defender John Egan was singing from the same hymn sheet: "I don't feel we've got the results we've deserved. The performances have been there, and we believe the tide will turn. As a group, we fully believe in ourselves and each other. We've got a philosophy and the belief is there, and the appetite is there to go and get the results we want."

It is important to note that, from the quotes provided by key players, as well as from Dean Smith, there was a calmness and demonstrable reassurance taken from the knowledge that the man at the very top didn't have his finger hovering over a panic button. Myriad other club owners would been thumbing through their book of managerial contacts, or asking the CEO to start preparing a severance package, at this point. Brentford's players knew they had to continue doing the right things, week in week out, to create more of those big chances in front of goal, then the tide would turn.

However, the mood on the Griffin Park terraces was not helped by what was seen by supporters as a fire-sale-like transfer deadline day at the end of August – where instead of strengthening in a bid to end the winless run – Brentford instead sold Jota, Harlee Dean and Maxime Colin to Championship rivals Birmingham City. Brentford fans watched the transfer updates on Sky almost in disbelief as, one by one, Birmingham City returned for another, then another, then another of our players throughout the afternoon and into the evening. Predictably, the online message boards and social media became a toxic place to visit.

Brentford fanzine, Beesotted, wrote the following on deadline day: "Bees fans have grown used to our best players moving on to chase Premier League football, or at least Premier League sized pay packets that BFC cannot compete with, and nobody can dispute that every time it happens, despite sticking on a philosophical hat, it feels like a royal kick in the nads. Surely, if we really are serious about getting to the top flight, we'll have to buck the trend and start holding on to the very best of the best.

"But take one look at the transfer market and the prices being quoted, and the wages being touted, then you start to realise how easy that is to say, but how difficult it is to achieve. Once a players' head is turned, there's precious little a club our size can do, especially with a contract in its final year. I personally consider Jota to be the finest player I've ever seen pull on a Brentford shirt, and I will be devastated to see him go, especially when all the player's assurances of 'staying unless a top flight club came in' for him seem to be well meaning tosh.

"Harlee (personally again) I'm less bothered about – both parties needed clarity and closure… he was a very good player for Brentford and all fans thank him for helping us on the journey to the Championship, but it was time for him to move on in all probability and I hope he's happy with the deal to St. Andrews. Maxime Colin's departure, unless Brentford intend to bring in new faces, which looks unlikely, even with recent developments, will set alarm bells off – okay, we have made numerous signings during the summer transfer window – but many will be asking how the poor start to the season can be rectified with (possibly) three first team regulars heading for the door. Who knows how the rest of today will pan out?"

Bees fan Jon Restall agreed that it needed a certain amount of vision to have taken the sale of the trio to St. Andrews without raising at least one eyebrow: "Friends who supported other championship clubs laughed and shook their heads at our decisions to sell our best players. But that was the plan and we stuck to it. Sell at peak and reinvest. It was something, as a fan, that it was hard to get your head around. But I consoled myself with the knowledge that we'd got to watch real talents, rather than journeyman chancers on their way back down the leagues, which had been the old tradition. Don't get me wrong, I loved some of them too... There's always a place in my heart for Paul Evans, Chris Hargreaves and Lloyd Owusu... but if I'm honest I enjoyed the flirtation with Jota even more. Jay Tabb can stay in my heart though, he was special."

It didn't help, of course, that Brentford had held a (admittedly rather one sided) grudge against Birmingham City since the 1994/95 season, when both teams were vying for the one automatic promotion spot in Division Two (third tier), and it was the Brummies who clinched it after manager Barry Fry was handed an almost limitless cheque book and seemingly made a new signing each week. The same club went on to derail two of Brentford's most promising subsequent promotion bids by signing first Nicky Forster (1996-97) and then DJ Campbell (2005-06) in January transfer window swoops. Now, Birmingham were waving their cheque book about again, and Brentford fans weren't happy about them signing three players who had been key figures in Brentford's rise over the past few seasons.

What wasn't clear at the time, however, was the fact that the directors of football viewed all three as players who had reached their maximum potential with Brentford and who were replaceable within the squad. Indeed, we have it on very, very good authority that the directors of football couldn't quite believe their luck when Harry Redknapp kept coming back with his cheque book at the ready for another player they were more than willing to let go. And although all three, initially, did well for Birmingham, only Colin sustained that form over the long term, with Jota and Dean both leaving the Midlands under a cloud and with the latter having numerous less than savoury spats with Blues fans on Twitter.

Dean would earn the wrath of Bees fans too, for some unfortunate comments made in an interview with his new club that insinuated Birmingham City were a 'ten times bigger' club than Brentford. On leaving, he also revealed his frustrations at what he saw as Brentford not being able, at that stage, to take the next step and fulfil his ambitions of playing top flight football. "It's not 100 per cent about the financial side of it – it's about the dreams and aspirations of me getting to the Premier League and being at a club where I feel I'll have more of a chance of doing it," he said. "I don't think there are many better teams football-wise in the league, but I've been there a few years and it's been the same each season. We've played well, but we're never really there or thereabouts, and I found that quite frustrating. I want to be challenging up at the top and have something to play for at the end of the season." However, he added: "With Dean Smith in charge, I can only see the club going from strength to strength. He's one of the nicest men and managers there is. He's been great with me and gave me that extra confidence that I probably lacked for a little while and he got the best out of me."

Despite being voted Birmingham's Player of the Year and Players' Player of the Year for the 2020/21 season, to date, in Harlee's five years at Birmingham City, the Blues have failed to finish the season in the top half of the Championship on a single occasion and, in 2019, were hit with a nine-point points deduction by the EFL for breaching Financial Fair Play spending rules. Birmingham had posted a loss of nearly £49m, £10m over the FFP ceiling for a three year period.

Smith also defended the deadline day dealings, saying as far as he was concerned, Brentford had completed the business they wanted earlier in the window, and that the potential loss of players had already been factored in. "I was in bed by half nine that night," the head coach said. "We've done a lot of our deals early and are pleased to have got in Henrik Dalsgaard, Neal Maupay, Luke Daniels, Ollie Watkins and Kamo Mokotjo. It was done knowing we may lose players as well, but for players to leave, clubs needed to match the valuation. We are very fortunate we've got an owner who has the foresight to put the strategy in place and the financial clout to bring players in knowing there was a chance players would go. What's surprised people is that three players have gone to the same club in the same league, but we're happy with the squad we've assembled."

Nevertheless, they would remain hollow words to the fans until the team started picking up some wins, and the longer the winless run went on, the more concern there was on the terraces – if not in the boardroom. Once again, where many clubs would have chosen to twist, Brentford opted to stick, and Smith found himself thankful for being at one where patience was a virtue and success was not (again) measured on the league table position alone.

"There's pressure in the game – you'll hear about it if you haven't won two games – we haven't won in seven in the league, but that doesn't bother me," he said in a heart-felt interview with GetWestLondon as the search for a three point haul went on. "I'll be consistent in what I do and make sure we're doing it in the right way, and I've got a great belief that we are doing things the right way. It only needs a couple of finishes to go in, a slice of luck, but you can't rely on that. All you can do is control what you control, and we keep telling the players that. It's the way the football club is run. I've always felt comfortable here – and the supporters, the players, the staff and the board – there's a connection. I don't think you get it at many other clubs. I have great faith in what we're doing and how we play the game. You look at the players and they're not short of confidence. As long as they're getting the same message from us and go out and perform as they are, things will change.

"I speak to Matthew after every game and the conversations are normal. We concentrate on the performances, and the performances have been good. We haven't had the results with them, but we can't control the results. We can control our performances, but there are too many random things that can be involved in results. The Crystal Palace manager lost his job after four games – what they've learnt after four games I don't know – that's a very harsh dismissal in my opinion. If I sensed that there was a dip in confidence then I'd deal with it, but looking at the performances we're getting, I don't see that.

"There's disappointment in the dressing room and frustration, but you do a debrief and show them the little details we can get right to prevent the goals we conceded. You can't get emotionally high or low in this game, I think. It's a random game at times and, I feel the players need to see from the head coach that we're doing the right things. If I come in today and say we need to change everything, then what we've been doing before is a waste of time and a waste of energy. You lose people then. They see people believing in what we're doing, and they believe in that as well. There's a great togetherness at the football club, but because we haven't won the games, from the outside, more pressure gets exerted from that."

Smith was certainly singing from the same page as those in the boardroom – taking emotions out of decisions; not getting too high when things were going well and not getting too low when things weren't going to plan. Brentford's patience was rewarded when, on 23 September, goals from Yoann Barbet, Nico Yennaris and Ollie Watkins saw the Bees finally pick up their first three points of the season with a 3-0 win at Bolton.

Wanderers' boss Phil Parkinson was another who could see beyond the results at what Brentford were building, calling the Bees an "intelligent side" who can "hurt you in possession of the ball" after the game, before praising the club's recruitment by adding "they have brought in players who do well in that system". He concluded: "The quality of the goals they produced was excellent, and if they are going in like that every week, you can't see them being around the bottom end of the table for long."

If the first seven weeks of the season had been another famine under Smith, the feast was about to return as the Bees embarked on a run of nine games without defeat, including five wins, then lost just two more games in the remainder of the calendar year. One of those wins was a pleasing – considering what had happened two months earlier – 2-0 win at Birmingham City, in which Jota and Maxime Colin both started against their former side, while Harlee Dean cut an unhappy figure on the bench for Brum.

Before the game at St. Andrews, Dean made an attempt to explain the 'ten times better' comments he had made on his arrival at Birmingham, which Bees fans had taken as an unwarranted and inaccurate insult to their club. Whether or not it's what he intended to say the first time around, Dean looked to douse the flames by saluting the progress the club had made since it first came into the Championship. "Football is a matter of opinions, and I think the Brentford squad is ten times better (the number ten obviously being one of his favourite digits) than the squad that finished fifth (in 2015)," he said. "When we finished fifth, we had no experience of the Championship. We were a team that came up from League One and we excelled and made the play-offs. We weren't adjusted to the Championship or experienced in it.

"The squad has now been there for four years. Brentford have three, four seasons of Championship football; they've got experience and internationals. We were an unknown quantity when we finished fifth, and now people know what Brentford are about. The current squad deals with it by doing what they do, day in day out, and by playing football. That's why the squad Brentford have now is stronger than the one that finished fifth. It's evident for anyone playing Brentford what they're good at and how good they are at it. They like to control the ball and control the game. I'll be honest and say all of them can hurt you."

Dean would, for some years, become a figure of fun with Brentford fans – not least when "Cheer Up Harlee Dean!", sung to the tune of The Monkees 'Daydream Believer', rang around Griffin Park as the Bees breezed the return match 5-0 a few months later. But he has also been generous in his praise for his former club since and should perhaps not be judged too harshly. Dean and the rest of the 'Birmingham Three' have moved on, and so have Brentford. But, as the Bees were soon to find out, despite discovering how to win again, things still weren't quite right on the pitch, and they were going to have to go back to the drawing board once more.

CHAPTER NINE

Regardless of the plaudits Brentford had been receiving from opposition supporters and other Championship managers, from the likes of Phil Parkinson and Ian Holloway, for their footballing style and recruitment culture, there was still something not quite right with both. It is fair to say that although the Bees were blessed with an ability to play delightfully going forwards, there remained a soft underbelly to Smith's Brentford side and the defensive frailties, which plagued the team under his leadership, seemed set to stay.

These failings were never more evident than during a 2-2 draw at Loftus Road against rivals QPR in the final match of November. Brentford were cruising at 2-0 up, enjoying a lead which really should have been more, but the hosts smelt blood and piled pressure on the visitors' goal going into stoppage time. Matt Smith pulled one back for the Rs in the third minute of added time before the inevitable happened when Brentford crumbled and handed Luke Freeman an equaliser five minutes into time added on.

Vociferous chants from the away end, that had been telling Holloway he'd be "getting sacked in the morning", were suddenly caught in their throats as the handful of home fans still left in the stadium went wild. The most frustrating aspect for Bees supporters was that the implosion wasn't all that surprising. Holloway, who had again been complimentary about the club before the game, afterwards accused Brentford's players of being disrespectful and thinking the game was won, but Smith, while defending his players, also laid some of the blame at the door of the officials.

"Tonight was down to the officials in my opinion," he said after the game. "People talk about losing from winning positions, but you need the officials to be having a good game as well. I felt more disappointed when I lost 3-0 here two years ago. It's part and parcel of the game – we should have walked away with three points tonight but we didn't. We have to take it on the chin. He (Holloway) doesn't know my players – he can make as many accusations as he wants, but I'm not going to get involved with his players."

That match would prove to be something of a watershed moment for the team, with obvious efforts made to avoid being perceived as a soft touch – although it would still take a few more years before the defensive and leadership issues were properly addressed. For striker Lasse Vibe, however, the anger amongst the travelling supporters was matched by the mood of the players back in the dressing room. There may not have been a full inquest as seen at Stevenage in 2014, or Norwich in 2016, but harsh words were certainly exchanged.

"It's such an angry and devastated dressing room," the Dane said post-match. "We've won some tight games, but losing points is what we're worried about. Everyone is getting involved and everyone wants their say, and that's better than everyone being quiet. We're not making it easy for ourselves and we're not seeing games out. We're going to have to look at that. But this is the first season where I've seen consistency in what we do in a positive way."

For Brentford supporter Harry Carney, writing a fans' column on GetWestLondon, the problem went back as far as August, when Brentford had conceded an equaliser in the eighth minute of injury time in a 2-2 home draw with Bristol City – another game in which Brentford's dominant performance should have seen them out of sight way before they chucked it away in the last throes.

"This Brentford side is both extremely talented and supported by a strong team of backroom staff, which makes it all the more confusing that we can't shut out these games," Carney wrote. "The decision making has been atrocious. After conceding the first goal on Monday, we rushed to restart the game and gave the ball away almost immediately. We seem to have no real leaders in the team. No one was able to step up and pull the team together after the first goal, we just collapsed straight away once more. Nico Yennaris and Dan Bentley are both loud, but don't have the armband to go with the voice and John Egan is too busy organising a haphazard defence to pull the squad together most of the time."

Smith later reflected that he had indeed been trying to rectify the problem for some months in the run up to that QPR game, adding: "We were reviewing it after the Bristol City game to be honest. We were looking at ways to make sure it didn't happen again. We know what we're good at and we have to maintain that when we're leading. It is the responsibility of the whole squad and the whole of the coaching staff. The disappointing thing is we were so comfortable at 2-0 and didn't take all the points."

It wasn't something evident only in West London either. Twice during the 2017-18 season, the Bees would come up against their future centre-back, Ethan Pinnock, who would sign for the Bees in the summer of 2019, but was then plying his trade for Barnsley. Looking back at playing against Smith's class of 2017-18, Pinnock certainly felt he had the measure of a team which could be incredibly exciting going forwards and dominate possession, but which could all too easily see the tables turned when things weren't going their way.

"The first time I played against Brentford for Barnsley, it was at Griffin Park (December 2017's 0-0 draw), when I came on in the second half," said Pinnock. "I remember Brentford dominating the ball but just lacking that final pass and final threat to score. Even though we weren't in it, we hung in the game. Brentford dominated everything possession-wise, but we felt we were comfortable holding out for a draw. We then played at Oakwell (April 2018, 2-0 defeat), and I remember for the first ten minutes, Brentford came firing out the blocks and we could barely touch the ball. Then we scored on the counter when our striker tried to cross it and it looped in, and we went on to an easy 2-0 win. From then on, I could tell Brentford were a top quality team, but maybe that mentality of when things don't go your way, or you don't score when you're on top, was missing. And if other teams could hang on in the game, they've got a chance of getting a result."

That late Loftus Road capitulation was hardly the way Smith was hoping to celebrate his 100th game in charge of the Bees. Brentford had certainly made progress under him – the toxic atmosphere from 2015 had gone, the club had stabilised, the team were playing some great attacking football and the new club culture had started to properly take shape. But there were still concerns about the side's backbone and inability to put consistent runs together. Looking back at that first century of games, Smith said he was particularly proud of the emphatic performances in the home wins over QPR (3-1) and Derby (4-0) at the tail end of the previous season, but was most pleased with the 3-0 home win against Aston Villa a few months earlier. He added there were a few games where he had "stood and felt powerless" – one of them being QPR away in March 2016, but interestingly, not the more recent shambles at Loftus Road.

Smith said of his ton-up landmark: "It's great to get there and to show the continuity of the club – we see too much change in the Championship nowadays… I've been very thankful for the owners I've worked under and the people I've worked with. The people here are good people to work for. You're always on your toes to get better, and people are looking to push you as well. I feel I've got better as it's gone on. We've evolved in the way we train and look after players. You can see a cryotherapy chamber in there, to make sure the lads are recovered for the ongoing games.

"Players have moved on when valuations have been met, but it's not stopped our progress. We've recruited well but developed well, and that's part of our model. The development of our young players has been pleasing, not just at first team level, but also in the B team. I don't look back and regret, I review and reflect, but that's part of my learning process as well. The consistency we've shown this season has pleased me. There's an identity to the club in how we play and how we do things. I feel our squad is stronger and I feel we can change things on the bench.

"From the start of the season, we've never got too high or too low following results. I know some people were looking at me as if I'd gone mad when I was saying how good our performances were, and that we had to continue and believe in what we're doing. There's a big character, and they're a robust lot. We've been through a lot at this stage in the season: losing three players on deadline day, Ryan Woods' tragedy (he and his partner losing their newborn) and the concussions (John Egan suffering two) as well.

"They've been through a lot, but they're resilient and a together bunch, I have no qualms about that. I think it's about creating the culture that you want. You have to have good people here first and foremost, and then you have to recruit good people. If anyone steps out of line, I'd expect them to police it rather than myself. If I had to step in all the time, they're probably not the right people for this club. Fortunately, we don't have that."

Considering what he had been through emotionally, Ryan Woods continued to be a shining light for Brentford. Having been one of the few success stories from the infamous 2015 transfer windows, he had barely featured under Dijkhuizen, but flourished under Carsley and Smith, and grew to become one of the most important players in the Brentford side of that time.

Here, Woods gives a good insight as to why he felt Smith was a good fit for Brentford, despite the ongoing concerns about whether he would ultimately be the man to take Brentford forwards. "He's just generally a good guy and a nice guy to have around the place," Woods said. "He's very approachable and someone you can talk to about other things away from football, and he's a good motivator. It's always good when a manager wants to have a laugh as well, and you know you can have a laugh with him. We like the way we play football, and it's important you buy into the way the manager wants to play. You only have to look at the technical ability of the lads here, which you need to play this style of football."

Looking back at that period, lifelong Brentford fan, Lou Boyd, feels that Dean Smith's reign was, "oddly consistent for Championship football, but without it ever feeling like he would be the man to take us up to the next level". He went on: "Smith may have made a great jockey – he knew how to sit patiently in the space behind the leaders and those tearing up around him – however, the potential of the 2017/18 season felt like it never really kicked in despite a creditable run of only two defeats in 12 between Halloween and New Year.

"That said, the start to the New Year saw a lot of us fans travelling up in good numbers to Barnsley in April, with a shred of hope that wins for us, and an incredibly favourable series of results above us, might have seen us snatch sixth place. That period you could describe as classic 'Dean Smith'... runs of good wins followed by a few disappointing results, then repeat. I had thought those good and bad runs went on for longer, but we seemed to get a month of good, then the other way around. Consistently inconsistent over the long term you could say. In truth, we were certainly not going backwards under Smith – the football was really good, the team was improving and we continued to take the scalps of the so-called big boys."

Another significant event transpired that month – as Smith was marking his 100th game in charge and Brentford's shortcomings were being cruelly exposed at Loftus Road – with Andy Scott departing Griffin Park for a third and final time. You'll recall that since returning to the club in 2015, Scott had worked as a scout, then chief scout and, finally, head of recruitment. His successes had been noticed by Watford technical director Filippo Giraldi, who coaxed Scott away to become the Premier League side's new UK football recruitment director.

"Looking back to when I left, it was probably a bit disrespectful to Matthew and Phil, because they gave me a chance and I left at the first opportunity," said Scott, reflecting on his departure. "Hindsight is a wonderful thing, but maybe I should have done things differently. There were no hard feelings – it was a job in the Premier League and they didn't want to stand in my way. The Premier League is where you want to work, and I was ambitious. Phil and Rasmus were the directors of football, so I knew I wasn't going to get to that level (of role), because they are excellent at what they do and know the club inside out. Maybe I was a bit impatient and wanted to prove I could still achieve things. That was probably my biggest problem as a manager, like when I went to Rotherham straight away without taking some time to reflect and have some time out. Since retiring, I'd never had time off to get my head together and reassess.

"There were no grudges or ill feelings from Matthew, Phil or Rasmus, they were fantastic about it and still are. I don't regret leaving, but maybe I'd have made a different decision now that I'm older and have had a chance to reflect on my life and career. Watford was a brilliant experience for me and I'm really proud of some of the stuff I did there, and it gave me a chance to broaden my knowledge as sporting director. It was just a difficult place to work at times, and that's something I should perhaps have done due diligence on, as it was never going to be a long-term relationship."

Looking back at his biggest successes while working in the Brentford's recruitment department, Scott added: "You go back to some of the first ones that came in like Henrik Dalsgaard and Yoann Barbet – they were real test cases as it cements the fact you can bring players in who are good, builds trust and gives you a bit more gravitas at the club to push forward. We brought in some really good players, Ryan Woods was excellent and sold for good money, and you start a process when you're generating money.

"I always say I didn't find a player, I scouted them. The data leads you in directions, or you watch a game and then go to the data and come back. People like Ollie Watkins, Neal Maupay – they don't work if the club's not set up like it is – the sports science, the medical, the coaching, the environment, the time, the ability to play games, the structure. As a scout, you're bringing players in knowing that's what they're coming into. I've seen plenty of good players, but they're not Brentford players – they wouldn't come in with that mentality of learning, and so you have to do a lot of work on the person.

"Again, I scouted Watkins, Maupay and Dalsgaard, then recommended them – but if they didn't have the coaching of Dean Smith, Thomas Frank, Chris Haslam and all those guys behind the scenes, they wouldn't be the players they are now. It's up to the club to make them the players they become, so it really frustrates me when scouts say they signed this or that player. It's a club signing, you scouted them and recommended them. Ollie Watkins was bought for around £1.5m and sold for £30m, and everyone at the club contributed to that. My job was to recommend players, then the sports science's job is to make sure they're physically capable of performing for England. There's a lot of players I'm proud we brought in, but I'm most proud I was part of that group that helped get them where they are now."

On the pitch, the post-QPR dressing room tête-à-tête seemed to do the trick, and the Bees made no similar mistakes in another West London derby the following week, comfortably dispatching Fulham 3-1 at Griffin Park. That victory started a run of four wins in six games in December, including three successive three-pointers over a memorable festive season. A 2-1 win at Carrow Road showed how far Brentford had come since their 5-0 hammering in Norfolk a year earlier, while Aston Villa, beaten by the same scoreline, once again discovered that history and the size of your crowd or stadium counts for nothing when taking on the modern day Brentford.

Before that Boxing Day game, Villa boss Steve Bruce had commented that one of the factors that he felt was helping Brentford keep the pressure on the Villains in the chase for a play-off place, was the lack of expectation compared to that at his own club. Somewhat ironically, given his next managerial role, Smith said after the game: "He's probably right to be honest, but it works in our favour because opposition supporters see us as little Brentford and are surprised when they see the standard of our football. Our expectation is to finish in the top six, and we know that will be difficult because of the size and finances of other clubs in this division, but we have had two defeats in 17, and that is tremendous in this league."

As 2017 turned into 2018, the New Year ushered in what was, for once, a quiet transfer window. Future play-off final hero Emiliano Marcondes came in on a free from Danish side FC Nordsjælland, in a deal which had been completed some months previously – Marcondes was the leading goalscorer in the Danish Superliga and had been voted the Player of the Year at the 2017 Danish Football Awards, and was billed as an exciting capture.

The only departure came after the English transfer window had closed, when popular striker Lasse Vibe left for Chinese side Changchun Yatai. Smith said at the time: "I am happy, as for the last couple of years, it's been a distraction at times. In the 2015/16 season the talk was about Alan Judge leaving, and it was Scott Hogan last year. This month has been very quiet, so long may it continue."

At the time of Marcondes signing for Brentford, Danish TV station TV3 produced a documentary about the transfer, and how the Bees saw off a lucrative offer from Brondby to land his signature, which provided an insight into how Brentford conduct their business behind the scenes. The fact that Matthew Benham and Dean Smith were at the initial meeting with him at the Brentford Novotel, as well as Rasmus Ankersen, impressed Marcondes and his agent, and helped the Bees get the deal over the line.

During the meeting, Benham told Marcondes: "We saw on our model that you get on the end of loads and loads of chances, and the level of your team since Christmas just went up – a huge, huge jump." An impressed Marcondes then tells the camera: "They are good at selling their business. I can really tell that they are professionals – businessmen that are good at selling their product and their club, and convincing you

Emiliano Marcondes, John Egan and Andreas Bjelland celebrate Henrik Dalsgaard's winning goal at Nottingham Forest

that this club would be the perfect choice for you. They spend a lot of resources talking to you about how you play and the role you will get. It tells me that they really want me."

A meeting with fitness coach Chris Haslam at the training ground the following morning talks Marcondes through the individual development plan the club has already tailored for him, which is followed by a meeting with head coach Dean Smith and chief scout Andy Scott at Griffin Park. There, Scott explains that the club has had six different scouts watch him play in 20 different games already.

Scott tells Marcondes what the club sees as his chief attributes (seeing goal scoring opportunities and getting into the box), and explaining how his technique under tight pressure will work well in the Championship, where teams sit tight against Brentford. Scott then identifies an area for improvement, which is being more consistent in his finishing, and saying the positions Marcondes gets into should lead to a lot more goals. Smith then explains how the club will make Marcondes a better player and says analysis is a big part of what they do. Marcondes comes out of the meeting convinced that Brentford's style of play and training methods will be totally suited to him.

With a lucrative offer from Brondby also on the table, Marcondes agonises over the decision but is left with "a really good impression" of a club which "feels like a family" with "people who really want to develop you all the time". He adds: "You can feel they want to make you better straight away, and that is just the way I want it. It's been really positive all the way. You can have a director that really wants you, but where the manager does not know you and has not seen you play, but that is not Brentford."

Marcondes made his debut in a turgid 1-0 home FA Cup exit to League Two Notts County six days into the New Year, which followed a 3-0 defeat at Wolves, as the Bees started 2018 in disappointing fashion. Things picked up with wins over Bolton and Reading, before the month ended with a home defeat to Norwich. Smith spoke, once again, about the importance of being given time to build the project and develop players, saying: "I think it's very important, and the only way to achieve evolution is having time. We feel we're building as a club. The foundations were in place, and we're just adding to that."

Smith went on to underline once more that his progress, as well as the team's, is measured on more than just results, and how the club looks to use innovative ways to plug the financial gap between them and their rivals. "If it was all about finances, we may as well pack it all in now," he said. "It's about 11 players going out and battling and we believe we can find different ways to match the resources of the bigger clubs. The players are well coached and have a lot of potential. They have good attitudes, and with that, their potential grows and harnesses a great team spirit, and you can go a long way with that.

"The club, we believe, is in a good progressive place. The team has been very consistent this season. We haven't got the wins that our play probably deserves, but my role as head coach is to make the players better as players and people. Along with that is also getting results, but I'm thankful I'm at a club that doesn't always look at the outcome. We look at the progression not just of the team, but players individually as well."

Somebody who agreed with those sentiments was Sky pundit, and former striker, Don Goodman, whose comments often received a mixed reaction from Bees fans, but who told Sky's EFL Matters podcast when discussing Brentford early in 2018: "They've just kept belief in what they were doing. They were playing very well but losing or drawing games, and Dean Smith was saying it was some of the best football they played all season. They kept faith in what the manager wanted them to do and they've turned results around. Brentford were my dark horse to do a Huddersfield (get promoted to the Premier League) of the 'unfashionable' clubs, after what I saw of them last season. After the first seven or eight games I wasn't really sure, but now they're right in the mix."

Unfortunately, Brentford's form was still too inconsistent to make a proper push for the play-offs, but they continued to make people sit up and take notice with some impressive results against teams that had been assembled with the aid of much bigger budgets. Although February was book-ended by defeat to Derby and Leeds, in between, the Bees put five without reply past a Birmingham side fielding all three of the players Brentford had sold them six months earlier, and put in a very impressive performance to win 2-0 at Sunderland, who had been in the Premier League less than a year earlier.

Both opposition managers were complimentary of the Bees' methodology. Birmingham's Steve Cotterill said: "It takes years – then you recruit numbers rather than players. A number six for them will do a certain job, the nine will do a certain job, the seven and eleven will do certain jobs. It's easier to recruit numbers rather than just collect players and then think 'right, how are we going to fit them into a team?' Their DNA has been clear for a few years now, which is good."

Sunderland's Chris Coleman, meanwhile, would be ultimately proved wrong in his prediction that Brentford's model would never see them get promoted to the top flight. However, in the rest of his assessment, Coleman gave what was probably a fair assessment of where the Bees were at the time. He said: "They've done well, they've got a certain model. They're a good footballing team and a good passing team, and Dean is a good manager. They're a well-oiled, well-tuned Championship team. I don't think they'll ever get promoted – I could be wrong – because they don't have the finances, but if they keep doing what they do, they won't be relegated either. For Brentford to be where they are, given the size of the club, Dean's doing a really good job, and they're a good little outfit." On the flip side, Sunderland, armed with big crowds, a magnificent stadium and Premier League parachute payments, finished the campaign rock bottom of the Championship, below Burton and Barnsley, who were also relegated to League One.

The Brentford hierarchy clearly agreed that their head coach was doing the job they expected, rewarding Smith with a one-year contract extension in February. Upon signing, Smith admitted there were still areas for improvement. He said: "I think it's important. We make a big noise about not letting players' contracts go into the last season, and likewise for the coaching staff, and the message reverberates at the club that it's a long-term plan, not short-term fixes. I've felt this has been as consistent as we've been this season and our performance levels have been very good. We need to improve on things, whether it be recruitment, tactically or style of play. We're looking to improve as coaches and how we deal with players as well."

Rasmus Ankersen hammered home the point that the club, despite some often-frustrating spells on the pitch, was happy with its progress under Smith, highlighting his leadership and man management, while also recognising the impact Thomas Frank had had on the coaching team. "We have been pleased to see the progress the team has made this season," he said. "We strongly believe we are on the right path, and with the new contracts, we can now continue the hard work with stability in key coaching positions. At Brentford, it is not about the individuals, it is about the team and the togetherness we need to compete in a very tough league. Dean is not just a strong leader, but also a real team player who buys into Brentford's way of doing things. His man management skills have been critical to the progress the club has made, and we believe Dean will be a key component in achieving our ambitions in the years to come. Thomas has now been with us for a year and he has brought to the table exactly what we hoped he would –attention to detail and an extensive experience in developing a clear style of play."

Going into March, Brentford still harboured top six ambitions but just couldn't put a good enough run of results together to break into the pack. The month started well enough, with a solid, if unspectacular, win at Burton Albion, but the four games without a win that followed, including back-to-back defeats against Millwall and Cardiff, put an end to any lingering hopes of extending the campaign. Nevertheless, following a 1-1 home stalemate with Middlesbrough, Neil Warnock was another opposition manager to recognise Brentford's strengths, although in doing so, perhaps gave too much credit to the head coach rather than the recruitment system, something the wider football world was perhaps still guilty of too. Warnock said: "They're a decent side and Dean Smith has done a smashing job here. He keeps producing good players, sells them and produces new ones."

Although consistency continued to elude the Bees under Smith, his team did finish the season, once again, with something of a flourish, losing just one of their final nine games and putting together a run of four wins out of five in April. Among them was a memorable 1-1 draw at Fulham in which Neal Maupay headed an equaliser in front of the travelling Bees fans four minutes into injury time that cost Fulham automatic promotion. Last minute goals against the Cottagers had become something of a thing.

The late equaliser at Craven Cottage saw Smith, a man recognised for his ability to keep his emotions in check, have a rare moment of 'losing it' whilst celebrating on the touchline, after which he explained why he normally keeps a lid on such exuberance: "I think it was a celebration as I felt it would have been an injustice to lose – I thought we'd played well enough to get something. It was nice to share my happiness, but if I'm out of control on the sidelines, it gives players permission to go out of control on the pitch. I try to contain my emotions and keep calm – you need to be thinking clearly." The scenes in the away end, however, were even more out of control.

Ryan Woods, Neal Maupay and Florian Jozefzoon spark wild scenes at Craven Cottage after the last minute equalizer

A week later, Brentford made up for their late horror show at Loftus Road earlier in the season, as goals from Sergi Canos and Florian Jozefzoon earned a 2-1 win over QPR at Griffin Park. After the QPR game, Smith looked back to the first match between the two sides and insisted – despite leading to concerns about Brentford being a soft touch and being unable to see out games – it had been a blip more than a sign of a fault in the system. He said: "We look back at it and there wasn't much wrong. It's easy to fix a two minutes lack of concentration – if we were getting pummelled for 45 minutes, it'd have been more of a worry. We were all disappointed at Loftus Road with the way that the game finished, but we showed today that, at the moment, we are better than them."

QPR boss Ian Holloway – another individual viewed in a negative light by many Bees fans but who has, in fact, often been complimentary about the club – admitted he had been wrong in tipping Brentford for relegation at the start of the season, which was good of him! He explained his thinking had been based on the club constantly selling its best players – particularly the strikers. To be fair, it was a grumble often heard on the Griffin Park terraces, but it was a scenario that would continue going forwards. Maupay, Watkins and Benrahma would bring in a combined £70m including add ons – sales that are clearly inextricably linked to funding Brentford's climb into the Premier League.

"What they've been doing – as a QPR person, I don't want to admit it – but it's been very good," said Holloway. "At the minute, you're trying to get in an even better place – with the scouting network and what you're doing, with your manager who's taken and embraced the way you've played and moved it on another level. If he hadn't lost the Hogans of this world, where could you be? If you didn't lose the Jotas of this world, where could you be at the minute? But well done to them. All I said is they might not do well if they keep selling their best players as it's not a good strategy, I had it done to me at Bristol Rovers, and if you lose all your strikers, it ain't going to help." As a wise man once observed, you can explain things to people a million times, but you can't make them understand.

As the season wound down to a disappointing defeat at relegation-threatened Barnsley, which officially killed off Brentford's top six hopes, then a 1-1 home draw with Hull, which confirmed a ninth-place finish, speculation intensified linking Smith with the managers' job at Premier League strugglers West Brom, a role that had been vacant since Alan Pardew's departure in April.

Following the Hull stalemate, Smith swatted aside those rumours, saying: "There's always going to be speculation about managers or players when a side does well, particularly when it's a club our size. But there is a long-term plan at this club, and I'm acutely aware of what I have got here and that is always a big factor. It is a proper family club and a good football club and I'm enjoying my time here. On the playing side, I have no idea if we will lose players in the summer, but they have developed as young men, individually and as a group. It's a privilege to be their head coach. If you leave, it's not always rosy, and the grass isn't always greener."

Romaine Sawyers, who had followed Smith from Walsall to Brentford, and a player who was finally being recognised for what he brought to the side, added his voice to those imploring the head coach to stay put. "It's a testament to the whole club, identifying him when he was at Walsall," said Sawyers. "He's come here and assembled a squad of young boys, but also mature men. We're trying to play the right way, and everyone can see him doing that. It's a testament to his character. I've been with him for five seasons now, and I'd want to keep him alongside me for as long as possible."

What would become the most instrumental transfer window in Brentford's post war history was still a year away – 2018's was a relatively quiet one, certainly in comparison to what would follow, but still saw some interesting movements. For once, Ryan Woods aside, there were no big departures – Chris Mepham's £12m move to Bournemouth would come in January – however, John Egan moved to Sheffield United and Florian Jozefzoon made tracks for Derby County.

Egan would notably help the Blades into the Premier League the following season, leading to questions about whether Brentford had been too hasty in letting him go. But after initially impressing at Brentford, the Irish defender then struggled to hold down a place in the side – and it should not be overlooked that it was his departure that ultimately allowed for the emergence of Mepham. Another defensive replacement after Egan left was Charlton's Ezri Konsa, who a year later would net Brentford a profit of around £10m when he moved to Aston Villa.

Although some saw Jozefzoon's departure as disappointing, he was replaced with another upgrade, with Brentford unveiling Said Benrahma from Nice for £3m. The Algerian maestro would go on to become arguably the best player ever seen in a Brentford shirt at that stage, lighting up Griffin Park for two years with his breath-taking skills and spectacular goals before netting the Bees another handsome profit – of up to £27m including add-ons – when he moved to West Ham in 2020.

Other arrivals included the low-risk return of Warburton alumni Moses Odubajo which, due to recurring knee injuries, didn't really work out and proved the old adage of 'never go back', while another low-key entrance was that of Josh Dasilva from Arsenal's Under 23s. Josh, however, would defy all expectations to become a key figure in Brentford's eventual promotion to the Premier League, before cruelly having his chances of shining in the top flight first season ruined by a career- threatening hip injury.

Interestingly, despite the previous campaign having highlighted, at times, the lack of leadership in an otherwise talented Brentford squad, the club took the bold decision in the summer of 2018 to dispense with the traditional captaincy model. It was another typically Brentford move, flying in the face of football's closely-guarded traditions, but unlike the transition from the manager to head coach model and introduction of statistical player analysis a few years before, Brentford were not as roundly slated in the sporting press this time round - perhaps a sign of acceptance from the wider footballing world that there was indeed some method to the perceived madness.

Since the long-serving Kevin O'Connor had hung up his boots in 2015, the likes of Jake Bidwell, Harlee Dean and John Egan had worn the armband, but following Egan's departure, no replacement was appointed. The captaincy would instead be shared by a leadership group of around half a dozen senior players, as Dean Smith explained at the time.

"It's something we've been thinking about for a while and something we've had discussions about internally," Smith said. "I think there needs to be a collective responsibility around leadership within football. I think I would have done exactly the same even if John Egan had stayed because it's something that has been at the forefront of my mind. What better opportunity for us to try and develop leaders by not having a captain?

"The players can name somebody to go and toss the coin each game and start taking responsibility as a group. I know for a fact I've got five or six players who I could have named captain this season, and I think it's probably unfair that I do name one out of those five or six. The job of a leader within the group is to help create other leaders and not followers. I think sometimes when you name that captain, he becomes that leader and people start to follow him rather than become leaders themselves."

It was an experiment which lasted a single season, with Romaine Sawyers taking the armband for the following campaign, while Pontus Jansson has been its custodian since 2019. It appeared to be a stroke of genius at first as Brentford opened the season with a 5-1 thrashing of Rotherham the start of a run of just one defeat in their first eight games – including further wins over Sheffield Wednesday, Nottingham Forest and Wigan Athletic.

The only loss during that time was a 1-0 reverse at Blackburn Rovers, on the same day on which Ryan Woods finally departed following protracted speculation. Woods joined Championship rivals Stoke City on a loan deal with the intention of making the loan permanent the following January – a precursor to Benrahma's transfer to West Ham two years later. It was a move which didn't really work out well for Woods, with the man who brought him in, Gary Rowett, sacked soon afterwards. Woods barely featured under Rowett's replacement, Nathan Jones, and later said: "Obviously I came from Brentford – pure football, that's the way the whole club is run – and they only sign players with that philosophy. It was really important to me, the philosophy of the club. I went to Stoke hoping to be able to change their philosophy slightly, and it just wasn't to be."

Woods would later reflect on his time with Brentford as the best days of his career, telling London News: "I was signed when Marinus Dijkhuizen was there but he only lasted six weeks. Lee Carsley took over and that's when I started playing a lot of games. Once Dean Smith came in I never really looked back, I started playing my best football. Dean had a lot of belief in me and tried to get me on the ball as much as possible. Brentford wanted to bring in young players they felt could improve and sell on for a much higher fee. Their culture and style was very important to me. The Shrewsbury team I was in played the best football in League Two and perhaps even in League One, and I wanted a club that had the same philosophy of how I like to play. I probably had my best two seasons there, I seemed to be getting seven or eight out of ten performances week in and week out."

As Woods packed his bags, the old frustrations were to return as feast once more turned to famine, and the Bees' good start became a distant memory as they went the next eight games without a win. It was during the middle of this run that Dean Smith left the club – landing a dream job as manager at his boyhood club, Aston Villa, despite having just led the Bees on a run of five games without a win. Rumours had been circulating with Smith's name seemingly becoming a natural link. He was by no means Villa's first choice to replace Steve Bruce in the hot seat, but he would end the season taking Villa back into the top flight, through the play-offs, after a three-season absence.

The move to Villa Park was still not an easy decision, apparently, with Smith claiming: "I had to give it some thought, which was down to the fact that Brentford have been very good. They're a great football club to work for with very good people. Throughout the process they've been class." He remained proud of his time at the club, adding: "People see the progression of the football club – the style of play is eye-catching and entertaining, and we've become more consistent. Four top ten finishes in one of the hardest leagues to get out of in the world is testament to that."

Ankersen paid tribute to his departing head coach, but also fired a reminder that, unlike at some clubs, the head coach's role is not the be all and end all, and that structure remains the most important thing at Brentford. "He's someone who has contributed a lot to the football club over the last three years and he has earned a lot of respect, not only as a coach, but as a man, and that's why we let him leave on good terms," he said of Smith. "That said, like I said to the staff and the players at the training ground, I think it's also a compliment to us, because Brentford is not a one-man band. It's a football club which has a structure and a strategy, and all of the players and the staff get this opportunity as well.

"It's not the first time a big club in this country has come in for our players, or our coaches, I think it's a compliment to Brentford. There's a lot of things you can buy in football, but there's a lot of things that you can't buy, and despite the head coach leaving, as a club, we feel in a strong position. I think the main thing for us is that we can see a person fitting into our structure, someone who buys into our project and someone who's able to execute the strategy we have and add to that."

That man, a week later, turned out, unsurprisingly, to be assistant head coach Thomas Frank – as Brentford's succession planning kicked in. Frank, by that stage, had been at the club for two years, and was clearly ready to be a head coach once more. In fact, he admitted he'd never wanted to stop being a head coach after leaving Brondby, but that after hearing what the project at Brentford was all about, decided he had to be a part of it. "After a few interviews I thought this suited me and who I am – my values, my philosophy," he said. "I've been lucky to be in charge of Brondby, where the board and the sports director allowed me to build the club in a similar way and structure. We search for every small margin that we could turn to our advantage every single day."

Frank then looked back at his first two years, waiting in the wings, and what he had brought to the table so far, saying: "The three of us together – me Dean and Richard – discussed ways of playing and had the same philosophy about football. I have detailed structures in the way I see training and developing a style of play, it's about every single drill needing to be aligned to create a style of play. It's not just a possession game, I like to press forward and defend from the front, so that's the detail we've been working on the last few years. I will continue that and try to add a little. We had a strong relationship and we had the same philosophy – we wanted to dominate and press high."

Looking ahead to where he wanted to take Brentford, Frank added: "Now it's just up to me to push to the next level. I think one of the biggest strengths of this club is that we have a clear strategy. The second thing, that is pretty rare in football, is the people in charge take calm decisions. Because we have that strategy and cleverness and coolness we have a top opportunity to just push forward and hopefully go to the next level. If we do this in every area in the training ground – if we just do a little bit extra every single day – we have the opportunity to go to the next level."

Frank also paid tribute to the off-pitch set-up, which had allowed the club to flourish, saying: "For me, one of the most important things is that both directors of football take care of the recruitment. Of course, we do that together, but there are a lot of things that you don't have to be aware of. As a manager, you need to manage the staff, which is no different to a head coach. I think Guardiola is spending a lot of time on the training pitch, so I think it depends on who you are and how you do it. I think the person defines the role, so maybe you have a title as a manager, but if you're very focused on detail and coaching, you do that more. I think I'm more of a head coach than a manager."

However he defined his outlook for the new role, Frank took over a side which hadn't won in five games, and things were about to get a whole lot worse, with the Dane's first three games in charge of the Bees all ending in defeat – at the hands of Bristol City, Preston and Norwich. A 2-0 win over Millwall at the start of November provided brief respite, but the supporters were left wondering if the right decision had been made when Frank's men then went six more games without a win – including defeats to QPR, Middlesbrough, Sheffield United, Swansea and Hull. Had the wheels come off, were we back in Marinus Dijkhuizen territory, or had other sides rumbled the Bees' style of play?

Seasoned Brentford journalist, Jim Levack, writing for the Beesotted website, asked the very same questions – to which he answered; "For me, the answer lies closer to home and has nothing to do with the man at the helm, be it Dean or Thomas."

He continued: "No. The big miss is the absence of Ryan Woods. A departure that has adversely affected us more than I'm sure anyone at the club will publicly admit. He wanted to leave for family reasons, the club wanted to sell to maximise income and that, after all, is how our model works. No problem with that at all. But the lack of a replacement is a loss that needs to be addressed in January. Brentford playing at pace with one touch zip-and-zing are virtually unplayable. But without Woods, our metronome, our tempo has dropped and we aren't the formidable opposition we were before his departure. Kamohelo Mokotjo, Romaine Sawyers and Josh Dasilva all bring different qualities to the side but don't possess a surge, that rapid and powerful change of gear over the first five yards, to make things happen from deep going forward.

"Woods was a 'busy little xxxxxx', he brought an urgency to proceedings and was often a catalyst to make something happen in a game that had been predictable and far too one-paced, like recent home games. There's now more pressure on Sergi Canos and Said Benrahma to provide the spark for Ollie Watkins or Neal Maupay to hit the target, and let's face it, if they don't score we hardly have prolific finishers elsewhere in the side. Maybe another area for January's shopping list?"

He also felt that match officials hadn't been giving the Bees the rub of the green during the dismal run of results, suggesting that: "Referees will continue to be poor, sides will continue to try to kick, niggle, time-waste and hit on the counter because to take us on at football is a much tougher ask. Bottom line is, the only way to combat that is to play football even better. And quicker."

For Rico Henry, Smith's departure was a case of losing the man who he had developed and flourished under at both Walsall and Brentford. But no longer having Smith by his side was eased by the fact that the club's succession planning meant the players were already familiar with his replacement. "I had a feeling Dean would leave as he was a Villa fan, and if they came in for him, he'd take it," said Henry. "There was a lot of speculation at the time, but I'd played under Thomas as well, and we knew he'd take over pretty much straight away.

"We have principles at this club, where if someone leaves there is always someone ready to step in and fill the role, and it's the same out on the pitch as well. At the start it was quite similar as they had worked together before, and Thomas didn't want to change anything too soon, but he gradually introduced more running and fitness into the team. If you look at us now, we're one of the fittest teams in the league."

Nevertheless, as Christmas approached, relegation was looking an ominous possibility, as the Bees went into the festive season just three points off the drop zone. Yoann Barbet told his fellow players after they conceded a late winner at home to Sheffield United that the buck stopped with them. "Of course we believe in him (Frank)," said the defender. "He was really good as an assistant, and now he's the manager, and I think the way he wants us to play is a good way. We have to be better. It's not his responsibility, he's not on the pitch. We just need to stick together and stop the spiral."

The mood at the club had not been helped, during the midst of that run, by the truly tragic and sudden passing of technical director Rob Rowan. The much-loved Scot, who had begun his coaching career with Celtic's U21s before landing his breakthrough job as sporting director at Stenhousemuir, had been with Brentford for four years and had, only nine months earlier, been promoted from head of football operations – where he had overseen the transition from an academy to B team structure – to his new role.

The loss of Rowan, at the tragically young age of 28, hit the club hard. Not only was he a popular figure amongst all the staff, but he had played a big part in the development of many of the young players at the club – players like Chris Mepham, who was rapidly developing into one of the most promising young defenders in the country, and who would be making a £12m step up to the Premier League with Bournemouth in a couple of months' time.

One who perhaps put it best, explaining just how devastating an impact Rowan's passing had been at the club, and those who worked with him, was midfielder, and skipper, Romaine Sawyers. "Losing Rob, a person who meant so much to the club, had a massive effect on everyone at the training ground," he told the matchday programme a few months later. "The club took a big hit during that spell, dealing with the tragic loss of Rob in the midst of the poor run that we were going through.

"It's testament to everyone that we rallied together and got through it. We've got a good group of players and staff – we've got no bad eggs and no bad attitudes. We're a tight-knit group and no one takes anything too personally. As captain, I've always tried to remain positive, regardless of how things are going. That's with complete respect to Rob's family. People deal with loss differently. Meps [Chris Mepham], for example, was really cut up about it."

Rob was clearly a much loved and highly respected man. Warm, friendly, loyal and genuine – he was somebody who was regarded as a footballing visionary with a long and successful career ahead of him. He had already played an instrumental part in the transformation of the club off the pitch and there was so much more to come. For Brentford, losing Rob was perhaps inevitable at some stage – Glasgow Rangers had already tried to tempt him away from Griffin Park – but not this way. He will not be forgotten and his legacy is the growing list of B teamers that have graduated into the first team at Brentford, which is celebrated on the Robert Rowan Debut Board at the Jersey Road training ground.

CHAPTER TEN

To say that Thomas Frank's first few months in the Brentford hot seat had been difficult would be an understatement. Eight defeats, with just one win, from your first ten games in charge is not the stuff managerial dreams are made of. In fact, the much-maligned Marinus Dijkhuizen had a superior record from the nine games he was head coach for in 2015 (two wins, two draws, five defeats). However, it was not a situation that bears comparison. Sure, you'd be hard pushed to find a Brentford fan who didn't have any concerns as Christmas 2018 approached, but the club had taken a big stride forward and was in a much better place than in 2015.

As with some of the difficult spells the team went through during Dean Smith's tenure, Brentford again chose patience where others may have pulled the trigger, which was eventually rewarded with a turnaround in form. Neal Maupay scored the only goal of the game at home to Bolton in a pivotal win to stop the rot just before Christmas, with the Bees seeing out 2018 with useful points on the road at Bristol City and Birmingham. The New Year started with another draw, against Norwich, before three wins in a row, against Stoke, Rotherham and Blackburn, showed they were heading in the right direction once more. The Blackburn win was particularly memorable, the Bees having let old habits creep back in by going two goals down inside seven minutes, before roaring back to hammer Rovers 5-2.

Thomas Frank reflecting on his difficult start at Brentford

Looking back, Frank insists he never felt any pressure, or suffered any sleepless nights, during that tough opening spell to his tenure in the hot seat, due to the structure of the club from top to bottom. For all that, he admits that even he would have started looking over his shoulder had the winless run continued through the festive season and into New Year. "I never feared it (the sack)," he said. "Of course it was tough – you're going in and taking over, you want to perform but you lose the first three, lose eight out of the first ten. But after that we didn't lose for ten games. You learn a lot about yourself in those spells. It's tough losing because you blame yourself and ask if you could have done something different, but I never feared for my job, and Matthew, Phil and Rasmus were very supportive. I wasn't stupid though, I knew I couldn't lose 16 out of 20.

"But I'm very pleased we went from losing eight out of ten to going ten unbeaten. You don't do that by luck or coincidence, it means what we had been doing over the last three and a half years works – the consistency, the same message, the structure, building the culture – that's why we flipped from eight losses to ten unbeaten. I clearly remember the Bolton game, both teams were close to the drop zone and we had to win, and I changed that game from a 4-3-3 to a 3-4-3, and we played well and won 1-0. That was a big release that day.

"We also had a lot of injuries when I took over. Julian Jeanvier was our most experienced centre back. Chris Mepham and Ezri Konsa were two brilliant players but they were young and lacked experience. Nico

Yennaris and Kamo Mokotjo were out injured, as was Said Benrahma. John Egan had a concussion, Ollie Watkins had a broken toe, so a lot of our top players were out through that spell. Rob Rowan also died during that period, a key member of staff. So many things were going wrong, which didn't help, but we got through it.

"I very rarely have sleepless nights. The only time I really remember was when I was at Brondby and we also started badly, we didn't win for the first eight games. The day we won the adrenaline was going round my body. That helped massively as we then went nine games unbeaten, so it was the same situation. I believe more and more in the things I'm doing in terms of consistent messages, clear plans, a clear structure and a clear style of play – try to build that culture. Every single day it's the small bits. Small momentum shifts in games also define results, so I've always been a big believer in that, even before Brentford, in all the other teams I have managed. And it was a perfect match with Brentford, so that helped."

As the hammering of Blackburn at Griffin Park testified, the attacking trio of Benrahma, Watkins and Maupay was starting to reap havoc with Championship defences, with a new-found confidence starting flowing through the side. There was suddenly a feeling that if the Bees fell behind in a game, rather than heads dropping, calmness would reign and it would only be a matter of time before they got back into a match. And, if they were defending a narrow lead late on, it was no longer inevitable that panic would set in and pressure invited onto themselves, but a confident mindset would instead see out the game or even seek to add to the lead. They were principles which would become increasingly evident in Brentford's march towards the Premier League, and ones which Brentford's steady progress had been built upon, without always having had the personnel to execute them.

Much of the credit for the turnaround must go to Frank himself – particularly for a formation change which helped shore things up at the back with the introduction of three central defenders, which also allowed the wing-backs to get forward and make the most of Brentford's embarrassment of attacking riches. Sawyers, in the same interview in which he spoke of Rob Rowan's tragic passing, said: "After a tricky start, Thomas recognised that we had problems and changed the formation. He gave it a lot of thought and then translated to the group exactly what he expected from us. Thomas has always been demanding, even when the previous head coach was here, but he really stepped that up when results weren't going our way.

"We've always had the ability, and it's not like we made five or six new signings in January that've come in and made a difference, it's a change in mentality that's made the difference. Thomas is constantly on to us about our concentration levels in training, in analysis and anything else we do during the week. He didn't have a power trip when he got the job. Thomas is still quite relaxed – he's a people person. We don't have to call him gaffer, and I think that's a real indication of how relaxed he is. He makes us feel comfortable. He's made the transition easier for the group; he could have started throwing his weight around, but he chose not to."

Another important factor around this time was the addition of Brian Riemer as first team assistant coach – a man who has been credited with helping tighten up the side defensively. Looking back, Rico Henry feels both the formation change and Riemer's arrival played key parts in Brentford's change in fortunes. "Because I'd played in a back five under Dean Smith at Walsall I was quite comfortable with it," he said. "The losing streak obviously wasn't good, but that's what made us learn, and as soon as we went to a back five we did well – we were solid at the back and scoring goals. Brian Riemer helped us a lot defensively too, and we didn't have that before. He always says if we defend back to front and as a team, we will always score goals at the other end, and that's what's happened."

Riemer, having started his coaching career with Hvidovre IF, joined Brentford following a decade with FC Copenhagen, first as U19s manager and then assistant first team manager. Riemer, speaking to Danish podcast Mediano in February 2021, gave an interesting insight into the situation he found on arriving at the club. "Thomas had two games before I arrived," he said. "They lost to Bristol (City) and Preston. Then I arrived and we lost 1-0 at Norwich. Then we won 2-0 against Millwall and that's when we all thought 'here we go'.

"However, that was not the case, and we hit this awful run with just one win in 11 or 12 games before we beat Bolton in a vital game at Griffin Park. Bolton was rock bottom and we had to win that game, which we fortunately did. But there was never any internal pressure from higher up. Quite the contrary actually – Phil Giles often came down after a loss and said, 'we deserved to win, keep going, it will come eventually'. He was completely calm – it was only Thomas and I who were a little nervous – especially me because I had only just arrived. I didn't know many people in the club but, looking back now, I know I had nothing to worry about. They are all great people, but I didn't know that at that time. It was only pressure we put on ourselves.

"We obviously knew we couldn't keep losing without getting fired, but it was never something they told us. They gave us the peace to work that we needed, but to be frank, it was not a nice time. The change of formation was very much connected to the players we had and the fact that the spirit we have in the team now wasn't there at that time. Our defence was hopeless. We conceded 56 goals in a season, which means you have to score a lot of goals if you want to win games. On our best days, we'd play fantastic up front but lose 3-2 anyway because our defence was rubbish. So, we chose to change the formation to get an extra defender to close the gaps."

Riemer went on to comment on the facilities he encountered at Brentford's Jersey Road training ground – a swathe of land nestled between the hubbub of the London approaches of the M4 and A4 and directly under the Heathrow flightpath – but nevertheless offering the tranquillity of the nearby National Trust treasure of Osterley Park. Jersey Road had come a long way since the club first moved there in 2004, but it was still a long way off being the kind of training facilities offered by most of the club's Championship rivals. For Riemer, however, this worked in Brentford's favour.

"We have five full-size pitches, and all the buildings are what they call portable cabins, which are basically shipping containers," he said. "Then there is one tiny 'real' house, with our kitchen and two changing rooms. That's all we have, but we don't need anything else. We have Smart-TVs, touchscreens, equipment for the players, but it's not exactly 'state of the art'. Everything is a bit rough, a bit cold and not very nice. However, I honestly think once you get past that 'oh god' period, it's actually something that strengthens our togetherness. No one is here because we have the best facilities and the best pitches in the world, they are here because we're on a common mission towards a common goal. I think the facilities have a positive effect, because when you don't have the best facilities, everyone will get a little closer to each other on the team bus. So yes, it is a unique place, but we actually like it like this.

"Brentford chose to say 'what is it that will make Brentford competitive? Is it spending all the money on the best facilities?' There is a natural limit here, Matthew (Benham) is not Abramovich, he doesn't have unlimited funds. So, the club decided to spend the money where it really counts – good players, managers, and staff. They chose a method, with which I completely agree. Scouting has been, and still is, an essential part of Brentford's recent success – spending money on the right players and minimising the possibility of buying the wrong players for the team. The scouting has both contributed to the finances as well as the success on the pitch. Brentford is a club where we all work closely together, and where we firmly believe in solid craftsmanship, thorough analyses, football knowledge and financial knowledge.

"So, going back to the facilities, I wouldn't trade any of the Premier League facilities for how this club is run. This is not a club where the upper management panics and will fire people because of a few bad results. They understand that there are underlying factors, and they know we will face challenges. In short, they are very calm and collected, which not many Premier League, nor Championship clubs, can say. I think that's exactly where Brentford differentiates itself the most. A calm and competent owner with two equally good directors of football who work with facts and not feelings. That is a massive strength to have compared to many other clubs."

On the pitch, things were definitely perking up for the Bees, but the side remained, undeniably, a work in progress. February saw Dean Smith return to Griffin Park for the first time with Aston Villa, who Neal Maupay saw off with a roof-raising, last-minute winner – while Said Benrahma further underlined just why he was quickly becoming a fans' favourite, scoring a hat-trick in a dazzling 5-1 demolition of Hull City. But, in between those two impressive performances, came a televised 4-1 humbling at Swansea City in the FA Cup, during which the Bees' defensive frailties of old came back to haunt them with the young, rocket propelled, Dan James causing all kinds of problems with his blistering pace on the flank. Brentford would eventually become Swansea's play-offs nemesis, but it was the Welsh side who looked better equipped to make the step up at that point in time.

Around the same time, Brentford welcomed a new chief executive as former Bees season ticket holder Jon Varney, who had previously worked with Pitch International and Premiership Rugby, was appointed as the replacement for Mark Devlin, who had left the club at the end of 2018. What he found when he arrived was, off the field, "very much still a League One club playing in the Championship". With key departments spread across TW8 rather than working together in one place, and the move to a new stadium just over a year away, Varney got to work quickly.

"My immediate impressions was there were a lot of good people there, but it was quite disparate, and I think a lot of that was due to the geography and layout of the organisation," he said. "You had the playing squad down at Jersey Road, the chief executive's office above the Braemer Road car park, finance down the other end of Braemer Road, sales at the Heritage Walk Centre – and when people aren't together they start to work in silos, so they're only really focused on their own patch. It was really important to get everyone together. Our training ground was built on togetherness and we needed to do exactly the same with the off-field organisation, so we started that journey straight away really.

"I think we were in a bit of a holding pattern as we knew a new stadium was coming down the track, but it was clear we needed to do something pretty damn quickly and be ready for when we moved into it. The first thing I did was jump in the car, drive to the Lionel Road site and look for offices where I could house everybody under one roof. The Sega building was there, and I knew the company on the sixth floor were looking to get out, and when I got into the building I was allowed to get onto the top floor, which overlooked the new stadium. You could watch it being built, and for me there was no other option, we had to get that space. At one point we were going to move the whole off-field team down to Jersey Road and develop there, but it was becoming apparent that with our aspirations of getting into the Premier League, we were never going to be able to house everyone in one site at Jersey Road, so it became very clear to me we needed that office space.

"That was a really key moment for me, and the first 12 months of my time at Brentford was focused on that migration work, making sure we got the right people into the right areas of the stadium. You don't always get things 100 per cent right, but I genuinely believe the team did a phenomenal job in doing this. In a way, the new stadium mirrors Griffin Park. The North Stand is New Road, and what we've really done is flip the Ealing Road with the West Stand, so that was a really complex bit of work, but something I think we will reap the rewards of for many years to come, because a lot of the migration process was playing into that great atmosphere we have."

While things were starting to move off the pitch, March began on it with a pleasing 3-0 swatting-aside of QPR to avenge the 3-2 reverse in Shepherd's Bush four months earlier, then a 2-1 win at one-time bogey side Middlesbrough, during which the Bees, once again, came from behind to bring home the points. Then followed a run of just one win in eight games, as the Bees' impressive record of a top half finish in each of their Championship seasons looked under threat. However, wins over Leeds United, Bolton Wanderers and Preston North End in their final three games saw the Bees climb from 15th to 11th and keep that proud record intact.

It was, however, also the club's lowest finish since being promoted to the Championship. Each time they had faced adversity, Brentford had shown a poker face, ignored those who criticised their approach and slowly and calmly rebuilt. But, for all the exciting, attacking football and admiring glances from rival fans unable to comprehend why their own clubs consistently failed with much more impressive budgets and facilities, Brentford still looked like a club not quite ready to take the next step. There remained a flaw in the Brentford diamond.

All that was to change over the summer of 2019. The departures of Neil Maupay, to Brighton, and Ezri Konsa, to Aston Villa – along with that of Chris Mepham to AFC Bournemouth six months earlier – had banked Brentford well over £40m. This allowed for some serious reinvestment and in came the spine of the side with which Brentford would eventually win promotion with. The Brentford Revolution now had the funds to become a reality.

Christian Norgaard arrived from Fiorentina, Ethan Pinnock from Barnsley, David Raya from Blackburn, Matthias Jensen from Celta Vigo and Bryan Mbeumo from Troyes. However, the big statement signing, which made all football fans sit up and take notice, was the capture of Leeds United's skipper Pontus Jansson – who had seemingly fallen out with United boss Marcelo Bielsa.

Rico Henry noticed the difference straight away. Asked if that summer's recruitment seemed like a turning point for the club, he said: "With Pontus coming in, definitely, although I didn't know a lot about the Danish lads. But we saw big characters coming into the changing room, and we knew straight away we'd be challenging. They were leaders, and that's what we needed at the time, it just clicked. Our team was young as well, so there wasn't much maturity. Suddenly we're getting a big, experienced centre-back like Pontus, and it definitely helps."

Pinnock, meanwhile – having reflected previously on how when he had played against Brentford they had been impressive in everything but mentality – quickly realised he had been brought to the club as part of the solution. "We knew the club attacking-wise had a lot of quality players – good on the ball, good technical players – it was that defensive steel, and having that mentality when things weren't going great to stay in the game, that was needed," he said. "That other side of the game, the grit, the leadership. Sometimes the importance of that can be overlooked, but that summer we signed quite a few older players, different to what Brentford traditionally went for. But having the balance of youth and energy together with the older heads and leaders worked really well."

Looking back at that transformational window, Rasmus Ankersen said: "We were always trying to improve, and 2018 was more an extension of the strategy we had the previous year. We brought in pretty low fee players, like £1-2m. We felt we would improve, but it wasn't a big push to get promoted. That moment came the season after, the season we sold Maupay and brought in Norgaard, Jensen, Jansson – that's the year. A few weeks into the window, we realised we could be one of the biggest spenders in the Championship, which was crazy because there were so many teams that tried to go too quickly and spend so much money and couldn't spend any more. We realised this was a big opportunity, and we had the funds after selling Maupay, Konsa and Mepham. We were on the front foot for the first time and could buy with what we sold, and that's what we did. We said this year, we could make a push."

Andy Scott, having left Brentford two years previously, was preparing to make his next move, from Watford to Swansea – and while he was no longer involved with Brentford's recruitment, he nevertheless remained an interested observer. "The season after I left saw a bit of a change in terms of finances and the type of player we brought in," he said. "I always felt Brentford needed a bit more steel and experience, and while the general strategy was to bring in younger players, Jansson and Norgaard came in – solid pros who could grind it out – whereas before we were playing our way. Sometimes that meant we would get turned over, and sometimes we would beat teams easily. I think it was clever of Matthew, Phil and Rasmus to bring in some solid citizens to solidify the group and allow the younger players to play the way they want to play. You could see it was inevitable after that, that they were head and shoulders above the majority of sides in the Championship."

That summer also saw the return to Griffin Park of one of Scott's alumni, midfielder Marcus Bean, who had just hung up his boots following seven years with Colchester and Wycombe after ending his Bees playing days. Bean was initially brought back as a consultant scout, then promoted to head of emerging talent two years later. What he found on his return was a very different club to the one he had left in 2012.

"The rise has been amazing, from the time I was here as a player to when I came back, I could see the difference in the direction it was going in – you could see it had the potential it had," said Bean. "Not just the new stadium, the difference now at the training ground from my playing days is amazing. We used to eat dinner with tiny partitions, with the gym work happening next to you in a tiny pavilion – the facilities have improved so much. But everything has changed, there's nothing that has stood still, the club is always evolving. Yes, it was a surprise to see us make the Premier League, but when you look back at all the things being put in place at the early stages, maybe it shouldn't be too surprising, as we've got such clever people involved.

"When I first arrived in 2008 there was no real structure here, it was just Andy Scott and Terry Bullivant, and that was it for the scouting department really. Now there's a very clear structure and a clearly defined philosophy which everyone is working towards, and that's the hallmark of any good organisation. You need principles and a philosophy you stick to, and that's what we've got now. It's a different beast now, multiple people, but still not as many as at some Premier League grounds I go to, where there's more staff than players. We haven't got to that level yet, we're still a tight knit bunch in the grand scheme of things. I watched Spurs U23s in the FA Youth Cup, and they had 30 staff and 12 or 13 players. We're not at that level yet, but miles away from what we were in League Two, that's for sure. One thing you do notice working at this club is everyone is really on it, nobody is getting carried or pulled along. I always wanted to get into recruitment, or have a director of football role eventually, and I realised one route into that is mastering recruitment. I was at Wycombe at the time, and I always admired the nature of Brentford's recruitment, so I thought it'd be a great place to go and learn after playing football."

Another of Scott's former players to return in the summer of 2019 was winger Sam Saunders who, just like Bean, had seen out his playing days after leaving the Bees – in this case, two years previously – with Colchester United and Wycombe Wanderers. Having also just hung up his boots, Saunders came back as a B team coach, and despite having only been away for a couple of years, also saw significant changes to when he had last been at the club.

"By the time I came back the players had improved, as every year the club improves," he said. "Thomas had managed to get the team playing the way he wanted and it just keeps moving forward every year. The recruitment changes and the players are of a better level, the training ground improves, and all these things that have gradually been building since Brentford were in League Two. Every year they try to move forward, and they're consistent in their methods. For me, when I got the opportunity to coach the B team, I thought it would be the best place to start my coaching journey. We try to work as closely as possible with the first team to create a real pathway and an opportunity to be seen as part of the first team. We work on the pitches next to each other so we can see and hear each other, and they're in and around each other."

That summer also saw several players leave the club – individuals whose performance levels had dropped off after initially impressing; who had never really impressed in a Bees shirt; or those who had been decent but were never going to get Brentford to the next level. Dan Bentley, Yoann Barbet, Josh McEachran, Lewis Macleod, Moses Odbuajo, Josh Clarke and Tom Field were among those finding new clubs. Odubajo had been one of the heroes of the Bees' debut Championship season, while Clarke and Field will forever be remembered for their impressive derby performances, in particular, against QPR and Fulham respectively, but there was no room for much sentiment if Brentford were serious about building for a genuine push for the Premier League.

Of the departures, the most notable was the sale of Romaine Sawyers, whose boyhood club West Brom had come calling with a £3m sized wad. The likeable midfielder had unquestionably been a 'Marmite' player in his time with the Bees, cutting a frustrating figure in his early days after arriving from Walsall, and more than once was booed off the pitch by sections of the crowd, which divided supporters at times. But as Brentford progressed as a side, it soon became evident what Sawyers brought to it. Admittedly, he would never be one for blood-and-thunder challenges, that simply wasn't his game, but he emerged as one of the slickest passers of the ball to grace the Griffin Park turf, and one described by Alan McCormack earlier in this book as "a Rolls Royce of a player". Here, Sawyers gives an interesting insight into his on-pitch demeanour and another example of the club looking past the obvious when judging players.

"My body language can be deceptive at times but it's my playing style and part and parcel of who I am," said Sawyers. "It works the other way too – in some people's eyes I can make things look easy because of how laid back I am. I've had to deal with criticism before – it's not something that plays on my mind. In the nicest way possible, the people who are important know what my game is about. I won the Players' Player of the Year award last year. No disrespect to the other awards, but when we're here to work for ourselves and for our team-mates over the course of a 46-game journey, most players would say that award means the most.

"Thomas knows me personally and he's the one who picks the team. Sometimes he will show me footage and say, 'look, you're walking here', and I'll be the first to admit when that's the case. We have a great sports science department, so the statistics are always there – you can't hide from those numbers. I can look as laid back, lazy and languid as you like – whichever word you want to use – but the numbers are there to show that such an impression of me is not accurate. It's funny at times, how Marmite I can be. If I was an insecure person, I'd love to sit down with those who think I'm lazy and ask them to justify their viewpoint."

The departures of Bentley and Sawyers, following that of Egan a year earlier, saw the back of the last of the UK-focused signings from summer 2016. Bentley and Egan had both faded somewhat after initially shining brightly for the Bees, while Sawyers was the opposite, having come through some difficult times initially to become one of the most important players in the squad. And although many of Brentford's key signings were now coming from overseas, they weren't about to give up on the lower leagues either, according to Phil Giles. "We have signed some great players from overseas – Benrahma, Maupay, Norgaard and Jensen, to name just a few – but I think our hit rate in the lower leagues in England has been pretty high too," he said. "There's not been too many players we've taken from League One or League Two that have failed and we've had to sell them on – even players that haven't necessarily played much for us, like Dru Yearwood, who didn't really break through, but we made a profit on him. So, we'll continue to keep looking in the English leagues as one of our priorities."

Going into the new season, Brentford opted to stick with the 3-4-3 formation, with new boys Jansson and Pinnock slotting into two of the centre-back spots alongside Julian Jeanvier. Up front, having failed to replace the Brighton-bound Neal Maupay, Brentford instead switched Ollie Watkins from a wide role in the front three to a central position. It was a move which would eventually pay big dividends as Watkins finished the season with 26 goals, but it took some time for Brentford's new look forward line to settle. Eventually, the season would be remembered for the Bees' famed 'BMW' front three of Benrahma, Mbeumo and Watkins. However, they didn't play together until a 3-0 home win over Derby at the end of August, by which time the Bees had already lost three and won just one of their opening five games, with Sergi Canos and Emiliano Marcondes filling the other front roles.

"So, we finished the (previous) season with this 3-4-3 formation, and it worked really well," said Riemer. "We primarily closed the gaps defensively while we kept playing really well offensively, perhaps even better than we did before. We were more in control of the games because we had an extra player in the central positions, and we dominated with the ball. So, we started the new season with 3-4-3, but there was no flow in our plays. We were still solid defensively, but we needed more players who were good on the ball. With all due respect to the defenders, there were too many who didn't have quite what it took on the ball. Benrahma was injured and we really just needed someone who could make a difference on the ball. So, we went back to our 4-3-3 formation.

"We'd scouted new players for the 3-4-3 formation. We knew Maupay was going to be sold, and we knew changes were going to be made. Our top priority for the transfer window was a top-quality striker, for which we searched for a very long time. We found two possible targets we went all-in on, and we were so close to closing the deal, but they both changed their minds at the very last minute. At that point, we were in Austria on our training camp and thought 'what are we going to do now?'. Then Thomas and I decided to use Ollie Watkins as a striker. His actual position is winger, and he had never played as a striker – maybe except a few minutes if we were behind and needed an extra man on top. We talked about how he has all the qualifications to play as a striker – he has the physique, he works hard, he is good in the box and has proven he can score goals.

"It was a huge risk we took, but I felt it was the right decision. We really worked hard to get him ready to play as a striker, but obviously, none of us knew Ollie would go on to score 20-plus goals and be sold for more than £30m. However, we really felt he was the type of player we wanted and needed upfront. We weighed our options – either we go for our third or fourth choice on the transfer market, who we don't really know, or we go with a player we know really well. It was a big decision, and those big decisions were throughout the transfer window – Mathias Jensen, Christian Nørgaard and Bryan Mbeumo joined us too. Everything in the transfer window was scouted for the 3-4-3 formation, which we then changed."

Perhaps that goes some way to explaining why Brentford took a while to get going that season with a squad which, looking back, was one of the most talented the club has ever had, and certainly one armed with the quality to have been challenging for automatic promotion. After unveiling the BMW front line six games in, the Bees still won just one of their next five games, and were sitting 17th in the Championship table when Millwall came to Griffin Park in the middle of October.

Two goals down midway through the second half, there was plenty of unrest on the terraces and questions being asked of the team and man-

As soon as Brentford's BMW clicked into gear, they stormed up the league

agement. "You're getting sacked in the morning!" could be heard, sung from the back of the Ealing Road terrace, which shouldn't be overlooked at this stage.

Then came a massive turning point, not only in the season, but in Brentford's recent history. Josh Dasilva pulled one goal back with a sweet strike from the edge of the area from Benrahma's lay-off, before Mbeumo equalised with two minutes of normal time to play, cutting in from the right before beautifully finding the top corner with the aid of a helpful deflection. As if that wasn't enough drama for one afternoon, in the fourth minute of stoppage time, Rico Henry's cross from the left was played back across goal by Mbeumo for Watkins, who had earlier missed a penalty, to sweep home for a dramatic winner. Bedlam erupted on three sides of Griffin Park as Brentford fans celebrated wildly, having witnessed a quite remarkable turnaround. Thomas Frank was not sacked in the morning.

There was no looking back for the Bees now as Swansea and QPR were both swept aside in the following week, with the Bees winning 3-0 and 3-1 on the road. Wigan soon had three goals put past them on their own patch too, and although there were narrow defeats to Blackburn and Huddersfield, Brentford displayed their new attacking confidence to maximum effect with a 7-0 hammering of Luton Town at the end of November – Josh Dasilva taking home the match ball following a superb hat-trick.

It all changed that Saturday against Millwall as far as Riemer was concerned: "Sometimes there are these key situations where you can pinpoint, this is where it started, which probably isn't entirely true, but sometimes it feels like a specific win was the turning point. And this particular game, against Millwall, was our turning point. Actually, there were two things. First, Nørgaard didn't really fit into our 3-4-3 formation, he's best when he plays as number six with two midfielders in front of him. He wasn't bad the first six games, but he wasn't at his best, and we knew that. Mathias Jensen, too, is better when there are three central midfielders.

"Something wasn't working with the formation, and we didn't create enough chances. We also knew that Pinnock, Jansson and Jeanvier were good in a formation with four backs. There were so many signals that told us we should go back to 4-3-3 if we wanted to get the most out of every player. So, we played this game against Millwall. We were down 2-0 at home in front of a sold-out Griffin Park, and our start to the season had been quite poor. It wasn't a catastrophe, but it certainly wasn't good either. Then in the 84th minute, we score, 88th minute, 2-2. And then, far into added time, we score the winning goal. Something happened that day. The team just exploded, we got a massive confidence boost and the team sort of realised how good they actually are."

Although that famed Millwall comeback is generally seen as Brentford's turning point that season, Frank himself points to a game a few weeks earlier, when an Ollie Watkins hat-trick earned the Bees a 3-1 win at Barnsley having fallen behind in the first minute. "Those players who came in that summer were sold the idea of getting promoted – five top players, the spine of our team – and I remember thinking we can compete for top six," he said. Some people forget we didn't bring a striker in, but we believed we could convert Ollie to a striker, which is a risk of course. Top six was my aim, and we started slow again, lost 1-0 to Birmingham after we absolutely destroyed them, which tells you everything about how random a game is. We changed the system one more time to 4-3-3 for Barnsley away, and we won 3-1. We now had three good midfielders, so that definitely helped, and from there on, we more or less didn't look back."

Although December started with a narrow defeat to Sheffield Wednesday, the Bees easily dispatched Cardiff, Fulham and Swansea, and while 2019 ended with a disappointing defeat at Millwall, Brentford started 2020 in style by hammering Bristol City 4-0 at Ashton Gate before yet another derby win over QPR. A home defeat to Forest rounded off January, while February was ushered in by another huge win on the road, Said Benrahma scoring a hat-trick against Hull for the second successive season as Brentford ran riot on Humberside to win 5-1, before then edging past Middlesbrough 3-2 at home.

January saw the Bees strengthen with a double swoop for Oxford duo Tarique Fosu and Shandon Baptiste, as well as Turkish international Halil Dervisoglu from Sparta Rotterdam, all of whom would go on to become somewhat fringe players over the coming years, but all have had moments where they have contributed when called upon. It was an unusual amount of activity for that time of year for a club which, normally, shunned doing much incoming business in the January window due to a perceived lack of value amongst the panic buys and bun fights.

Ankersen said: "In the January 2020 transfer window, we had deal terms pretty much lined up with a winger we wanted to bring in, but eventually we decided there was not enough value in the deal, which is often the case in January. We had to weigh the price and the costs financially against what improvement you expect that player to make – how much that player is actually going to increase the probability of promotion – and it tends to be a lot less than people think. So, if it's one per cent or two per cent, then what's worth paying for that?"

At this point, in early February, Frank's men sat in fifth place, just two points off the automatic promotion places. Then followed five games without a win as the Bees were held to stalemates by Leeds, Birmingham, Blackburn and Cardiff – sandwiching a turgid 2-1 defeat at a Luton side determined to avenge their seven-goal hammering just three months earlier. By the time that run was over, the Bees were still in fifth but the gap on top two, Leeds and West Brom, had grown to 11 points, and automatic promotion looked like a fading dream. In fact, not even a play-off place was looking assured, with the gap on seventh place a mere three points, meaning there was little room for error. As the fans slipped away in the snow following the Kenilworth Road defeat, Brentford's chances of promotion felt as bleak as the weather.

However, the Bees were to end that run in style with a 5-0 hammering of Sheffield Wednesday at Griffin Park, but there was little time to celebrate what proved to be an untimely return to form. With Brentford due to leave their ground of 116 years at the end of the season for their new home at Lionel Road, the Sheffield Wednesday game proved to be the last one at Griffin Park in front of the fans, and the supporters' concerns turned away from the Championship promotion race and towards the Covid-19 pandemic that was rapidly taking a hold on not just the country, but the entire world.

As Covid spread alarmingly, Brentford's televised trip to Fulham six days after the Sheffield Wednesday game was postponed, quickly followed by all that weekend's fixtures. These alarming developments soon led to a blanket shutdown of the EFL until early April, as the emergency services battled to get the virus under control. Frustrating as it was for a Bees side, who had seemingly just turned the corner with a brilliant performance against the Owls, there was now a bigger picture in play. It was an unprecedented time for both staff and players – mindful of the need to keep fit as well as staying healthy in the midst of a pandemic – but not knowing when they would actually be taking to the pitch once more.

Frank said: "Kevin, Brian and I, plus the goalkeeping coach, had four of five players we were responsible for at that time, so we tried to communicate with them every week, especially if they were young and alone with no family. We created a fantastic culture, so the players when they came back were really in a good place, in better shape than last year in fact. That showed us the culture we had been creating was fantastic. We came back in a good place, all the players were fit and we had our best XI available." Rico Henry added: "We had programmes we had to do by ourselves. We still had to run and stay fit, and that fitness helped us at the end of the season."

In the event, it was three and a half months before Brentford were able to take to a pitch once more, but they, like all other clubs, would have to see out the season behind closed doors. Griffin Park took on a very different feel for the post lockdown matches with the remaining home fixtures played out in a sterile, training ground-like environment, devoid of the usual passionate support from Bees fans. Printed images of supporters' faces and large banners and flags were used to cover the empty seats and terraces – it was certainly not the way anyone had envisaged leaving Griffin Park.

Brentford finally returned to action on 20 June, with that postponed trip to Craven Cottage. Late goals from Benrahma and Marcondes not only sealed a 2-0 win, but kicked off an astonishing run of seven successive wins, which pulled the Bees right back into the promotion race. Crucially, six days after the Fulham game, Ollie Watkins scored the only goal of the game against one of the teams they were trying to chase down, West Brom, and that was followed by wins over Reading, Wigan, Charlton, Derby and Preston, as Frank's men all of a sudden looked unstoppable.

Going into the penultimate round of games, the Bees were just a single point behind the Baggies, and when West Brom lost at Huddersfield on the evening of Friday, 17 July, Brentford knew a win over Stoke the following day would put them into the automatic places with a game to go. Unfortunately, as had happened so often before, Brentford blew it when the stakes were at their highest, and Lee Gregory's goal seven minutes before half time proved to be the only one of the game.

"Absolutely impossible to prepare for," Frank admitted. "We played every third day, and we had no idea if they would drop points and if we could catch them or not. We went into the Stoke game meeting on the Friday at 6pm, eating dinner on the bus, playing the next day at 12.30 to minimise time together. We were jumping around when Huddersfield

Brentford smash Sheffield Wednesday 5-0 in the last ever game with fans at Griffin Park because of the Covid lockdowns

scored, then they equalised just before we left on the bus. Huddersfield scored again and people were jumping around and running up and down the bus. I tried to play it down that evening and told them it didn't change anything, but it was impossible to get the players ready for the Stoke game after that.

"No matter what first time experience you have in your life – the first time you drink a beer, the first time you get pissed, the first time you have sex, first time you sit an exam or whatever – you will always be nervous, you can't prepare for it. Another big thing was we got that message (the West Brom score) at 10pm, then had to go to sleep, get up early and play. There were definitely three or four players that didn't perform, but I hate people saying we bottled it. I agree we didn't make it, but if you look at it and randomise that game against Stoke, six or seven times we're not losing that, 100 per cent if you look at the chances. And even a draw would have kept it in our hands."

Speaking on the Mediano podcast, Riemer was in agreement. "If I could change one thing, it would be that we could play Stoke at the same time as West Brom played their game," he said. "When we heard that West Brom lost, I talked to some of the players after the season and they told me that they couldn't sleep the night before our game. It was all suddenly so close – too close almost. We had fought all season, we were the chasing team and now it was ours for the taking, and it couldn't possibly go wrong. That was the feeling we all had.

"Bear in mind, this team is built around young players who haven't experienced a lot yet, so being in a situation where all the focus is on you, and you have everything to lose. We were nervous and people didn't cope well. It, unfortunately, meant that the entire team performed several levels below standard. We previously talked about how the Millwall game was the positive turning point early in the season. Well, this was the negative turning point. The players suddenly realised the consequences and it changed everything."

All of which meant, going into the final game, at home to Barnsley, Brentford had to better West Brom's result against QPR. The Bees were one point behind, but had a superior goal difference. Unfortunately, Thomas Frank's men were up against a Barnsley side who had looked a dead certainty for relegation for much of the season, but were now gearing up to pull off a spectacular great escape.

What followed was certainly not the glorious swansong for Griffin Park that Bees fans had hoped for. They watched nervously on lockdown prescribed computer and television screens as their heroes failed to break down a stubborn Barnsley side, then found themselves in the unusual position of cheering QPR taking the lead, as Ryan Manning's goal at The Hawthorns not only put the Rs in front against West Brom, but also put Brentford into the automatic places.

Brentford's stay in second place was all too brief, however, as seven minutes later, Callum Styles gave Barnsley the lead at Griffin Park four minutes before half-time. Over in the Black Country, Stephane Diagana levelled for West Brom a minute before the break, and when Callum Robinson put them in front four minutes into the second half, the watching Bees fans knew the dream was over. Even Eberechi Eze's equaliser for QPR just after the hour mark only raised half-hearted cheers.

A flicker of hope was sparked when Josh Dasilva drew Brentford level on 73 minutes – requiring a QPR or Brentford winner – but there was a feeling that the game was already up. And so it proved when, going into injury time, Clarke Odour turned in a low cross to snatch a victory which kept Barnsley up by a single point and saw Brentford miss out by two, consigning the Bees to the lottery of the play-offs once more.

Thomas Frank said: "The Barnsley game was another crazy scenario, although we were more prepared for that one. They just came with a style of play that is extremely difficult to play against. Leeds played them the game before and were lucky to win 1-0, Barnsley had destroyed the best team in the Championship. We faced a team in form and still had massive chances when it was 1-1. For me, it was randomness plus that little bit of experience in terms of being chased, the pressure and so on."

Rico Henry agreed, and reckons Brentford were hampered by not being able, due to Covid, to see club psychologist Michael Caulfield, who had joined during Dean Smith's reign and was credited with helping the mental development of many of the players. "At the time a few of us were quite stressed out and overwhelmed by it all, and nervous all of a sudden," said Henry. "We knew we had to play those last two games as cup finals and give it our all, and I think we did do that, but we were also a bit anxious and nervous where we needed a cool head. That's where a psychologist perhaps would have helped – I don't think our psychologist could come in at the time due to Covid."

Riemer added: "Barnsley had had a terrible season, but they brought in Daniel Stendel who completely revolutionised them, and they went into the last game being one of the best performing teams in the league, despite being in the relegation zone. It was high-intensity and high-pressure all over the pitch throughout the game, almost Bielsa-style football. We tried to play short passes and play it out of the defence, but they were really good at applying pressure and marking us tightly, which resulted in a bad pass which they converted into a goal. That didn't exactly help our nervousness. Then we got the news from West Brom's game, so we knew if we won, we would be in the Premier League. It just resulted in a horrible game.

"I remember Thomas and I talking about how 'evil' it was that we didn't win and West Brom didn't win either. Had they won, the disappointment wouldn't have been as big. Everything worked out to our advantage, and it was right there for us to take it, but we couldn't finish the job by winning just one out of the two games against two teams at the bottom of the table – it hurt like hell. Looking back at those two games, they were different in many ways, but I have never seen a team wanting something that badly. I saw grown men crying after that last game, it was horrible. There was nothing they would rather want than to get Brentford promoted. It was so cruel, and losing to a team that we, on paper, should beat nine times out of ten, while our rivals, for once, helped us by drawing at West Brom, doesn't make it any better.

"At that time, you can say many things and you can do many things, but in the end, it doesn't really matter. There are things you can't control as a manager, like how players will react to situations like this – it is so difficult to do anything about. And with only a few days between that ending before we had to play the first play-off game against Swansea, we primarily focused on recovery and saying a few things about refocusing, getting back on track, reminding the players of how well they have performed in the season. You also have to remember that back in lockdown, we would have been more than happy with a play-off spot, which we tried to tell the players. We felt there were three teams left and we were better than all of them – we had every chance of finishing what we set out to do."

Brentford's last ever league game at Griffin Park thus turned out to be a huge anti-climax, not only due to the manner of defeat in such a crucial match, but also the lack of supporters to see it. Leaving a beloved stadium behind is always hard for the fans who have filled it week in and week out for decade upon decade, but even more so when circumstances prevented it from being given a proper farewell. That sense of loss was summed up by chief executive Jon Varney, who was unable to execute any of the plans he had for the old girl's last stand.

"Not being able to give Griffin Park its proper farewell was one of the saddest things to happen in my career," said Varney. "I'm so pleased we had that Sheffield Wednesday game, and all the fans left that day on a real high as hopefully their last memory of Griffin Park. We'd done a deal with Barnsley to have a reduced ticket allocation, which would have been a nightmare in the end because it was a do-or-die game for both of us. We planned bells and whistles, everything, but Covid took hold and everything had to be put on hold. It was absolutely brutal and genuinely sad for the fans. I think the players were really upset too that they were leaving the stadium the club had been in since 1904 and hadn't had that moment. I grew up at Griffin Park and I loved the atmosphere and the smell of it, the quirkiness of it, but we could never have carried on in there or reached the ambitions we're currently enjoying. But it will be a horrible scar forever that we never got to say goodbye to Griffin Park properly."

And so to the play-offs once more, where a late Jordan Ayew winner and a harsh, later to be rescinded red card for Rico Henry, left Brentford facing an uphill battle going into the second leg of the semi-finals against Swansea. Some 14 years earlier, in the second season under Martin Allen, it was the Swans who had knocked Brentford out at the same stage in the League One play-offs. On that occasion, Allen's troops had performed magnificently in Wales to come back to Griffin Park on level terms, but were fired down by a Leon Knight double in an anti-climatic second leg.

After finishing the regular season in such depressing fashion, Bees fans were left fearing more of the same when the Swans travelled down the M4 for the return leg three days after the first, but they found a Brentford side in an irresistible mood, having recaptured the form which had taken them on that magnificent post-lockdown run. The Bees simply blew Swansea away in a stunning first quarter of an hour in which Ollie Watkins finished off a superb move involving a quick throw from David Raya and a sublime through-ball from Mattias Jensen, before Emiliano Marcondes – who a year later would score an even more crucial goal against the Swans – nodded home Said Benrahma's cross to put Brentford in front on aggregate. Bryan Mbeumo extended that lead a minute into the second half, and even when Rhian Brewster pulled one back for the visitors 12 minutes from time, there was never a feeling that it would be anything other than Brentford's night.

Watching from the sidelines that night was, of course, Andy Scott, who you will recall, having left the Bees for a third time in November 2017, had spent two years as UK football recruitment director and then sporting director at Watford after, before taking up a role as head of recruitment at Swansea. "The good thing that came out of that match was I was able to be at Griffin Park for the last ever game – which was obviously nice, even though we lost," said Scott, looking back at the clash. "Brentford just blew us away in the first half hour and we struggled to get back into it, so it was bittersweet really, but nice to be there and experience that at the end – fate really."

Outside the stadium a fairly large gathering of Brentford fans had assembled from the neighbouring pubs to mark the win, as well as the final ever game to be played at Griffin Park. Strict Covid regulations meant that the party was a limited affair, but emotions ran high as the floodlights were turned off, one by one, for the final time, bringing an end to 116 years of football at the proud old ground.

Having swept aside Steve Cooper's Swansea in style, could Brentford now take that form into the final? It was perfectly set up; a winner-takes-all battle against West London rivals Fulham, albeit still played out in front of an empty stadium. The Bees had already done the double over the Cottagers that season, indeed, since promotion to the Championship in 2014, Brentford had beaten Fulham six times compared to just two wins for the men from SW6. History was against Brentford, however, with seven previous play-off campaigns all having ended in defeat – three of them in the final.

Looking back to the weeks leading up to the final, Benham admitted despite a cool and calm exterior, and introducing a club culture based around rational thought ahead of emotional decision making, even he couldn't help but think like a 'normal' Brentford fan at times. "To be perfectly honest, the week leading up to it was miserable," he said in his 2022 Bees United interview. "The nerves are so horrible in the week leading up to Fulham, as they were leading up to Yeovil (2013 play-off final). In fact, I'd say Yeovil was even worse. I could honestly say that it was so horrible that by the time we got to extra time against Fulham. I was just thinking, 'I want this to be over, at least in an hour's time it's going to be over one way or another'. And I got into that state even after five minutes against Swansea (2021 final). I thought, 'at least in two hours this is going to be over'."

In the event, a dull match against Fulham produced no goals in normal time, and for the first half of extra time it looked for all the world as if it would be going to penalties. Only in the second half of the added 30 did the game finally spark into life, and unfortunately for the Bees, that breakthrough was provided by Fulham's Joe Bryan, who saw David Raya

Thomas Frank tries to console Sergi Canos after the Wembley defeat

off his line whilst sizing up a 105th minute free kick. With Raya expecting a cross, Bryan instead smashed the ball towards goal from 40 yards out, and despite desperately scrambling back, Raya couldn't keep the ball out of his net.

As Brentford threw men forwards in search of an equaliser, gaps appeared at the back, and Fulham took advantage by adding a second, again through Bryan, with three minutes left. Henrik Dalsgaard pulled one back for the Bees with a close-range header deep into injury time, but it was too little too late. The Brentford play-offs curse had struck once again – this time in the cruellest way imaginable.

After the game, Benham was back to his usual rational self, and his overriding concern was the now inevitable departure of two thirds of the BMW, Ollie Watkins and Said Berahma. On a positive note, Watkins' reaction to the defeat, despite knowing he would be leaving, confirmed for Benham that the club had got the character assessment aspect of its recruitment spot on – the 'no dickheads' policy was coming into its own. That's not to say there were any bad apples back in 2013, but for Benham, the reaction to this defeat, compared to back then, was pronounced.

"I saw a documentary about Mary Decker and Zola Budd (who clashed in the 1984 Olympics 3,000m final)," he said. "That really puts things into perspective. Decker was just too young in 1972, she was injured in 1976, and in 1980 there was a boycott, so 1984 was her final chance. If she doesn't win this, she's never going to win it again. That put it into perspective for me, that it wasn't like that was our one chance. I always knew we'd have more chances.

"To be honest, my rational way of looking at things was if we go up, we've got an 80 per cent chance to stay up, and if we don't go up, then we've got a 60 per cent chance to go up the next year. So rather than being all or nothing, it was 80 versus 60. I mean, the thing that really stung was losing Ollie and Said. That's because they were so integral. I was very confident we would get there at some point because we were the second best team in the league that year behind Leeds, and we'd been pretty damn unlucky, so I didn't feel that's our one chance of getting to the Premier League gone. It was more like, 'what a pain in the arse', we're going to have to deal with the sales of Ollie and Said.

"After we lost to Yeovil, I was surprised at the after-party as some players seemed quite chipper. It felt as if they thought, 'Okay, Brentford ain't gonna be in the Championship, but I will be'. Someone like Ollie could have been forgiven for thinking number one, 'I'm going to be in the Premier League come what may', and number two, 'I'm going to be better off financially if it isn't Brentford'. But Ollie was absolutely crying his eyes out all night. Phil Giles saw him in the morning and he was still crying."

For Thomas Frank, there was little to choose between Brentford and Fulham, and a toss up between two very evenly matched teams was pretty much decided by a goalkeeping error. "The final, of course, there were nerves, but it was a 0-0 game," he said. "We'd destroyed them at Griffin Park, and it had been even at their place, when we got two late goals. I knew that game would be a flip of the coin, and it should have gone to penalties – then the best keeper in the division made a mistake."

Riemer said: "We tried to the best of our abilities to take it as a regular game, where we just had to go out there and do our jobs. Having said that, everyone knows what was at stake, and you can easily feel and see that. The game was characterised by nervousness. We beat Fulham both games in the regular season, but in the final they were the better team. Scott Parker had definitely learned from his mistakes and had prepared his team well. He made some tactical adjustments in the midfield, where they played with four players in sort of a box. That really hurt our three midfielders, and it was really hard for us to apply pressure and close the gaps.

"With that being said, it was a very close game, and you just had the feeling that the game would be decided by the smallest margins. It all ended in extra time where they scored directly from a freekick. It's a freekick on one side of the pitch, and 99.9 per cent of the time, it will be a cross towards the tall players in the box. Then suddenly Marcondes has a small brawl with Mitrovic, and at the same time as they take the free-kick, the ref blows his whistle because he wants to have a talk with the two players. That kick was a cross. But because he blew his whistle, they obviously had to retake the free kick. While the ref gets a talk with Marcondes and Mitrovic, Fulham's goalkeeping coach calls Joe Bryan, the free-kick taker, over to tell him something. Then Thomas and I realise that they are going to do something. So, we start looking for unmarked players or gaps in the defence, but everyone is marked, and we are organised properly. But what Fulham had seen was that our goalkeeper, David Raya, who had had a fantastic season, was standing relatively far out in the box because he anticipated a cross. So, Joe Bryan chooses to shoot from an obscure angle and relatively far out, and unfortunately, it's on target and Raya can't reach it because of his initial position. I mean, what are the odds? The ref blows his whistle after their first kick, they retake it and shoot from that angle... It's the smallest of small marginals that decided the game.

"After the game, we drove back to Thomas' house. They have this sort of split house, where Thomas and his family lived in one part and I live in the other part. We felt as if we had let down people, it was awful. We all met up the day after because one of our coaches was leaving, and we felt we needed to say a proper goodbye. When I woke up the day after the game, I felt as if I had the worst hangover, and I hadn't even had a drop of alcohol. People came in with tears in their eyes, looking down, and no one knew what to say to each other. It was one of those situations where there are no proper ways to do it. Thomas said a few words, and after some time, people went home. And trust me, people really wanted to go home, also because we only had eleven days before we started again."

Thomas Frank had spoken about the randomness in play during one of the final league matches, the away defeat to Stoke, and Phil Giles reckons it played a part in the final against Fulham too. "There's just a lot of randomness in football," he said. "Yes we can point to decisions we made, or in-game decisions and selections by Thomas, and to the players we did or didn't sign, but actually, so much also comes down whether you get the rub of the green, or players staying fit. There are such fine margins, and we were so close to going up against Fulham.

"I think you can sometimes over analyse and try to pick out lots of things you could change, but actually, we know where our underlying level is. I think we're pretty strong at understanding where that is and acknowledging that random things can happen that are out of our control. Let's not overreact to them and let's just keep going, and eventually this season, next season, the season after, we hope we'll get there. That's more or less it, it's no more secret than that, I don't think."

Giles also spoke about a sense of relief amidst the heartache, as it meant, with a new season kicking off in just a matter of weeks, he could finally get on with putting together a squad, knowing which division Brentford would be in. He went on to say that the short turnaround due to Covid probably helped the club in the long run, as it meant there was no time to dwell on the disappointment of Wembley, and instead a need to get straight back on the collective horse.

"In a sense, when the final whistle went, it was also nice, because I'm sitting there thinking what are we going to do about the summer? Are we promoted and trying to build Premier League players or staying in the Championship? The final whistle did provide a bit of relief for me as I could actually get on with my job. I said straight after the game to Matt, who wasn't in an overly good mood, right, tomorrow, we'll get on with getting Ivan Toney. We knew we'd have to sell Ollie and Said, and we knew we'd be getting Ivan, so we just got on with the job. When I got home that night I did lay on the couch in the kitchen, on my own as the family had gone away, ate a bowl of cornflakes and went to bed. That was it.

"We went into training the next day and Ollie was in tears, feeling he had let us down. He didn't really want to leave, he wanted to stay as he loved it here so much, but knew he had to go for the good of his career. Ollie was tired and emotional – the staff and players were all disappointed – but it was important for me to take myself above that and not get sucked into it. After the game, I went into the dressing room and chatted to Pontus, Dalsgaard, Kevin O'Connor, and said we're in a great place to start the season in two weeks. That probably helped as instead of moping, we can go right, season starts in two weeks, we think we're the best team in the league, let's deliver it. That's not something you want to necessarily hear at that point, people want to talk about how terrible it is, but I took myself out of that emotion. We weren't actually allowed down there due to Covid rules, and we had to lobby the EFL, but there was no way the Fulham guys weren't going down there – we said the winning side are going to want to celebrate, the losing side needs to commiserate."

For Rasmus Ankersen, there was no clear reason for Brentford's defeat, making it all the more frustrating. "The media, and maybe the fans to some extent, wanted to build a narrative around why we didn't go up," he said. "But sometimes it can be dangerous to create them, you have to be sure about having the right narrative if you want to make big decisions based on them. And sometimes it can just be random, and it can be really frustrating if there is no clear narrative for why."

However, looking back, Andy Scott reckons the defeat, hard to swallow as it was at the time, was best for Brentford in the long run. "In a weird kind of way, losing to Fulham in the play-off final laid the foundations, as the team was good enough – but to go up to the Premier League with no fans would have been crap," he added. "It's like it was meant to be. The foundations off the pitch have been solid for the last few years." It was a belief which would finally translate into the Bees finally achieving their ultimate goal.

For Rico Henry, with the following season just a matter of weeks away due to the delays Covid had caused, there was little time for reflection or dwelling on the disappointment. "Going into the final, we were all excited and thought we would do it," he said. "It was a bit of a slow burner of a game, nothing was really clicking for either side, a bad day for us overall. Straight after the game, the gaffer said next season is just around the corner, and on the first day back in, he said fresh start, we're going to do it this year. And in truth, we had a lot of belief going into the new season."

From the fans' perspective, there was a sense of bewilderment and sadness. Brentford had provided a wonderful and much needed distraction to the awful backdrop of Covid deaths and financial uncertainty. The stunning seven straight win run, that had hauled in West Brom and made automatic promotion a possibility, was a real shot in the arm. But would the Bees really come back as strong and finish the job off? I'm not sure everyone thought they would. However, the summer signing of Ivan Toney certainly perked up the fanbase after the inevitable loss of Benrahma and Watkins.

CHAPTER ELEVEN

With more than three months of the previous season having been 'lost' to Covid-related lockdowns, and with the footballing authorities attempting to realign the traditional season schedule timings, Brentford's players found themselves back in pre-season training just 11 days after that heart-breaking play-off final defeat. Another 11 days on, and the players would be trotting out for their first pre-season friendly, a 3-0 win over Derby County at the St. George's Park National Football Centre.

Six days after that, sandwiching a 2-1 friendly defeat at West Ham, Brentford completed their brief and somewhat shortened pre-season with a 2-2 draw against Oxford – the first game at the new Brentford Community Stadium. Sadly, as with the Griffin Park farewell a month or so earlier, ongoing Covid restrictions meant supporters had to watch from home as the club's shiny new home saw its first action – Sergi Canos bagging a second half brace before Derick Osei replied with a late double for Oxford.

"Thomas and I took 11 days off, and after that short break, we met up with the squad and started the preparations for this season," said Riemer at the time. "So, for almost two years, we only had those 11 days off. And the same goes for the players. To do that and still demand the players to keep their sanity, you have to find gaps in the schedule to take a day off."

The Bees now had another 11 days – an increasingly familiar number – to prepare for their Championship opener, although in between there was a penalty shoot-out win over Wycombe Wanderers in the first round of the EFL Cup. Although technically still with the club, the absence of Watkins and Benrahma from the pre-season friendlies spoke volumes about where they were expected to be once the season kicked off again in anger. Watkins was indeed, within a week, an Aston Villa player, as a tidy £28m made its way from the Midlands to TW8. Replacing him, and having made his debut in that Oxford friendly, was hot-shot striker Ivan Toney, bought in from Peterborough United, where he had scored 49 goals over two seasons, for an initial £5m. He was a player with a deadly mixture of natural ability and unswerving self-confidence, Toney seemed a Premier League player in waiting.

Looking back at the transfer, Phil Giles admitted the Bees had tried to sign Toney six months earlier, and had to go through a real tug-of-war with Peterborough before landing their man. "In my experience, I don't think clubs treat Brentford any differently – the one exception I'd say is when we tried to sign Ivan Toney from Peterborough in January 2020," he said. "Rasmus led on that one, and he had a bit of back and forth with Darragh MacAnthony, who I don't know personally, but seems like a good guy. Some of the messaging was good, so we made an offer and he came back and just said, 'I know what you're up to, you're gonna basically take him for peanuts, sell Watkins for massive money and do the same with Ivan'. I said to Rasmus, you're gonna have to basically reply and say, yeah mate, our game's up on that one, we can't deny that!"

Ankersen added: "I went to watch Ivan with Lee Dykes, our head of recruitment – it was on a really, really cold January day and Peterborough were playing Wycombe. We had a meeting before the game with Darragh and his three co-owners – we had been trying to get the price down, but they stuck to their £10m valuation. We left the meeting feeling it would be difficult, but then after five minutes Ivan scored. Ten minutes later, he made an assist. At half time I went to the washrooms, where I bumped into one of the co-owners, and he said to me, 'Hey, did you see that, so that's another £1m for the goal, then another £1m for the assist'. I said to Lee, let's get out of here – we left at half time and realised the deal had broken down, and I don't think we felt it would come back to us again – but fortunately it did. But the standard reply, every time you send an offer to Peterborough, no matter what the offer, is 'I looked at your offer and I thought it was April Fool's Day'. That's their standard reply."

If the pursuit of Toney proved to be somewhat protracted, Said Benrahma's exit was fast turning into a real saga, and as speculation mounted over a move to West Ham, which dragged on into the start of the new season, the Algerian was left out of Thomas Frank's first two matchday

Ivan Toney scored the goals that made Premier League dreams come true

squads, as the Bees kicked off with a disappointing defeat to Birmingham for the second successive season, before giving the new stadium a proper welcome as it hosted its first league game, during which the Bees brushed aside Huddersfield 3-0.

Benrahma returned as a late sub in the next game as the Bees were held to a 1-1 draw at Millwall, a game in which Toney got off the mark with an equaliser from the spot. The game saw Ryan Woods turn out for The Lions, who before the game declared his former side as one of the favourites for promotion. "They've lost Ollie Watkins and will probably lose Said Benrahma, but they are still a very good footballing team and they don't sign players unless they fit into the culture," Woods told London Online. "I always look out for Brentford's results. It is a club that I hold dear to me, I had three great years there. I moved on to go to probably a bigger club in terms of stature in Stoke – hoping to play in the Premier League – it didn't work out that way. I think you have to put Brentford up there [as one of the favourites for promotion] after the success they had last season. They have lost two of their best players, but how many times have you seen that over the years? They've always gone out and found more golden nuggets."

Although Benrahma's final Brentford game came against Preston on 4 October, again as a late sub, his proper farewell came a few days earlier, when he scored two brilliant goals as Brentford – having already dispatched Premier League sides Southampton and West Brom – made it a hat-trick of top flight scalps in the League Cup with a 3-0 fourth round hammering of Fulham, gaining a small modicum of revenge for the play-off final defeat.

Eventually, Benrahma finally left the hive and signed for West Ham on a season-long loan, with a view to making the move permanent the following summer. Sad as it was to see another hugely talented player depart, for an eventual fee of around £22m, there was also some relief that the protracted saga was finally over. There were concerns, however, over how the Bees would cope without their wing wizard – especially as his final game had seen a return to the bad old ways with 2-0 half time lead at home to Preston being wiped out by four Lilywhites goals in 18 devastating second half minutes, earning the visitors the spoils 4-2. The defeat was partially explained by the loss through injury of defensive midfield maestro Christian Norgaard which affected the team's balance.

His drawn out exit hasn't dampened the opinion of Bees fans that Benrahma is arguably the most skillful player to have pulled on a Brentford shirt prior to the arrival of Christan Eriksen. Although he was only at the club for two full seasons, you could fill several YouTube reels with outrageous pieces of skill and spectacular goals. It was certainly great business bringing him in from Ligue One side Nice for a reported £3m. Ankersen remembered: "Said was really keen on joining Brentford – we were the only place he wanted to go – so I don't know if it was the best negotiation in the world. But I remember during the first week of training I spoke to some of the players, and they were just like, 'wow, what a magician we've got in the camp'. His skill levels were unreal." Giles added: "I'd say Said surprised me the most, not because I didn't think he was a good player, but just the level he got to was incredible, and the money we got for him."

Without Benrahma, although the Bees recovered from that Preston defeat in his final game to beat Coventry 2-0 and Sheffield Wednesday 2-1 – with the increasingly impressive Ivan Toney bagging braces in both games – they looked anything but a side with promotion ambitions following a 3-2 loss at Stoke in which the Bees had been 3-0 down with half an hour left, before Marcus Forss pulled back two late goals.

However, after that reverse at the Bet365 Stadium, it would be another four months before the Bees tasted defeat again, as Thomas Frank's men embarked on an incredible league run of 21 games without a loss. In fact, the only time they found themselves on the negative side of a scoreline during that time was a 2-0 defeat in the club's first ever League Cup semi-final. Having knocked out Newcastle a few days before Christmas to claim the fourth successive Premier League scalp, the Bees were unable to make it five and book an historic place at a Wembley final. Covid limitations had seen the authorities make the semis one legged affairs, so there would be no return match back at Brentford to try and turn things around. It was also Brentford's first brush with VAR and Ivan Toney had a 'goal' chalked off that would have stood in any of the previous rounds. The Bees were, however, looking every bit a side ready to take their place amongst the elite, as that magnificent giant-killing League Cup run testified.

Things didn't click into place immediately, however, as four of the first five games in that 21-match run ended up in stalemates – against Norwich City, Swansea City, Middlesbrough and Wycombe Wanderers – with the only three-pointer coming against Luton Town at Kenilworth Road. Successive wins over Barnsley, Rotherham United and QPR then lifted the Bees from 11th to fourth, and they never looked back from there. Especially impressive was a run of eight wins in nine league games between mid-December and mid-February, during which Wycombe Wanderers became the second team to concede seven goals to the Bees in a game in as many seasons. Reading (twice), Cardiff, AFC Bournemouth, Luton Town, Bristol City and Middlesbrough were also left empty-handed, the only blot on the copy book being a 1-1 draw at Swansea.

Just before the start of that winning winters' run, at the start of December, a 2-2 draw at home to Blackburn saw an emotional moment as Sergi Canos, having missed nine months spanning two seasons through injury, scored his first goal in almost two years with a brilliant finish to put Brentford 2-1 up, cutting in from the left before curling a superb effort into the top corner from the edge of the area. It was Canos' first goal in almost two years – and with (a smattering of) fans allowed back inside Griffin Park for the first time since the start of Covid (before a second lockdown just before Christmas put paid to fans again), a tearful Canos celebrated not only his goal in front of them, but the end of the most testing time of his career.

"It all comes from inside," he said. "I suffered a lot, and it was a really hard time for me and my family. My family is happy when they can watch me play – that has been our life since I was a young lad – they come everywhere to watch me play, then that changed completely. I came back after the injury and we lost the final at Wembley, then had ten days off and straight back in. I started playing again with the team but you need that goal or something which gives you that lift again, but it wasn't coming. Thomas and everyone at the club trusted me as they kept putting me in the starting line up, but you feel you have to give something back. To have a winger, if the season starts in August, and to get to December without scoring a goal, it was always playing on my mind. So when I scored that goal, it just all came out. I released everything, like opening a wine bottle. It gave me the feeling that it was me again, but before that it was hell!"

For Riemer, the run of results was all the more impressive given that the intensity of a Championship season was difficult to prepare for under normal circumstances compared to what he knew in Denmark – never mind in a season congested by a late start and now with a cup run thrown into the mix. "In total, we're going to exceed 50 games at the end of this season," he said at the time. "There are days that I don't even know what day of the week it is, I just know we have another game in two days. I believe the Championship is one of the most intense leagues, not just because of the high amount of games, but also because of how the games are played. There is high pressure, hard tackles and the referees allow quite a lot in both set-pieces and open play. This means all the games are extremely intense, which requires a lot physically. You have to be ready for a game just three days after the last one.

"We do not have, like many other clubs may have, a squad of 28 players where each and every one has experience with fighting for either promotion or relegation to or from the Premier League. We have a small squad, which makes us very dependent on every single player. Not only do we focus on recovery, but we also often have days where the coaches have groups of 10-12 players and they have to make sure that they all run sensible and practical sessions so that when they have to play games, they haven't only practised possession plays, but they have actually taken the necessary steps to prepare for the next game. So, the many games and the little time for training and practice have forced us to think differently."

When the Bees finally tasted defeat again, they did it in style – losing at home to Barnsley on Valentine's Day 2021 before also losing to QPR and Coventry to make it three defeats in a row after 21 games without one. But any fears that the wheels would come off were quickly dispersed with wins over Sheffield Wednesday and Stoke, and although Norwich then took the three points at Carrow Road at the start of March, it would be the last regular-season defeat Brentford would suffer.

However, whereas Brentford had led the table at the end of their 21-game run, they were now playing catch-up to top two Norwich and Watford, and a run of six draws in seven games between mid-March and mid-April put a real dampener on any automatic promotion hopes. A 1-0 win at promotion rivals Bournemouth got the Bees back on track and sparked a run of four successive wins (also beating Rotherham, Watford and Bristol City) to bring the curtain down on the regular season, but it was too little too late for a top two place, as Brentford finished four points adrift of second-placed Watford. So, it would have to be the play-offs again. What could possibly go wrong?

When semi-final opponents Bournemouth carved out a one goal first-leg lead, then doubled it in the fifth minute of the second leg, it looked like the curse of the play-offs had struck again. But Ivan Toney equalised from the spot before Vitaly Janelt – a bargain €600,000 buy from Vfl Bochum in October as one for the future but thrust immediately into the Championship fray due to an injury to Christian Norgaard – continued his impressive form with a goal which levelled the tie on aggregate. All of which set the scene for Marcus Forss, in front of a (reduced capacity) matchday crowd once more, to hit a dramatic late winner, which sent the Bees back to Wembley.

Lifelong Brentford fan Sara Loewenthal was one of the lucky supporters able to attend the semi final against Bournemouth, as well as the final against Swansea. Here she shares her emotions about being able to watch her team again in that must-win clash with The Cherries. "To say I was apprehensive making my way to the playoff semi final would be an understatement. I'd been to every Brentford play-off final and every home play-off semi (apart from the Covid 2020 of course), and ultimately, we know only too well how those went. It would be my second visit to Lionel Road, having also been to the Derby bore-draw with fans finally able to attend before the second lockdown, but I felt more hope this time. I can't really explain why, I just did. Bournemouth scoring so quickly dampened my belief just a bit, but I still felt we were very much in it, albeit down 2-0 on aggregate. Toney's penalty and the confidence he showed under pressure made my heart jump but I was still guarded. Mepham's sending off settled my nerves though, then the sight of a swashbuckling Janelt charging in to slam home that brilliant goal made the heart race and I thought, 'we've got this'. Even Begovic's comical attempts at cheating wouldn't stop us – it felt like a question of when, not if. That moment seemed like a long time coming, but after Emiliano's cross and Forss's superb winner, I had such a feeling of relief and euphoria. Yeah, the final ten minutes seemed like an hour, and I had a few 'it's Brentford innit' moments, but I could see this was a team that was capable of doing it this time. They had a steel I hadn't seen in previous playoffs. This team wouldn't fold after an opposition goal, they were different. Later, on the bus to my car, a bee crawled up my Brentford scarf and left some pollen. That was surely a sign that this year was ours."

On co-host duties on the club's iFollow commentary for the second leg was former Bees striker Charlie MacDonald, who had been impressed with the impact of finally having fans inside the new stadium. "I was at the new stadium during Covid when it was empty and wondered if it would be able to create the same atmosphere as Griffin Park, would there be the same passion?" he said. "I did the commentary for the play-off game against Bournemouth – when there were only 5,000 fans, and I kid you not, I got goosebumps with the noise they were making. You don't realise how important the fans are as a player until they're not there. The impact of the stadium being full is fantastic, the fans definitely play their part in what Brentford are doing. They will be sitting there now watching their team play the likes of Manchester City and Manchester United, and credit to them, they deserve it, because the club have worked their socks off both on and off the pitch."

For chief executive Jon Varney, it was an emotional moment to finally see a decent-sized (if not capacity) crowd inside the new ground, after all the hard toil which had gone into transitioning from Griffin Park to the Brentford Community Stadium - especially during a pandemic. Looking back to that second leg, Varney was visibly pleased for those supporters finally able to (2,000 had been allowed in for two league games the previous December). "I've said before that leaving Griffin Park without a proper farewell was sad, but as brutal as that was, it was also brutal to open the new stadium without fans," said Varney. "That hurt the staff, because we'd worked tirelessly on that migration process for 18 months. That's why, for me, the stadium came alive for the Bournemouth game. We had 4,000 in there and the atmosphere was unbelievable. We had a desperate start to the game and came back to win it. Stadiums are bricks and mortar and steel and glass, but what makes a stadium is people and memories and occasions, and that was the first time that stadium had felt like home."

It wasn't all sweetness and light though, as Phil Giles' thoughts turned back to 12 months before. "The play-offs are honestly miserable, a horrible experience," he said, echoing the thoughts of most Bees fans before 2021 as well as the club's owner. "So, when we scored the third goal against Bournemouth at home in the second leg, Matt, who was sitting next to me, turned and said, 'Oh no...' or words to that effect. When I questioned his comment, he said that's another week of absolute stress and misery! Although to some extent, when we lost the previous year, after dealing with the players and coaches who were devastated, for me at least, there was clarity there. We knew where we were then, you can't change it. We just had to move forward knowing we had a great chance the next year. It was a case of 'we've got four weeks to get ready', so let's crack on."

Back at Wembley, Brentford would once again come up against Swansea City, who the Bees had conquered in the previous season's semi-finals. Whereas play-off finals had, for too long, been something to fear for Bees fans – scars still raw years on from a succession of past failures – this time it felt different. This time, it felt like everything was in place. That everything the club had been building towards culture-wise for the past 15 years was finally about to be realised, Brentford Football Club were finally ready to break free from the shackles of the past. The Revolution was about to happen and 5,000 gob-smacked Bees supporters were lucky enough to be able to witness it in the flesh.

From the moment Ivan Toney, Brentford's penalty-taker extraordinaire, opened the scoring from the spot just ten minutes in, after Bryan

Mbeumo had been brought down by Swans keeper Freddie Woodman, there was no looking back. The Bees were comfortably in control, and even more so after a fantastic move turned defence into attack ten minutes later – Mbeumo making the hard running and laying the ball off to Mads Roerslev, who had matched his lung-bursting efforts. The young Dane held the ball up before picking out a late run into the area from Emiliano Marcondes, who calmly slotted the ball past Woodman to send Bees fans everywhere into raptures.

Toney almost added a spectacular third when his long-range volley crashed back off the underside of the bar, but it mattered not as any limited resistance Swansea put up disappeared when they were reduced to ten men midway through the second half – Jay Fulton receiving his marching orders for chopping down Mattias Jensen. Some watching on were able to enjoy the rest of the proceedings, safe in the knowledge that it was different this time – this was new Brentford and negative history counted for nothing on this day of days. Others, not quite able to leave the past fully behind, were scarcely able to believe it and wondered just how the Bees were going to mess up a two-goal lead against ten men – even going into injury time.

When the final whistle blew, it felt like those nine previous failed play-off campaigns – not to mention three Football League Trophy final defeats – had finally been laid to rest. Who would have thought, when Wigan lifted the Freight Rovers Trophy under the twin towers in 1985, that the Bees would go on to lose six more finals – both at Wembley and the Millennium Stadium – before finally winning one? And who would have thought, after being frustrated by Eric Nixon and knocked out in the semis by Tranmere in their first experience of the play-offs in 1991, that it would take nine more before the Bees would triumph in one. But this final was bigger than them all – not just for the right to play in the Premier League, but to do so in front of their fans, as Covid restrictions gradually eased. This was the big one, and Brentford had finally done it.

In the last chapter, we looked at Benham's reactions around the final against Fulham the previous season, and how, despite basing his whole success story around rational thought over making emotional decisions, being a long-standing Brentford fan had naturally forced doubts to creep in. He was no different this time round. "At half time against Swansea, when we were 2-0 up, I couldn't sit down, I was pacing around nervously," he said. "Ras said to me afterwards, 'you'd prepared yourself that we were going to lose, even though I knew we had a 70 per cent chance to win'. So, I'd mentally prepared myself to lose, and all of a sudden, I was having to come to terms with, 'shit, we might win'. Even when they got the red card, my main thought was, 'how terrible is this going to be if we don't go up now? And if we don't go up now, we'll never ever recover from it'. About 30 seconds from the end, I realised, 'shit, they're not going to have time to score, and then score again'."

For Sergi Canos, there was never any doubt on the day. He said: "If I'm honest, we knew we were going to win since the play-offs started. The mentality we had at that time was crazy. I remember the walk before the game was very calm, we were 100 percent confident. There was no option, either we win or we win, and we started the game like we were winning already. We started fighting and creating chances straight away. There were some nerves obviously, but it was a fantastic day, and it felt like everything was connected for us to win."

One who was sadly watching from the sidelines that day, due to injury, was their longest-serving constant player (Canos had signed for his first spell earlier but left and come back), Rico Henry, who reflected on the journey he had been on with the club over the previous six years. "When I signed, I honestly thought it would be a stepping stone to the Premier League rather than Brentford being in the Premier League," he said. "But coming into the club, I realised how much togetherness there was, and that's when I started realising it could happen. Probably not the first season, especially with the injuries where I lost a bit of self-belief, but when I got back from the injuries and had a season where I played every game. The season we lost the play-off final is when we started really believing, we definitely knew we would do it.

"I was on crutches for the final, and carrying crutches around is annoying in general, but especially at the play-off final. I tried to throw them away but the doctor was having none of it. It was frustrating at the time but I got a real buzz watching the team, celebrating with the players and physio when we scored the first, and when we scored the second, I knew we'd done it. I remember being 2-0 up with time running out, everyone around me just saying, 'wow, we're going to the Premier League'. It didn't sink in until maybe a week after."

Ethan Pinnock had been at the club for a far shorter time than Rico Henry – but he too was surprised at how quickly Brentford had become genuine contenders in his two years there. "You always think it's possible," he said. "Before I signed, I looked at where Brentford were finishing, comfortably in the top half for maybe four or five years. But how quickly we managed to progress and establish ourselves as one of the top teams in the league could be seen as surprising.

"The brief was we were looking to get into the play-offs and go from finishing in the top ten to the top six and go from there. I think after two to three months, once the team had settled and learnt each other's games, you really start to see the potential – some of the games we were playing and results we were getting away from home – you just think we can go all the way here. Obviously there will always be little

No more Wembley heartache – the Bees make it to the Premier League

patches that don't go right, so we didn't manage to get into the top two both years, but in terms of quality, we were right up there both years."

Thomas Frank, reflecting on the previous 12 month, brushed aside any suggestion that Brentford hadn't been ready to go up the previous year, but was bursting with pride at the way in which his side – just as the club had seven years earlier – had found triumph through adversity. "I think the team was completely ready (in 2020)," he said. "We had two of the best offensive players in the league, both would have loved to have stayed and the BMW would have been kept together. But things happen for a reason, and I love Ivan.

"In life, if you get a million quid, then another million, but you don't have to work hard for it and never have to experience failure or disappointment, you don't get that drive to keep going. Learning from that year, which was so tough, I was even more proud of what we did the second year. We played 57 games in nine months. When we played Spurs in the League Cup semi final we were the team who had played the most games in the whole of Europe. Little Bees, the bus stop in Hounslow, and we kept performing, performing, performing – with no private jets and all that, because we had top staff who do a top job.

"So that experience, after being massively disappointed, selling our two best players, bringing in an unknown guy from Peterborough and then getting promoted. Fulham were a better team than Swansea. I knew before the (Swansea) game that if we performed, we would win, and we did, which was fantastic. It looked easy after that. At 2-0 we were jumping around and I was thinking 'have we done it?' telling yourself to stay cool, but your head is spinning."

There wasn't much time to celebrate for Rasmus Ankersen, however, as he went about preparing Brentford for life in the Premier League – which included the decision not to offer a new contract to Wembley hero Emilano Marcondes. "We were proud about what we'd achieved – it was a bit surreal the first couple of days – it didn't really sink in," he said. "We had a great party after the game, and I think we enjoyed it, but this is our (directors of football) peak season, we always try to be rational about our decision making. It's easy to be emotional about these things, to hand out big contracts to everyone who's done amazingly and help get us here, but I think it's important we stay hungry – to recruit and prepare for where we want to go, not where we were or where we are."

Asked when he knew Brentford had actually done it during the final against Swansea, Ankersen echoed the views of so many Bees fans too familiar with past failures, who had been still biting their nails right up to the final whistle, when he added: "In the 95th minute! But seriously, we are human beings too, and even though we were two goals up, it was 11 playing 10 and three minutes into injury time, you're still paranoid. So it was not over before it was over. But the strange thing was, when we were 2-0 up at half time, it felt like we were there. It was an emotional experience for us because we couldn't affect the decision making during the game. Maybe we looked rational and calm, but that was not necessarily the case."

Co-director of football Phil Giles agreed, harking back to that infamous game at Loftus Road three and a half years before, when the Bees had conceded twice in injury time to throw away a 2-0 lead. This time, it was a very different Brentford, but as Giles admits, even the coolest and most rational of minds can let doubts in from time to time, especially with so much at stake. "We all remembered QPR away a few years before, where we had our fingers burned late on," he said. "But I kept telling myself towards the end of the game, 11 versus 10 men – even if they score then they'd have to score again, and even then, in that heat in extra time, I thought we could step it up. In fact, I thought we stepped off a little bit from about half an hour onwards and didn't keep possession as well as we could have. But I always felt we could have raised the tempo again had we needed to go into extra time. It would've been a big ask to lose the game from that point."

Andy Scott, for the second year in a row, had seen his former club beat his current one in the play-offs and the man who had led Brentford out of the bottom tier was now watching them winning a place in the Premier League. He said: "We knew we'd be up against it. Brentford should have gone up the year before, they had strengthened, and we just knew they were the better side. We knew they had to have an off day and we had to have a good one. We started badly, and in a weird kind of way, by the time we had a man sent off, I was resigned to the fact we were going to lose and they were going to go up. It wasn't nice from a working environment point of view, because you want to be in the Premier League. But to feel like you've been part of the journey that's enabled Brentford to get to the Premier League – I still see it as my club. They're the club I look at and like going back to. I like to think I played a part in that and was involved in that process."

For Alan McCormack, having by that point hung up his boots after seeing out his playing days with a third spell at Southend, it reminded him of the situation he found when he first joined Brentford. For him, the manner in which Brentford had put the 2020 play-off final defeat behind them, to come back stronger, showed parallels to their recovery from the Doncaster and Yeovil earthquakes in 2013, and says a lot about the psychology installed at the club. "They stepped up to the promised land, and deservedly so," said McCormack. "Everyone I spoke to about Brentford knew it was going to happen – the way they went about their business, not buying the league but doing it their way, sticking to their philosophy, trusting it and getting the rewards. It's a rare bravery in football to keep trusting the system.

"They could have gone up the previous year, but as a parallel to when I first signed, they took strength from adversity. It's a very difficult thing to do, as lots of clubs that have been in the final, one year, have been relegated the next, because it's difficult to kick on again when you've been so close and had it snatched away. To have that mental strength and the energy to come again is such a tough thing to do, but Brentford have done it twice, and that's credit to everyone there now and before. It was always a big thing at the club to try to be better than you were yesterday, to be the best you can be every single day. They look for that in players, they love the psychological aspect of a player."

For Richard Lee, the psychological aspect was something which had been building at the club for many years: "Psychology is such a broad term – trying to get a group of lads to buy into an idea and a process rather than game by game – the mentality needed just for that is so key," he said. "Ultimately, it's about setting a culture, and I started to notice that quite early, under Warbs in particular. Uwe as well, but certainly under Warbs. I remember some of the central ideas that started to get implemented at the time, which for me were quite new – even the idea of not holding the ball up in the corner if you're winning 1-0 – because of the negativity associated with that. You'd see teams go 1-0 up and the whole flow of the game changes, but we'd look to go 2-0 up and 3-0 up. They were simple things that were being brought in back then, and no doubt looking at them now, they've just built on them."

While many clubs had suffered – and are still suffering in some cases – from the financial difficulties presented by Covid, and games being

Pontus Jansson lifts the trophy as his Brentford team celebrate at Wembley

played behind closed doors for the best part of a year, Brentford were well placed to cope with it due to their financial model. That was the opinion of football finance expert Kieran Maguire, speaking on his Price of Football podcast towards the end of the 2020-21 season. Maguire said: "One of the clubs that did remarkably well during the pandemic was Brentford, and again, this was because the club was not hugely reliant on matchday income. It had a player development and recruitment model, and it utilised that to ensure it could get promoted on a sustainable level."

On a previous podcast, Maguire said: "The Brentford model is an intriguing one. They lose money on a day-to-day basis and their wage bill is higher than their income, but what they've done every year since they've been promoted from League One to the Championship is to find players and spot talent. That model works as they have made about £130m in profit from selling players. As a business model, it's a really clever approach. They're making more money over that five-year period from player sales than practically everybody else, and they do it because they believe in the data and identify particular characteristics. They always go for younger players with a view to moving them on within a couple of years, and they're very, very good at this particular approach to football."

Hindsight is indeed a wonderful thing, though, and returning to Sergi Canos, the long-serving Spaniard admitted even he'd had doubts in the past over whether the club would ever make the promised land. Like most supporters, it took time to have faith in the system, and like them,

Canos looked on year after year, with the club's best players being sold, and wondered what the end game would be.

"I never thought it would be like this," he admitted. "When I first came to the club, yes the ambition was the Premier League, but if you ask 18 out of 24 Championship clubs their ambition, they will say Premier League too. So having that ambition is one thing, then at the end of the season we'd sell our best players. I have nothing against how we do things as we do things fantastic, but when I came at 19 years old and signed a long contract – you see Jota leaving, Harlee Dean leaving, Judgey leaving – all the big players leaving and you stay, you wonder what the ambition really is. But it was fantastic to have Thomas (Frank) on board and Brian (Riemer) as they were the difference we needed, the spark the club had to make to get to the Premier League."

One thing that doesn't perhaps get mentioned enough is the part Bees fans played, not just in terms of their support from the stands when allowed back in, but in helping the finances by – in many cases – the magnificent gesture of not claiming back the season ticket money they were owed for games they were not allowed to attend during lockdown. "The fans played a big part during the 2020/21 season, especially with the finances, because most of them left their season ticket money in the club," Phil Giles added. "That helped us get through and meant that we didn't have to raise cash for cash-flow reasons. So, it was a big team effort."

That view was echoed by chief executive Jon Varney, who added: "People leaving their season ticket money in during Covid was hugely important and showed just what togetherness there is at the club. Our fans knew we would be hurting financially, so it made a massive difference. People knew there was a lot of money going out in player wages and not a lot of revenue coming in, and we were still in the Championship, so the central money was pretty meaningless. Every penny we could keep in the business was really, really important, so we will always be grateful, and that's why we wanted to repay them by not hiking up our ticket prices when we went into the Premier League. We all enjoy the good times together and the tough times together." There had indeed been plenty of tough times during Brentford's journey to the top, but the good times were truly about to roll.

CHAPTER TWELVE

So, once the dust had settled, just how would Brentford approach their first ever Premier League season? We'll come onto their transfer window business later, but what would their targets for the season be? Would they have to adapt their style of play and hone in the attacking instincts that had served them so well? As far as Phil Giles was concerned, it was a case of sticking to the same script and trying not to step away from what had made Brentford successful in the first place. Speaking before the start of the new campaign, he said: "It's not like we suddenly flip to a new Premier League script or try to do things differently. We will try and do what we've always done, but one level higher. We really want to avoid setting an arbitrary target of wanting to finish second or 10th or 15th, or even to just survive. I think what we want to do is keep doing what we've done. Keep bringing players in, who are young, hungry, can develop and thrive."

He added: "I'd like us to contribute something to the Premier League. I'd like your average Premier League fan who sits and watches Sunday afternoon on Sky not to turn Brentford off when we come on, but to turn us on – to say that's interesting, this is gonna be a good football match, I'm gonna enjoy watching Brentford. For everyone to know who we are and that we've put ourselves on the map. That the whole profile of Brentford has been raised, not only in this country, but worldwide. That, for me, would be a good starting point. I'd like us not to be a club who just exists, or that ticks along picking up survival money – going around the Monopoly board and picking £200 up for just passing go.

"We have certain principles about how we play and we've said we want to make sure we keep those principles. The way we defend, the way we try to win the ball back, the way we attack – let's try and do the same, but at a higher level. Let's not say 'right, we're in the Premier League, we need experience, we need to defend another way'. Let's not copy anyone else, let's just do it our way. If it works, great, and if it's not good enough, we'll learn from it, and then we'll have another crack at it."

Rasmus Ankersen, who would end his eight-year association with the club midway through the season, leaving Giles as sole director of football, added: "We want to attack, we want to take risks, and I feel we need to go into Premier League with the same mind-set, because there is maybe a tendency in the Premier League where clubs just don't want to get relegated. It's a negative motivation, isn't it? I think we got here because we've taken risks. Yes, we may get relegated, but I want to see us take risks and try to be Brentford – to be true to our model. That may be more of a process target, but if we do that, we have a really good chance of establishing ourselves there."

Considering Brentford were going into their debut Premier League season with a squad boasting just 14 minutes experience at that level in total – Ivan Toney's five minutes as a late sub for Newcastle against Manchester United in 2015, and Sergi Canos' nine minutes off the bench for Liverpool at West Brom the following year – the Bees had a fairly understated transfer window in the summer of 2021.

Norway defender Kristoffer Ajer was purchased for a club record £13m from Celtic, and would start the season as the furthest right of three centre-backs, but Ajer really came into his own as a marauding right-back when Thomas Frank switched formations later in the season. Brentford also paid £8m to Matthew Benham's other club, FC Midtjylland, for Nigerian international midfielder Frank Onyeka, whose enthusiastic, bustling style earned rave 'Frank The Tank' reviews early on, but who struggled to hold down a place in the side as the season wore on.

A similar fee of £8.5m went to French side Lorient for attacker Yoane Wissa, who was used sparingly at first after missing pre-season due to eye surgery following an acid attack in France, from which he made a complete recovery. After making an initial impact with three goals in two League Cup appearances, the DR Congo international earned a super-sub reputation for coming off the bench to score – firstly a late equaliser against Liverpool, then an even later winner at West Ham, which came in successive weeks in the autumn.

Myles Peart-Harris also arrived from Chelsea for £1.8m, but it soon became clear the promising youngster would be plying his trade in the B team before being considered for first team action, while keeper Alvaro Fernandez was picked up on a season-long loan from Spanish side Huesca, with a view to a permanent deal, as back-up to David Raya. Free agent Mathias 'Zanka' Jorgensen, a former Danish international, also came in a month into the season as defensive cover and filled in admirably when called upon, but soon suffered injury problems of his own. Aside from those, the Bees would pretty much be relying on the squad which had got them promoted. A brave move, but a calculated one. After all, Fulham had spent more than £100m after beating Brentford in the 2020 Championship play-off final, and all it had got them was an instant relegation. Few could argue with the gamble, given Brentford's track record – but all eyes were firmly focused on the new kids on the block.

For Rico Henry, in not rushing out and buying a load of ready-made Premier League experience, but sticking with the players who had got them there, the management team had cast a vote of confidence in the squad's abilities. "The gaffer said he believed in us as Premier League players, and if we trained well, he was going to play us, he wasn't afraid of that," said Henry. "Everyone had a good feeling going into the new season, and when we started preparing, that's when it kicked in. We prepared well and the gaffer had us running lots during pre-season. Everyone was fit and we were ready for it. Suddenly you're coming up against the likes of Adama Traore and Mo Salah though – you have to be always switched on in the Premier League as the tempo and intensity is a lot higher and the quality is a lot better. That's when I started realising you really had to step up now."

Ethan Pinnock was in agreement, saying: "It was a massive vote of confidence. You see that quite a lot, teams getting promoted to the Premier League and saying right, we now need X, Y and Z. Obviously we got a few new faces, but I think it was important that we didn't try to reload the whole squad. We just looked at what we felt were the main areas to get new players in, and that blend of the new players, with those who had played a lot of games for us, worked really well. As a team, that would have been our third year together as well, so everyone knew each other's game by then, and making that step up, we've all done it together. It just goes to show that even though it's the Premier League, if you have a good bunch of players who know their game, are willing to learn and take new things on board, anything is possible."

The majority of the footballing press had run articles and online predictions in which their journalists tipped the Bees for an instant return to the Championship. There was an almost unanimous consensus, despite Brentford demonstrating time and time again that succeeding as an underdog and excelling under the radar were traits not to be ignored, even in the strongest league in world football. So, it was clear, if they were to flourish in the Premier League, they would have to do so against a backdrop of apathy from the pundits.

Never-to-be-forgotten celebrations after the debut win over Arsenal

So, just how would this Brentford side, with less than a quarter-hour's previous Premier League experience, fare against the big boys? An emphatic answer was given on the never-to-be-forgotten opening day of the season, on a balmy Friday night in August 2021. All the pieces of the Brentford jigsaw fell into place – a night game, under the lights and in front of the Sky cameras, with a spine-tingling atmosphere created by the new stadium's first capacity crowd. An Arsenal side in opposition with a reputation for sometimes being brilliant, but at other times having a soft underbelly – and missing two key strikers. Yes, there were nerves as the home fans approached the stadium, but the pride and excitement pulsing through their veins was off the scale. Few could predict just how special that night would prove to be however.

For chief executive Jon Varney, it was the culmination of the best part of two years of toil to not only move stadiums during a pandemic (as mentioned in the previous chapter), but to now get it ready to host Premier League football. The eyes of the world would be on the Brentford Community Stadium, and while the players certainly delivered on the pitch, it cannot be underestimated just how much the off-pitch team did its bit too. "Premier League Ready was a sign plastered throughout the organisation," he said. "You come up with key mantras and messages you want your staff to buy into, and Premier League Ready was absolutely one that was written on every single wall.

"Were we ready when Arsenal turned up on that Friday night? Definitely not, but we had the persona that we were ready, and the ground the staff covered between getting promoted and the start of that season was quite incredible. Genuinely, it was probably the proudest I've been in my career of people that have worked alongside me and – the effort they put in was outstanding. To have been able to put that game on with the world's media there was a truly exceptional effort from everybody. You've got to remember the backdrop - we'd gone through a process of missing out the year before, Covid hit, you had to furlough staff, and that was emotionally wounding for a lot of people. We had to keep a core of staff together to deliver those matches behind closed doors, and then some of the others were clearly thinking why am I being furloughed?

"I think the scars of Covid will run forever. I think they'll be hard scars to heal, but the effort when everyone came back, getting promoted, and that whole process of getting ready for the Premier League – because the window was so tight to get everything done. You go from having a press conference for the Middlesex Chronicle and a couple of others to having the world's media down at Jersey Road. You've got to handle that, be ready for that, have the facilities for that. When we turned up for that game against Arsenal, the amount of broadcasters in the stadium that evening – and not just from 8pm when the game kicked off but from about 2pm – the whole operations team were absolutely phenomenal in very stressful conditions. Because of Arsenal's Covid situation, there was a very serious risk the game would have to be called off at the very last minute – I even called the Premier League and asked if it was worth us getting the burgers out of the freezer at one stage.

"I said before that when I arrived, off the field, we were very much still a League One club playing in the Championship. And in our first season after being promoted, we were a very good Championship club off the field playing in the Premier League. Hopefully this season, we've got a Premier League side both on the field and off the field. It's just the reality of the way we've grown. When Matthew arrived, his number one focus was on the on-field activity, because ultimately, if you want to drive more fans and get more people engaged, you've got to get up the leagues, so the sensible place to put all your investment is in the team. Naturally, the off-field team was always going to be behind.

"There also wasn't a lot of point investing massively in an off-field operation when we were at Griffin Park. I've gone on record thousands of times saying our fans are the best in the world at getting into a stadium at two minutes to three on a Saturday afternoon, because you couldn't have a pee and you couldn't get anything to eat, so you literally legged it out of one of the pubs and got into the stadium – match days frills didn't exist. I think it was inevitable the off-field operation was going to be behind the playing operation, but I think it's important the fans see the investment and backing Matt has given me to build the off-field side of the business as well as the playing side. That group of staff

Chief executive Jon Varney, owner Matthew Benham and director of football Phil Giles – delivering Premier League football at Brentford

are the unsung heroes who have to deal with the tricky stuff, but it's stuff that's important to the wellbeing of the football club."

The scene for the evening was indeed set before the match had even kicked off, with perhaps the loudest rendition of 'Hey Jude' ever heard (Glastonbury 2022 included), and the appearance of a home side clearly feeding off the atmosphere. If the pre-match singing rattled the rafters, the roof was truly taken off when Sergi Canos cut in from the left midway through the second half, evading one challenge, before slamming the ball past Gunners' keeper Bernd Leno. Christian Norgaard doubled the advantage with 17 minutes left, popping up to head home at the far post after Mads Bech Sorensen's long throw was allowed to bounce in the box – although it took a stunning save from David Raya to stop Nicolas Pepe pulling one back and making it a nervous finish.

Having ploughed tens of millions of pounds into building the new stadium, and having had to watch it play host to virtually empty audiences for its first year of existence, Benham was delighted to finally see it packed to the rafters for its opening Premier League fixture: "I mean, it was a bit of shame that for the first year it was empty so it was a bit of a letdown," he said. "We were still in the bloody Championship, and number two, it was empty. So, it was really only the Bournemouth game that I felt, 'oh, finally, finally', and then of course the Arsenal game, that was really memorable. It was incredible."

It was fitting that Canos scored the goal which started Brentford's Premier League adventure – a player who had been with the club for much of the journey to the top, sharing the ups and downs on and off the pitch, as well as fighting his way back from serious injury, and a subsequent spell of self doubt, to become a true Brentford legend. "First game in the Premier League with Brentford, first goal, first full stadium after Covid, having my family in the stands, I think everything was connected for it to happen," he said of his goal.

It became Canos' most important goal for the club – moving ahead of the sublime solo strike at Reading in December 2015, which had cemented his popularity at the club and became the subject of a terrace chant in the player's honour. Canos remains philosophical about his top goal-scoring moments, however, and thinks it's wrong that players are remembered for those achievements over their other contributions on the pitch. "The Reading goal was nice – but I'm a bit angry with football because right now you have to score, or give assists, for people to notice you, and everyone noticed me because of that goal," he said. "But I think football is more than just goals and assists, and I'm sad that people don't look at it (other aspects of the game)."

Christian Norgaard, scorer of the second goal, admitted, like the hundreds of thousands of fans who had walked through its gates over the years, that it was sad saying goodbye to Griffin Park, but also that the new stadium had become a cathedral of its own. "Griffin Park was a special place, away players hated it as they couldn't even close the door when they went to the toilet," he would later tell the BBC's Monday Night Club. "You couldn't get any privacy in the dressing room, and it was a fantastic feeling going into a game knowing they (the away team) had had a shit preparation. It wasn't the best stadium in the world, but there was this magical atmosphere, and I would definitely say the fans have taken that over to the new stadium. It was something I was a bit worried about, whether we could recreate that same intensity and loudness, but they definitely have. We have started to create new memories and history, and hopefully it will continue as it definitely gives us extra energy and is responsible for a lot of the points we have got at home."

As the match was the curtain raiser for the entire Premier League season, Brentford were able to bask in exclusive glory (not to mention being top of the table) for almost 24 hours as Sky TV's rolling sports news services and television stations around the globe repeated the scenes non-stop throughout the night and into the breakfast coverage the following morning. The elderly Bees fan, with tears rolling down his face at the final whistle, was beamed into a billion households – and the name of Brentford Football Club was in the conscience of men, women and children in even the remotest corners of the globe.

Pinnock said: "Making the jump up to the Premier League, as a new club, you're always going to be doubted and thought of as one of the favourites to go down. But from the first game we showed that we're not here just to make up the numbers, we wanted to really show what we could do. A lot of us had never experienced playing at stadiums like Anfield, Old Trafford or Stamford Bridge. For a lot of us, myself included, who had spent years playing in the lower leagues, it was always something I'd dreamed about, being able to compete in these stadiums one day. But once you get the chance to play there you just want to show you can play at that level, and a lot of us were thinking that."

Undoubtedly, it had been a stunning start to their debut Premier League campaign, but Brentford now had to prove it wasn't a flash in the pan, with two away games on successive Saturdays. They needn't have worried. The Bees showed they had the required mettle too, knowing how to grind out results at this level, by bringing a point home from both Selhurst Park and Villa Park. August done... unbeaten, so far, so good. The first disappointment came at the start of September, when Brighton snatched a late, late winner in West London – Leandro Trossard's composed 90th minute shot into the bottom corner showed that the Bees were not going to have it all their own way after all. How Brentford reacted to this setback would be crucial, and the answer came in the shape of an emphatic away performance, with goals from Ivan Toney and Bryan Mbeumo earning a 2-0 win at Wolves. Although the margin of victory could have been far greater, the travelling away supporters heading back to London were simply delighted with a first win on their travels.

It got even better a week later, when Jurgen Klopp's Liverpool side were the visitors to TW8 – again in front of the Sky cameras and a raucous atmosphere. Ethan Pinnock stunned the visitors when he scrambled home at the far post midway through the first half, before Diogo Jota ensured the two sides were level-pegging at the break. Twice Liverpool took the lead after the interval – through Mo Salah and Curtis Jones – but Brentford hit back on both occasions, through Vitaly Janelt and Yoane Wissa, to earn a well-deserved share of the spoils. The opening day win had earned the Bees many plaudits, having defeated one of the traditional big name clubs, but to have held a genuine title contender really made people sit up and take notice.

Pinnock, scorer of the opening goal against Liverpool, spoke of the different approach Brentford were taking in the Premier League, restraining the urge to always be attacking, but still being on the front foot. "A lot of games we started really fast, trying to make sure we had high energy levels and make it as difficult as possible for teams," he said, "We knew in the Premier League we would spend a lot more time without the ball, so our defensive structure and knowing when to press had to be a lot better. We tried to catch teams off guard, especially at the start of games, and once the momentum's with you and you're on the front foot, it's hard for the other team to change it. We always felt that if we got a good start and got in other teams' faces, it could help us, and in the early part of the season, it showed.

"Our ethos for the season was always to stay in the game, even if we go a goal down, or two goals down, the main focus was to get your minds back as quickly as possible, because at 1-0 or 2-0 you always have a chance, but at 3-0 or more the game is done. Do the things you do at 0-0, and the longer you can keep it 0-0, the better chance you have. Other teams go a goal down and the floodgates open. I think that comes from Brian (Riemer) as well, the defensive coach, who was really good with what he wants our principles to be, to maintain that focus even when you go behind.

"Liverpool at home and Chelsea away stand out, but Liverpool, with them being the team that they are – they've matched Manchester City in the last three or four years, two of the best teams in the world – we showed we can stand up against them even after going behind twice. That mentality spread throughout the team. I think I blacked out after scoring! I was expecting Pontus to finish it but he didn't get a touch, but I came in at the back post."

If the Liverpool game had made the wider footballing world realise that Brentford's initial bursting onto the Premier League scene had not been a fluke, it was even more evident a week later, when the Bees showed they could scrape points from lesser performances too. And at West Ham, the Bees took all three of them, despite a weaker display than the previous week, when Yoane Wissa came off the bench to strike a memorable injury-time winner. What followed was yet another scintillating performance in front of the cameras, as only keeper Edouard Mendy stood between Brentford and what should have been a memorable home win over Chelsea. The Senegalese stopper made a string of outstanding saves, while Brentford – Bryan Mbeumo in particular – were also wasteful in their finishing. Ben Chilwell's first half strike for Chelsea somehow proved to be the only goal of the game.

It was another hard luck story the following week as Brentford went down to an undeserved defeat, this time losing 2-1 at home to Leicester, but worse news was yet to come as, a few days later, the club confirmed that keeper David Raya, having been injured saving at the feet of Leicester's Ayoze Perez in the dying minutes of the game, had injured the posterior cruciate ligament in his left knee and would be out for four to five months.

This was immediately recognised as being a massive blow, as Raya was so important to the way Brentford played for his distribution as much as his shot-stopping abilities that had promoted Klopp, after the

Liverpool game, to say Raya could just as easily wear the number ten shirt as his goalie's top. Raya's replacement, Alvaro Fernandez, would struggle to make his mark on the side – so much so that former Huddersfield keeper Jonas Lossl was brought in on loan from Midtjylland in the New Year to provide some back up and competition.

Richard Lee, a keen student of the game as well as a former Bees keeper, gave an insight into just how important Raya was to Brentford, and just how much he would be missed by his old club. "He's phenomenal and I love how he plays," Lee said of Raya. "I think he epitomises a lot about what the modern goalkeeper is now perceived to be. He plays very much on the front foot with an aggressive starting position and is very brave with his decision-making, comes a long way for crosses and corners and stops a lot at source. He's got good shot-stopping, is powerful and quick and moves well. His distribution is very good, one of the best in the Premier League. There's a realisation with teams playing a style of football like Brentford that it's not just about keeping possession, but a lot more than that now.

"Goalkeeping has gone to the next level now and everything is rehearsed, whether a goal kick or a back pass. With all the different patterns of play and the different exit routes, it's about having the ability to execute the right pass at the right time, into the full-back or to the chest of a striker or winger. You're effectively a quarterback, and it's about knowing when to use each play. I think it's certainly tough for anyone stepping into David's shoes, because in terms of being an all-rounder – catching crosses, making saves, distributing well – there's very few I've seen who are so skilled in all areas. When you have a keeper who's your outright number one, it's very hard when they're out for a long period of time to have someone step in, and you will see the change.

"David is that good, genuinely. It was going so well for Brentford at the start of the season, and he was such an important part of that. I may be biased, as goalkeeping is my passion, and I can see why people say strikers are the most important people on the pitch, but I would say that goalkeepers run them close. There's never been a team that's won the league without having a top-quality goalkeeper. With the way Brentford play, there's not many keepers in the world who can play the way Brentford needs them to, and David is one of them – which is why they've done everything to keep him at the club these last few years."

But it wasn't just Raya who would be missing from the forthcoming team sheets. Josh Dasilva was already a long-term absentee before the season had begun, while Kristoffer Ajer, already an important figure in the back four, would be out until after Christmas. Shandon Baptiste, having just started to establish himself as a first-choice midfielder, once again succumbed to injury, while key players like Vitaly Janelt, Bryan

Mbeumo, Ivan Toney and Yoane Wissa would all spend time either on the treatment table or recovering from Covid.

The result was a sudden transformation from a team which had been hailed as a breath of fresh air for the Premier League, and more than capable of mixing it with the big boys, to one playing more like strangers and starting to look capable of sinking like a stone. Back-to-back defeats, to Burnley and Norwich, were not only terrible performances but handed two teams below the Bees in the table their first wins of the season. A back line without Raya looked shaky and vulnerable, as was the replacement keeper himself, and as a result, the attacking instincts which had made Brentford a joy to watch had been severely blunted. The end of November brought some respite, however, as the Bees grabbed a 3-3 draw at Newcastle United in a game they could easily have won, having twice led, before Ivan Toney scored the only goal of the next game from the spot, at home to Everton, to earn a first win in six. It was by no means a classic, with two struggling teams toiling for much-needed points, but the relief in the home stands as the final whistle was palpable. The Bees could win again.

Rico Henry noted that Raya's absence, above all others, was having an alarming effect on the side, and was threatening to undo all the good work of the first few months of the season. "He was a big miss, we know what he's capable of, he wins us games, even with his feet," Henry said. "That's what we need to take pressure off – sometimes we need to keep the ball and sometimes we need to go long. Alvaro stepped up well, but David is an excellent keeper."

Defensive partner Ethan Pinnock added: "It was a difficult period. We had a few injuries, and David is obviously an amazing keeper. With him being part of the team for two years, without being out, once you're playing with a different keeper they have different tendencies, so a sudden switch is difficult, there's certain things you're unsure of. Credit to Alvaro, it was a difficult time for him, but he managed to keep his head in the game and had a few good games where he did really well. He tried not to let it affect him too much. We tried not to focus on the big picture too much and just looked at the next opportunity to get three points, with a game plan. Compartmentalising things that way makes it a lot easier."

Canos sympathised with his fellow Spaniard, Fernandez, admitting it was harsh on a young player coming into such an important position at such a difficult time. "It was a hard time for everyone as we started so well and then went down a little bit," he said. "But that's what football is like, you have an amazing time and then you have to fight and fight to get it back to where you were. We were up here (gestures high up), then big injuries happened and we were down here (gestures low down) when Alvaro came in, and the team's confidence was not the best at that time.

He's a young player coming into a new league, a new team, so I think everything was difficult, but he did have some good games. Not every game, but not everyone can play well every game. I remember one, Everton at home, he was outstanding. Newcastle away he was good, even though we conceded three goals. But if you score three goals away from home you need to win, so that was down to the team as well."

Alongside the post-Everton relief, however, was a distinct feeling that the win was papering over the cracks, and Brentford's shortcomings were indeed exposed four days later, when they visited the huge, brightly lit spaceship that is the new home of Tottenham Hotspur. The visitors actually put in an okay display considering the players still missing – well at least it wasn't a non-performance like the previous month's away game at Burnley and home game against Norwich – but the Bees were simply outclassed by a Spurs side who were, in truth, better in every department. Charlie Goode, who seven years earlier had been playing non-league football, and who had been thrown in due to the injuries to Ajer and Zanka, put in a solid performance to keep Harry Kane quiet. But such was the quality Brentford were up against, keeping the England captain under wraps wouldn't be enough with the likes of the irrepressible Son Heung-min about.

Brentford did, however, take the positives from that game into the next one, at Elland Road three days later, where after fighting back from a goal down, they found themselves within seconds of taking home all three-points… before Patrick Bamford grabbed a deflating equaliser for Leeds five minutes into stoppage time. A notable absentee from that game was top scorer Ivan Toney, who had fallen victim to the latest Covid Omicron variant sweeping the land. That meant a rare foray up front for Sergi Canos, who due to the injuries had been deployed at right wing-back – he responded to his return to a more natural forward position with his first league goal since that opening day stunner against Liverpool.

For Canos, who had been used, briefly, as a right back at times in the Championship, it was frustrating to be playing in an unnatural position against world class players. "It's been a hard year for me, because I showed against Leeds away that I can play forwards in the Premier League," said Canos. "They said a right back was coming in the winter window and didn't come, so I kept playing as a right wing-back, and it's been hard because it's not my position. I tried, and I think it worked out really well, and I've improved a lot of things in my game. But my strength is going forward, and I want to be closer to the ball and score goals and provide assists. To not be able to do that as much was frustrating, but the team achieved what we wanted to achieve and stayed in the Premier League and gave some big teams some really hard times.

"I'm never negative, always positive, but I've been basing my confidence on chances, goals and assists my whole career. So to get to that goal of being in the Premier League and not be able to do that as much was frustrating. I had to completely change my mind-set and mentality and base my confidence on blocking crosses, defending the back post and set pieces, which is not my natural thing. But I did it because I'm a fighter and I will fight for anything, and if they need me as a right wing-back, I'm there. That's my mentality."

Toney would also miss the home game against Watford five days later, with Bryan Mbeumo this time ploughing a lone furrow up front. But if he wasn't there in person, Toney was certainly there in spirit for Brentford's dramatic winner. Having gone into the final ten minutes a goal down to one of the teams below them in the table – and one widely expected to be a rival for staying out of the drop zone – it was looking grim for the Bees until, with six minutes remaining, Pontus Jansson chose, with impeccable timing, the perfect moment to score his first goal for the club. Vitaly Janelt's excellent cross to the right was flicked on at the near post by Marcus Forss for Jansson to nod past a prone Daniel Bachmann in the Watford goal. Then, in the sixth minute of injury time, Saman Ghoddos was clipped down in the area while latching onto Christian Norgaard's pass. Toney had carved out a deserved reputation as one of the country's best penalty takers, but for such a pressure cooker situation, he could only watch on, helplessly, from home. Up stepped Bryan Mbeumo, with Brentford's huge moment entrusted to a player who had already hit the woodwork an astonishing seven times that season. Nerves were shredded around the stadium, but if Mbeumo was feeling any fear, he certainly didn't show it, mimicking his strike partner in taking the most minimal of run-ups before picking his spot and coolly side-footing home. Anyone would think that they practise together.

That should have been the spark for a Brentford revival, but sadly, any momentum was lost when a home game against Manchester United four days later was postponed due to Covid cases in the opponents' camp, and had well and truly disappeared by Boxing Day, when the Bees put in arguably their worst display of the campaign, by losing 2-0 at Brighton. Not exactly ideal preparation for the visit of the reigning Champions and league leaders, Manchester City, three days later. City were a club which, during the time Brentford had been steadily making their journey through the lower leagues, towards the top flight, had been undergoing their own ascent towards the near-dominance of English football. Even less ideal, in terms of preparation for Brentford, was Rico Henry and Bryan Mbeumo joining the list of the injured – meaning rookie Dominic Thompson was thrown in at left-back as one of the best teams in Europe came to town. A midfield shorn of its three first choice players would also be fighting back the triple threats of Kevin De Bruyne, Bernardo Silva and Fernandinho – it would almost be amusing if it wasn't so frustrating. In the event, a ramshackle and cobbled-together Brentford side put in a performance to be proud of and were unfortunate to go down to the only goal of the game, scored by Phil Foden.

That was the end of a hugely memorable 2021, although 2022 started in promising fashion too, as yet another brilliant Yoane Wissa strike, then a winner from that unlikeliest of sources, defender Mads Roerslev, saw the Bees come from behind to beat Aston Villa 2-1. However, that was just the calm before the storm, as the Brentford side, which had been patched together week by week since late October, started to come apart at the seams. The positive flickers, which had provided hope during a brutal two months, looked to have been stubbed out as the Bees embarked on a run of eight games without a win. Ominously, seven had ended in defeat. The first, a midweek 4-1 capitulation at Southampton, was probably the worst of the lot in the eyes of travelling Brentford supporters, increasingly worried about the direction the side were heading in.

Coincidentally, it was Southampton's first home game since Rasmus Ankersen – who to the surprise of many had stepped down as Brentford's co-director of football in December – had taken on a similar role with the Saints. The transition was part of the takeover at the South Coast side by London-based sports investment company, Sports Republic, of which Ankersen was chief executive. Having spent eight years with the Bees, and having played such a big part in their upward trajectory, Ankersen admitted it was strange finding himself coming up in opposition to them so soon after leaving – but said he'd been planning to depart for some time.

"I'd had the conversation about doing this other (joint ownership) project for six months, and I'd been very open about what I wanted to do," he said. "My first preference was to do it at Brentford, and I thought I could raise the capital, but it would have required Matthew selling quite a bit of his stake, and although he was willing to sell some, it was not enough for the model to work. We'd love to have kept working together, but it wasn't to be, and who knows, maybe our paths will cross that way again in the future. It may have looked very sudden, but it had been going on for months. The first game after my departure was announced was Southampton versus Brentford, and at that point I thought I shouldn't attend as it was on television – I thought it would look strange me standing there clapping if Southampton scored."

Ankersen may have been preparing for his exit behind the scenes for some time, but the loss of such a key figure at the club couldn't have come at a worse time, as the injury-hit Bees struggled to recapture the positivity of the first few months of the season. Five days after having been handed their backside at Southampton, a Brentford side completely unrecognisable from the one which performed magnificently to give Liverpool an almighty scare four months earlier, were easily swatted aside 3-0 in the return game at Anfield. The hosts were dominant from start to finish and, although Bryan Mbeumo had a couple of great chances, Liverpool handed out a lesson in the realities of top flight football and their third goal will be remembered as one of, if not the, most calamitous the Bees would concede all campaign.

Three days later, Brentford hosted Manchester United in the game rearranged from December, and a much improved first half performance saw the Bees blow away their visitors with some brilliant attacking football, but they failed to turn their chances into goals. Particularly culpable was Matthias Jensen, who unfortunately found himself presented with a hat-trick of first half opportunities but was unable to take any of them. The Bees were made to pay after the break when United finally showed up, took control of the game and knocked in three goals, before Ivan Toney pulled one back late on. Four days on and a poor performance at home to Wolves, in a strange game delayed by about half an hour due to two concussions and the appearance of an unauthorised drone over the Brentford Community Stadium, ended in a 2-1 defeat.

It would be more than two weeks before the Bees would be in action again, during which time (and much to the concern of many fans who had only witnessed one victory since before Christmas) the transfer window had closed with Brentford's business limited to the capture of free agent Christian Eriksen (more on him later). Most frustrating was a late snub from Brazilian right-back Vanderson, who had reportedly verbally agreed to join the Bees from Gremio – thus solving what had become something of a problem position for the Bees – but he changed his mind at the 11th hour when an approach was made by French giants, Monaco.

"People had warned us, and lo and behold, it came to pass, that it gets harder and harder the higher up you go, that the agent situations get more difficult," said Benham. "Believe it or not, in the lower leagues, many agents genuinely want the best for their players, rather than saying 'let me cause disruption so I can engineer a move every year'. I read something about how we showed amazing calmness not to splash the cash in January, but in two cases everything was agreed with a club, player and agent, and then they fell apart. So, it's not always as calm as it looks, but these things happen."

February started with some respite from Brentford's league woes with an FA Cup fourth round trip to Everton, but despite the welcome return of David Raya between the sticks, there was little comfort to be taken as the Bees crashed out 4-1. With Chelsea having also provided a knock-out blow in the League Cup quarter-final in December, Brentford now had just the league to concentrate on, but up next was the return game against Manchester City. Just like in the home game, the Bees put in a performance to be proud of against the Champions-to-be, but again, it wasn't enough as City ran out 2-0 winners. There was certainly no shame in defeat at The Etihad that night.

A home game against Crystal Palace three days later was seen as the ideal opportunity to finally end the losing streak, and following a nervous performance, that's exactly what the team did – grinding out a goalless draw to stop the rot. It didn't exactly signal the turnaround in form hoped for, however, as Arsenal gained revenge a week later for their opening day defeat with a 2-1 win in the return game at The Emirates. February then ended with a 2-0 home defeat to a Newcastle side revitalised by their Saudi takeover and a resultant January spending spree. Brentford were now just a single point, and a single place, above the relegation zone and desperately needed something inspirational to help turn their season around.

Coming on as a second half sub during that defeat to Newcastle was Brentford's only January signing. While The Magpies had spent more than £80m of their new found wealth during the transfer window, the Bees brought in a solitary free agent. That freebie, however, proved to be arguably one of the best pieces of business Brentford have ever done, as Danish international, Christian Eriksen, was persuaded to make TW8 the scene of his rehabilitation and return to the foot all stage. Eriksen, who for many years had lit up the Premier League with some sublime displays for Spurs, had not played since suffering a cardiac arrest mid-game while playing for Denmark at the Covid delayed 2020 (2021) European Championships, which almost cost the midfielder his life.

Finding he could not return to Inter MIlan due to Serie A rules that prevented him playing with a pacemaker, Eriksen found himself on the hunt for a new club, but not many seemed willing to take the gamble, despite him being one of the world's best midfielders. Brentford – who already boasted a core of Danish talent, an owner who also had a Danish club and a head coach who had developed Eriksen as a youngster – secured the deal right at the end of the window, but it was another month before he was deemed fit to play.

Frank said: "I would like to say I was the main part (in Eriksen coming). Obviously it helped that it was the Premier League and in London, if I was in the Championship he wouldn't have been likely to come. I know a lot of other clubs were in contact with him, but I think maybe the Danish connection we have, together with other things, obviously helped. I called him up for a chat and asked him if he was thinking of coming to Brentford to play, he said he had thought about me and would like to give me a call, and I knew then we were in a good position. Then it took five to six weeks."

Benham added: "Obviously there's a pretty limited data set for players who nearly die of cardiac arrest and then go back to playing top level football. Thomas was very, very bullish – exceptionally bullish. It's not unusual for head coaches or managers to say, 'oh, this guy played for me ten years ago, and he was great then', not realising that times have changed, and this is a pretty extreme example of how times have changed. Thomas was absolutely glowing about Eriksen's personality, about his humility and modesty, which has come to pass."

Eriksen had done enough during that half-hour or so against Newcastle to be handed his first start the following week, at bottom club Norwich, in what was increasingly looking like a crucial match in Brentford's bid for survival. Ivan Toney may have hit a hat-trick in a 3-1 win for the Bees, but it was Eriksen who took the headlines, running the show from the middle of the park and providing assists for both Toney's opener, and for the move which saw Pontus Jansson fouled for the first of Toney's brace of penalties. It was a similar story a week later as Toney, again, netted twice, but Eriksen stole the show once more with an assist and a starring role in the middle as Burnley were beaten 2-0. What a turnaround it was from the first games against those two sides. However, it should be noted that while Eriksen had undoubtedly lifted the side and filled his team-mates with confidence, as well as adding a touch of class, the return of key players from injury was also playing a central part in Brentford's revival. All of a sudden, that single-point gap to the bottom three had opened up into an eight-point cushion and the dark relegation rain clouds had started to dissipate.

"We knew we'd get through it," said Rico Henry. "David coming back from injury gave us confidence, but we had a few other players returning as well. We knew we'd get out of it, we just needed one win to get everyone's confidence going." Ethan Pinnock added: "At that point, we got a couple of boys back from injury, and getting that first win, we got that extra boost and you're all bubbly on the training ground again. That winning feeling perked everyone up and gave us an extra ten per cent in every game."

The Bees hit a bump in the road in the next match, with a 2-1 defeat at Leicester – in a game that Eriksen missed with Covid and Thomas Frank's team deserved at least a point from – but what followed was the kind of monumental result that their fans would barely have dared dream of when coming into the Premier League. The previous time Chelsea were Champions of Europe, they had taken on the Bees in the FA Cup fourth round in what proved to be a memorable performance for Uwe Rösler's men who came within seven minutes of knocking out their illustrious West London neighbours. Eight years on, with Chelsea once more kings of Europe, as well as the World, the Bees made the journey to Stamford Bridge on a far more level, if still far from equal, playing field. The Blues had already beaten Thomas Frank's twice that season at the Brentford Community Stadium – undeservedly in the league, and perhaps a little more deservingly in the League Cup – but nothing could prepare the travelling Bees faithful for what was to come. Absolutely nothing.

Christan Eriksen's first start for Brenford ended in victory at Norwich

Following a goalless first half, Antonio Rudiger kept to the script by putting Chelsea in front three minutes after the break with a howitzer of a shot from fully thirty yards, but Brentford were back level just two minutes later when Vitaly Janelt finished superbly from the edge of the area following Bryan Mbeumo's lay-off. Four minutes later, Mbeumo was again in the thick of it, turning defence into attack by sprinting half the length of the pitch before teeing up Christian Eriksen to lift the ball precisely over the onrushing Edouard Mendy and into the back of the net. Janelt struck again six minutes later, Ivan Toney this time providing the assist for the young German to finish brilliantly at the near post from a tight angle – a three goal blast inside ten minutes putting Chelsea on the ropes. The knock-out blow duly arrived with three minutes remaining as Thomas Tuchel's side failed to deal with Christian Norgaard's lofted ball into the box, and Yoane Wissa slammed home the loose ball with the outside of his right boot and into the net. It was to be the stand-out result of Brentford's debut Premier League season, and what's more, they were worthy of the adulation which followed the 4-1 win.

West Ham were up next, making the return trip to TW8, and whereas the game between the two in early October saw the Bees steal perhaps an undeserved win on the balance of play, there was nothing fortunate about the three points they took at the Brentford Community Stadium. West

Ham may have been challenging for a place in Europe, but it was Brentford who dominated proceedings and left the Hammers chasing shadows. By now, Eriksen's influence on the side was obvious – one of those players seemingly always with time on the ball, and the ability to make what they did with it count every time. The mercurial Dane had clearly lifted every player around him and the Bees were back to playing with the sort of freedom and confidence they were at the start of the campaign.

Ethan Pinnock admitted the players weren't entirely sure what to expect from the arrival of a world famous star like Eriksen in their midst, but revealed the Dane had made them feel at ease around him off the pitch as well as helping lift their game on it. "As a player he's really humble," he said. "As he came in, the first thing he did was speak to us as a team and tell us not to worry about him – that he's been cleared by the doctors – and that helped break the barriers and allowed us to engage with him. It made everyone aware he was good to go, and after that it wasn't really a topic, it felt like we could move forwards and concentrate on playing the games.

"He's always willing to receive the ball from any position and always has a picture in his head. As a player, it helps when someone like that is constantly available to offer to take the ball and make that pass. His confidence spread throughout the team, which you could see in the performances. Rico Henry added: "Straight away in training, you could see the quality he brought to set pieces and crosses, controlling the middle, he was excellent. His stats were incredible, everyone knew he would bring quality to the team."

With West Ham sent packing once more, a first double of the season was soon followed by a second, thanks to Pontus Jansson's dramatic injury-time winner at Watford, before Brentford's new-found maturity was evident for all to see when Eriksen's former club Spurs came to town. A side which had given the Bees a harsh lesson in Premier League football five months earlier were lucky to leave TW8 with a point – Ivan Toney twice rattling the woodwork and Jansson seeing a header cleared off the line by England skipper Harry Kane as the Bees outplayed their top four-seeking visitors.

There was a blot on the copybook at the start of May when a Manchester United side suffering a poor season by their own high standards decided, belatedly, to turn it on for their own fans in their final home game of the season, sweeping the Bees aside by three goals to nil. But Brentford responded by gaining revenge for their 4-1 hammering at St Mary's back in January by easing past Southampton 3-0, then in their final away game of the season, showing true grit and determination by twice coming from behind at relegation-haunted Everton to win 3-2, thus earning a third double of the season.

The Southampton game saw a first return to the Brentford Community Stadium for former co-director of football Rasmus Ankersen, who even with his calm exterior, allowed himself to indulge briefly in a bit of sentimentality. "I was emotionally invested in both Midtjylland and Brentford for so long and still have very strong feelings for both clubs, and I hope they both do well, but your mind is where you are," he said following that game. "It was good to be back and see everyone. I've been back a few times watching games with Matt and still help him out with a few bits, we've not severed ties. We're still friends and speak to each other every week. I'd hoped for a Southampton win, of course, but if we had to lose 3-0 to someone, I would rather it was Brentford than another team."

Unfortunately, the campaign ended on a flat note when a Leeds side, desperately needing to win to be sure of survival, grabbed an injury-time winner at the Brentford Community Stadium. It was a game to forget, and particularly so for the player who, nine months earlier, had got their Premier League adventure off to a dream start, Sergi Canos. Having come on as a sub midway through the second half, not long after Leeds had taken the lead, Canos equalised with a spectacular header 15 minutes later before being booked for taking his shirt off in celebration. Three minutes after that, a second booking followed for a needless foul, and he was off. It wasn't the ideal ending, but it was a memorable season nonetheless, and a debut Premier League campaign to be proud of.

Looking back on the season with undoubted pride, Thomas Frank said: "I had an unbelievable belief in us, from the experience we had come from, and also having an idea of where we were among the other clubs. I was convinced we would stay up and perform, the players' mentality is unbelievable and we have good structure and work very hard for each other. I'd never have predicted we'd beat Chelsea at Stamford Bridge, which was like wow, or draw 3-3 with Liverpool at home. Our first season followed many other promoted teams, but I don't think many have done it as good as us. I know what Leeds and Sheffield United did, but Sheffield had zero injuries to their starting XI, so to do what we did with all our bad luck was incredible."

He does, however, share the frustration of Bees supporters as to just how much credit Eriksen is given in the media with keeping Brentford up. Sure, his brilliance on the ball helped get the confidence flowing once more, and his set piece expertise provided a number of important assists. But it was like, the way things have been reported, it was all a single-handed effort. Never mind the fact that several of the players who contributed to Brentford's magnificent start to the season were all returning from injury and fit again at the same time.

"It's bullshit to say Christian made us stay in the Premier League," Frank underlined. "He's a good player, he helped us and consistently performed, but we had a lot of good players coming back to fitness too. David came back, Ivan had been out for five games, Rico had been out. All our best players played, and that helped us."

Benham agreed with his head coach's analysis, saying: "We improved with him in the team, but as ever, there's a lot of randomness. We had this period of seven losses and one draw in eight games, and we actually weren't playing that bad at all. In fact, we had times, like the first half against Manchester United, and the whole game away at Man City, when we really played pretty well. And then maybe there were some wins subsequently, like away at Watford, where we weren't at our best, so the effect wasn't as extreme as people think. But certainly there was a positive effect.

"For me the highlights are Arsenal and Chelsea. Probably the two games that I remember most fondly for the same reason were Watford at home and Burnley at home. In each case, we were playing a potential relegation rival. Just before Ghoddos got us the penalty against Watford I turned to my wife and just said, 'blow the final whistle, please blow the final whistle, I'll take this all day'. And I think just before Christian crossed for Ivan against Burnley I said to Phil Giles, 'I'll take a point all day long'. And Phil, in his way said, 'I don't think I would'. Some of the results have a more special meaning because of the way we have been treated by particular individuals connected to those clubs along the way but I will keep those to myself. Fans will be able to guess those anyway."

CHAPTER THIRTEEN

Mission completed, but what was the next step to be for Brentford? How would they improve and build on a magnificent first Premier League season, in which they had not dwelt for a single minute in the relegation zone? According to former director of football Rasmus Ankersen, Brentford now have a big opportunity, with a second round of Premier League money coming their way. Speaking before the summer 2022 transfer window opened, he said: "Brentford has a very good opportunity as it has a low-pressure culture and Matthew has a lot of money to spend this summer, and if he spends it wisely, you could definitely push into the top ten. I don't think Brentford is maxed out, I think it has another push to make in the next few seasons.

"Getting into the top six or seven would be a top story, and there is a real opportunity there. The contracts we had in the Championship were cleverly structured and kept the salary structure low even when we got promoted, which is what gives the club the opportunity now, with cash in the bank to spend on improving the team. I'm very proud of what we achieved there. It's a bit of a miracle that Brentford got to the Premier League, I think, with the budgets we had and the teams we were up against, so I'm definitely very proud. The experience I had with Brentford allows me to do what I'm doing now, which is building responsible clubs across the world."

Brentford's summer transfer window was, indeed, impressive. Although Christian Eriksen could not be persuaded to stay on the levels of pay that the club could offer, instead heading to Manchester United for a bumper windfall and around £1m per month in wages. However, the disappointment of his departure was tempered by some impressive summer arrivals which neatly blend youth and experience. Firstly, in came Scotland international Aaron Hickey from Bologna, equally comfortable on either flank, but brought in mainly to solve Brentford's long-running right-back problem. He was followed by exciting young attacker Keane Lewis-Potter from Hull, whose YouTube highlights suggest a very exciting future for the England U21 international.

Albanian international keeper Thomas Strakosha, acquired from Lazio, should provide a more reliable back up to David Raya than last season and avoid a repeat of the sort of problems experienced in the autumn and winter of 2021, while Burnley stalwart, Ben Mee, should provide ample cover at centre-back while both Ethan Pinnock and Kristoffer Ajer sit on the injured list. Danish international Mikkel Damsgaard, scorer of a brilliant free kick against England at Euro 2020, promises to be a thrilling capture from Sampdoria. Alongside Eriksen, the only departures of note were fringe players like Marcus Forss (Middlesbrough), Dominic Thompson (Blackpool) and Julian Jeanvier (Auxerre).

Suddenly, it was commonplace for Brentford to be spending between £15m-£20m on a player. Imagine telling a supporter between the Ron Noades and Matthew Benham period of ownership – when debts of around £10m were threatening the club's very existence – that they would one day in the near future be spending that on a single transfer fee. For Phil Giles, however, the numbers are relative, and what really matters is the kind of investment they will turn into in years to come. "The money side, the actual numbers, is kind of irrelevant to me," he said of the summer of 2022 window. "If we paid £2m for Ollie Watkins and he goes for massive money, you get the satisfaction of it being a good deal. But I won't sit here thinking it's a shame we can't do £2m deals any more. It's all relative, and what we paid for Aaron Hickey will perhaps turn back into the same situation. Hopefully, in hindsight, we can look back and say yes it's eight times what we were paying four years ago, but actually, it's just a rescaling. Whether it's £2m or £20m is irrelevant. If it's £2m, but they're worth £8m in a few years if they play for us regularly, or it's £20m, and they'll be worth £80m if we get to the level we hope to.

"To some extent though, if you believe they're going to be a top player, you really have to push the boat out to get them in and do it as early as possible. We know how quickly young players can develop, and within six months they've got away from you. They've suddenly rocketed in development, and that's what Brennan Johnson did (who Brentford tried to sign during both the winter and summer 2022 transfer windows, but who opted to stay with Nottingham Forest). We put in a hell of a lot of work with Brennan, and it was quite depressing to see Forest then get steadily better and better as the season went on. We could maybe have got a better deal for Keane Lewis-Potter if we had hard-balled, but if we'd left him at Hull for another year, and he scores 16-18 in the Championship, suddenly he's a £25m-£30m player.

"We're not that big yet as Sampdoria couldn't spell our name right (during the Mikkel Damsgaard transfer), but obviously we're a lot more well-known because of the profile and platform the Premier League gives you, and most people who like football to a certain level will have heard of Brentford now. But what we've done is given ourselves the opportunity to sign certain types of player, not based on whether we're a big club or not, but based on the brand we've built ourselves – partly based on the Scandinavian connection. Like when we signed Christian Eriksen, I told Thomas we really should now be able to sell ourselves to any Danish player out there. Would we have signed Eriksen without Thomas? Probably not, but I would say it's more about the wider Danish thing."

Off the pitch, meanwhile, it was a sign of the club's ambitions that it, perhaps somewhat reluctantly, agreed to reopen its academy, starting with an U18s team, six years after the much-maligned decision to close it. If Brentford one day aspires to play in Europe, UEFA rules dictate that clubs taking part in its competitions must have an academy in place. That still may seem like quite a stretch at the moment, but it's certainly not beyond Brentford's long-term ambitions, and with European qualification possible with as a low a finish as seventh (or winning the Carabao Cup, which Brentford reached the semi-finals of two years ago) through the new Europa Conference, it's not beyond the realms of reality either. Certainly, if the journey from these last few years is anything to go by, you'd dismiss Brentford's ambitions to continue to grow and improve at your peril.

It's certainly not an admission of failure of the B team system either, which will continue to operate as the next tier down from Brentford's first team. Marcus Bean, now back at Brentford as head of emerging talent, insists the B team remains as important as ever to the structure of the club. "We want to maintain what we were always about, which is developing young players and selling them on, and maintaining a young age among the first team players," he said. "The dream is for our B team players to be the ones who become the next Watkins or Benrahma, and I think the dream will become a reality as we're now in the Premier League and able to attract even better players for the B team, plus they can see a pathway for themselves, which is important.

"It's a great recruitment tool when you can tell a player to come to Brentford and they will have a chance. The level has gone up again with promotion though, and it's about trying to find boys who are able to cope with the quality and intensity of the Premier League, as the higher up you go, the more difficult it is to get that. But even if they don't play Premier League football, it's about developing good players and human beings who can go on at decent levels in the Football League."

The B team certainly remains as important as ever as far as Phil Giles is concerned, with the director of football recognising the need to increase its quality in line with the first team's progress. "Clearly when you get the club higher, the B team players need to start at a higher level, as it's very hard to take a player from a lower level and make them a Premier League player," he said. "So we need to get slightly better players in to give them a genuine chance, otherwise you're running a squad with the best opportunity being to develop players for League One clubs, and there's no return on investment there. You do need a nucleus of real talent in the B team and a genuine opportunity, and if you've got players coming in from places where you weren't expecting that jump in level but you get it anyway – Fin Stevens, Ryan Trevitt have done incredibly well over the last 12 months from where they're come from – then they're extra positives."

As for the first team's ambitions, Thomas Frank was candid when asked if Europe was a realistic ambition, saying with a grin: "I think everything is possible at Brentford." But he was careful not to downplay their aims either, and just like the first season in the top flight, it will be about more than just survival. "We never mention just staying up, it's always aiming as high as possible and winning the next game, and it's the same aim again," he added. "Every time a club stays in the Premier League for six seasons they say now we want to be a top ten club. The minimum of course is to stay up, but instead of aiming for top ten we would like to be eighth. So many things can go well or go badly, so I like us to be a little bit better every season. Try to maintain and improve the style of play, try to add a few players, try to work on things so we constantly improve."

Thomas Frank's name has already started being linked to managerial positions at other clubs, and the Danish national side's top job must also be a medium/long-term ambition for Frank – would losing such a pivotal part of the machine risk rerailing the Bees? Well, it's not something that keeps Phil Giles up at night apparently, as he feels the support structure already in place is just as important. "We don't fear it, it's part of football, so there's no point worrying about it," he said. "Thomas is a great coach and a great guy, but also has good support and people around him. We appointed Ben Ryan (director of elite performance) and Justin Cochrane (head of coaching) in the summer. We've got good players in, but it's just as important to bring good staff in. If we lose him, we're in a great position, and we'd look at it like we did when Dean left, and with the same process we do with all staff members. What have we got internally, and how do we want to run this process? Generally, you will want to have a look at the best possible candidates, but maybe you'll settle on someone already in the building, and maybe they'll have a headstart on the process as you know how they work already and there's less risk associated with it. Whenever anyone leaves, you have to see it as an opportunity – how can we get better from this rather than how will it set us back."

Sergi Canos, meanwhile, is hoping for a more relaxed season, now Brentford have proved themselves to an extent and have little to be nervous about. "If we work as a team and do the basics we've been doing the last few years, we won't have any problems," he said. "It will be difficult, of course, because if it was easy, everyone would do it. We're going to need everyone on board and everyone working with us, but we don't feel like the second season will be downhill, we're still flying. This time last year we felt a bit nervous around teams like Arsenal and Liverpool, but right now we're quite calm, which can sometimes be good and sometimes bad. But this time I think it's good because we don't have anything to prove and will just enjoy every game again, it's a bit more relaxed this year."

For Benham, again, the aim remains year on year improvement, and not necessarily finishing higher than last season's 13th place, but keeping up the standard of performance. "Always the ambition is to get better and better," he said. "But having said that, realistically, at the start of any Premier League season, there are six clubs who hope to make it into the Champions League, and then the other 14 saying, 'please for the love of God don't let's get relegated'. Randomness is such that it can happen, and it has happened, that you could be maybe the tenth best team, but you get unlucky enough to get relegated. The main thing we look at is the club's underlying performance, and if that continues to improve, and we stay up, yeah, I'd be delighted."

Returning to Phil Giles, he insists that things like five-year plans – so beloved by company directors both inside and outside football – are not part of the Brentford DNA. One-year plans, yes, and two years at a push. "Normally, we look ahead one year," he said. "One of our board members, when I first started, said we need a five-year plan. I asked why, and said what happens if we don't do it and it's down to bad luck? You can make a five-year plan, but what does it actually mean? Nothing. Instead, we'll set out our principles and stick to them, and we'll make a one-year plan of what it would take to get promoted this year if at all possible. When we got promoted, that became a two-year plan, as we didn't want to come into the Premier League with a one-year plan. All the money would have been assigned to retaining Premier League status, and we didn't want such a negative thought process.

"Becoming an average team in the Premier League is a high bar to set, doing it in two years is more possible. Everyone bought into the idea of becoming a good, solid Premier League club, which is here to stay. If you speak to the players, they will say things like we want to get to Europe, that's a target. But it's not about getting there in three years or five years, it's about getting better every year. If you keep getting better, then your chances of scraping into European qualification, or winning a trophy, get better, and maybe that will happen. You'd put yourself in a position where it becomes an expectation rather than a pipedream."

Before the second Premier League season kicked off, many outside observers, rather lazily, predicted 'second season syndrome' awaited the Bees, pointing out that Sheffield United's impressive ninth place finish in the Premier League in 2020, following promotion, was swiftly followed by a last-place finish and relegation back to the Championship the following campaign. But it's an idle narrative used by those trying to make sense of Brentford's achievements last season without bothering to look deeper.

Never mind the fact Brentford and Sheffield United are two vastly differing clubs in terms of footballing style and recruitment. Never mind the fact, also, that there's been many more examples in recent years of clubs of a similar size and traditional league placing to Brentford's thriving for long spells in the Premier League after promotion. Brighton, probably the closest example in terms of culture and recruitment – and with an owner with a very similar background – are about to embark on their fifth successive season. And although clubs of a different nature, Burnley managed six in a row before finally succumbing, while Bournemouth and Watford both stayed up for five years after being promoted at the end of Brentford's first season in the Championship. Swansea also had an impressive six-season spell in the top flight not so long ago, and Wigan topped even that with a mightily admirable seven seasons at the top table as well as an FA Cup Final victory.

It could, in fact, be argued that second season syndrome isn't really 'a thing', and probably wouldn't even be mentioned if not for Sheffield United's recent exploits. It could be seen as nothing more than an attempt to draw a cultural parallel with the music industry, where people like to talk of 'second album syndrome', saying the follow-up to the often-brilliant debut album is the hardest. It makes for a neat comparison, but the facts don't bear it out. The Premier League celebrates its 30th year in 2022, and in that time, there have been just shy of 90 promotions to it. How many of those instances have ended in a second-season relegation? Only 11 – and two of them were the same club (Hull City).

Midfielder Christian Norgaard is certainly not a believer in the cliche either. Speaking on BBC's Monday Night Club, he said: "Our mindset has been very similar to last season, we want to improve and do better. We're sick and tired of hearing about second season syndrome and making statements on that topic. It's about keeping on improving and working hard. We have a strong culture built up through a lot of years, but we also know how little it takes for things to go wrong, and this league can really punish you if you don't have the confidence or luck with you, as we found for a spell last season. We had a really good first season, but we're not satisfied with it, we want more."

One of the hosts speaking to Norgaard on the show, New York Times chief football correspondent Rory Smith, added to the debate, saying he doesn't see Brentford struggling in their second season. "I think a lot of people looked at Brentford and talked about second season syndrome and said they may struggle, but I just don't feel it with them as they get on the better end of margins, and their organisation and recruitment is fantastic," he said. "They're a superbly organised team and know what their identity is. They're an advert for the fact that you can do it if you have joined up thinking from board to coaching staff, recruitment staff, players. If you do everything well, you can overcome quite a lot of the financial inequalities that exist within football. Fairytale is probably pushing it, but they're definitely a feel-good story."

An hour or so into the new season, it looked like the armchair pundits, rather than the likes of Smith and Norgaard, may have had point, as the Bees found themselves 2-0 down at Leicester, who had controlled the game and looked for anyone's money to be cruising to a comfortable victory in the season's curtain-raiser. But Thomas Frank, taking advantage of new rules which allowed teams to make five substitutions, rang the changes and Brentford slowly took control, pulling one back through Ivan Toney just after the hour mark. One of the subs, Josh Dasilva – who had missed most of the previous season through injury and at one point been told he may never play again – then completed the comeback with his own personal redemption moment, cutting in from the right to curl home a brilliant equaliser from the edge of the area with four minutes remaining.

Reflecting on the tactical possibilities opened up by the new substitution rules, Phil Giles said: "I think we used three different shapes in that game, 4-3-3, 5-3-2 and 3-4-3. Some of the subs were planned due to some players not being able to last 90 minutes because of the pre-seasons they'd had, and some were not planned, reacting on the spot to what's happening in front of you, and it worked well. But there'll be other times when we look to make changes and it won't work out or will make us worse, and that's okay too because it's important to try it and see if it works."

The opening exchanges showed there was still work to do, but the two-goal comeback, at a club which had beaten the Bees twice the previous season, showed a real resilience, not to mention a tactical masterclass from the head coach. A true test of Brentford's Class of 2022-23 was to come in the next match, however, as the mighty Manchester United came to West London – another team to have done the double over the Bees in their debut Premier League season. What transpired was beyond even the wildest dreams of long-standing Bees fans who had watched in astonishment 12 months earlier as their side had put Arsenal to the sword, or put four goals past Chelsea at Stamford Bridge the following spring. The narrative leading up to the match would, naturally, be around Christian Eriksen's return to TW8. Afterwards, what the footballing world was instead left talking about was an absolutely stunning result and performance from the Bees, as one of the world's most famous clubs were humiliated 4-0 in front of a delirious crowd at the newly-named GTech Community Stadium.

There may have been an element of fortune about the opening goal as David de Gea allowed Dasilva's speculative daisy-cutter from the edge of the area to somehow slip under him and into the back of the net, for the midfielder's second goal in as many games. But there was nothing lucky about the way Brentford took the game to their illustrious visitors, with Eriksen – booed by some sections of the crowd for the perceived manner of his departure – looking on helplessly as his new side were ripped apart at will by his old one. In fact, there was a delicious moment for the second goal when Eriksen, sold a hospital ball inside his own area by de Gea, was dispossessed by his former apprentice for both Brentford and Denmark, Mathias Jensen, who then clinically rolled the ball home.

Ben Mee added a third with a header from a deep corner before a magical fourth goal sealed United's humiliation. Jensen, scapegoated by many Bees fans for some ineffectual performances in the past, but now in fine form and having the game of his life, helped snuff out a United attack before turning 180-degrees and playing a sublime ball from inside his own area out to Ivan Toney on the left flank. Toney looked up to see Bryan Mbeumo making a run into the box and played a first time volleyed pass perfectly for his strike-partner to hold off a last ditch challenge before slotting past de Gea. Two brilliant passes had turned defence into attack in a matter of seconds, and Mbeumo, whose finishing had been called into question the previous season, completed a fantastic move with the perfect finish – it was all over for United. Four goals in 25 first half minutes had blown away the 20-time top flight champions, and in some style. The second half passed without any further embarrassment for United, scoreline-wise at least, while the Bees put in a professional performance to see out the game comfortably and preserve their first half heroics.

"To beat Manchester United 4-0, the biggest club in the world, with top class players, we made some remarkable memories for the fans – it's crazy and, in some ways, unreal," Thomas Frank said after the game. "But when I look at what we do every day – the staff, the players, we try to improve things – it's not a surprise to win as I know we're good. But 4-0, that's big. I understand the narratives (concerning Manchester United's decline), but I really hope people look at our performance and give us credit." Highlighting what seemed a glaring contrast in attitude between the two sides, Frank added: "We have a big value that's called togetherness. We can never take it for granted and we have to work on it every single day. We have people who care for each other and who will go through a brick wall for each other, and we're very proud of that value and togetherness. We have to keep building on it, because when you have that, you can create something very special."

Bees midfielder Christian Norgaard, speaking to the BBC Monday Night Club, revealed that the comeback against Leicester had given them added confidence going into the United game. He went on to say that even though they went into it believing they could win, the players themselves admitted being 4-0 up against such a team was a "crazy" situation, but insisted there was just as much to be proud of from the second half performance. "The Leicester game showed what we are about in terms of character, keep believing, keep out-running our opponents and pressing high," he said. "It almost felt like a win, coming back from 2-0 down, and we took that confidence into the United game.

"We trained a bit more without the ball as we knew United would have more possession than us, and we had quite a clear man-to-man structure, especially on goal kicks. It was important for us to set the tone from the first pass, and it was one of those days where everything clicked.

"We all found it a bit crazy. We went into it believing we could win, we always do, but it was a strange feeling walking in at half time being 4-0 up against United. The same cliches were flying around about being focused, playing it as a 0-0, and emotionally, I think we handled it really well in the second half. We closed them down, and I know we didn't create a lot, but we didn't have to attack, we just had to be solid and defend the lead we had. But we had to worry all the time, even at 4-0, with the quality of players they had. If they came out flying and got one back, then another, it would be stressful, so we were on our toes the whole time and it was a whole team effort.

"In the transfer window I arrived we bought myself, Mathias Jensen, Pontus Jansson, Ethan Pinnock, David Raya and Bryan Mbuemo, all within a three-week period and for about a tenth of what the United team we had just played cost – we have done very well on recruitment and are doing a lot of things right. Thomas is very parental with the players too and cares a lot about us and how we feel, which is a very important quality for a manager to have."

So, Brentford 4 Manchester United 0. Perhaps the greatest scoreline in the club's modern era – certainly since its last top flight spell – and one which would have produced howls of laughter from the travelling Bees at London Road to watch Brentford lose 7-0 at Peterborough if you'd told them what they had to look forward to 15 years later. That contrast was encapsulated by supporter, Lewis Holmes, who, once his hangover had worn off, wrote the following in his post-match article for Beesotted.

"The headlines are all about how far the famous Manchester United have fallen, but in every single headline you see our name. 'Manchester United humiliated at Brentford', 'Manchester United annihilated by Brentford', 'Manchester United blown away by Brentford', By Brentford. By Brentford. Brighton gave the mighty giant a bloody nose last week, we took him out at the knees and roundhoused him into unconsciousness. The narrative may be all about Man United but our name is absolutely everywhere. Everyone from the football obsessive, through the casual observer, all the way down to those who legit don't care (weirdos) will have noticed Saturday's result and our rampaging, dominant performance.

"I write this on Monday morning and it's still going on. I have LBC radio on while I work (fantastic background noise) and there was a government minister being interviewed about the cost of living crisis. Out of the usual back and forth babble Nick Ferrari suddenly thundered: 'Come on now, let's be honest: you lot are Manchester United and the Labour Party are Brentford'. Saturday's heroics have leapt out of the football world and into the wider national narrative. Ten years ago people would often mistakenly think I supported 'Brentwood' but there's just no chance of that mistake these days. When you become the go-to metaphor for an abject humbling, I think you can rightly claim to be #bigtime.

"From a purely footballing point of view, there are so many details from that result that put a big sloppy grin on your face. Thomas Frank basking in a tactical masterclass; the continued rehabilitation of Josh Dasilva; Aaron Hickey's beautifully impetuous bodycheck on Ronaldo; the real Mathias Jensen standing up; that fourth goal, which I've seen 167 times and it keeps getting better every single time I see it.

"In the wider context though, Saturday's result sees little old Brentford making more friends and influencing more people. Expect to see a few more stories about clubs who aspire to 'be like Brentford', expect to see a lot of juxtaposition between our happy, harmonious little club and the absolute skip fire we played off the park on Saturday. Don't hold your breath for all those experts who predict 'Second Season Syndrome' to backtrack any time soon, but they'll have seen that masterclass and they'll be quietly reassessing their rash forecasts.

"Where does it end? Who knows, certainly not this guy. Our lord and saviour Matthew Benham talks about continual progress, and after only two games we've already improved on last season – taking points off two sides who last season gave up nothing. Are we going to go one better when Liverpool show up? Could we even humble the mighty Manchester City? I don't know. But in an era of so many great memories for Brentford supporters, I wouldn't be surprised one bit – and the rest of the footballing world will continue to sit up and take notice."

Although the Brentford journey and its future potential remains as exciting as ever, it's perhaps a good point at which to end this book's Brentford Revolution chronicles on the pitch, and hand over to Jon Varney, for his take on where the club goes next off of it.

"I genuinely think we're a very pragmatic board, ownership, senior executive and fanbase," said Varney. "We haven't had a lot of great times up until recently, so everyone cherishes the moment we're in and understands the fragility of it, which drives us all on and puts us in a position to keep driving forward year upon year. It would be incredibly arrogant to try to convince anyone that what we're doing is right for everybody, because the one thing I've learnt in 30-odd years working in the sports industry is that every organisation is different. One size does not fit all, so what's right for Brentford is completely wrong for Chelsea. We know our subject matter, and we know we're not always going to get it right, but when we make a decision, we get on and do it and we back ourselves. The majority of the time we will get it right, we believe, but there will be occasions when we have a stinker. We've got to be honest about that and not pretend it was outside influences – we're pragmatic, but we're committed as well. Again, every club has its own identity, so there's no point in taking someone else's business plan, we have to create our own that is right for us.

"Being in the Premier League gives Brentford the best platform on the planet to go and project itself, and I think it's at that point that you need to be really careful about how you want to present yourself to the world. I genuinely believe we have stayed true to our core values of togetherness, being progressive and respectful, and I think if you try and overegg it when you're on a global stage and try to become something you're not, then you're going to trip up really quickly. I don't think we've changed our characteristics, we get on with our life and we do it with a smile on our faces. We work hard, and I think they're values people across the world respect and associate with.

"I genuinely believe if we carry on doing that, we will attract more and more people. We've still got a lot of work to do in our own market, and of course, we will look at international opportunities. I think we do that a lot with our corporate partners. Hollywood Bets (shirt sponsors) are an unknown entity in this market but they employ 6,500 in South Africa and have 120 betting shops which are also restaurants and bars, so the opportunity for us to go and get more exposure and affinity in South Africa is tremendous and something we should absolutely look at doing over a period of time. But the thing that will always be true with this club is it's about performance first. Where did we go on our training camp this summer? To Germany. We had opportunities to go to Asia, Australia, North America, but for our second season in the Premier League, it was about making sure we've got the performance right at the start of the season. We will never ever go for commercial over playing performance.

"The stadium's capacity is a challenge. With a 17,500 capacity you're not going to drive the same stadium revenue as one which has 30,000, but it just means you have to work harder in other ways. Broadcast income is so important, and we try to make it the best broadcast facility in the country, so when broadcasters are making those decisions of where to go, we're ready, able and welcoming, because every TV game earns you more money. Having a smaller capacity sharpens our mind and focuses on drawing revenue from other areas. Broadcast is one of them, so are commercial partnerships, and that's why our brand health is so important to us, as that's what attracts sponsors. Businesses want to align with other organisations that have good values, and that's why being true to ourselves, having a good DNA and having a respectful progressiveness driving us forwards, is really important."

So, how to conclude our journey, for the moment at least? For Brian Riemer, it starts with the man at the top, and that people like Benham are the future of sustainable football. "Again, this club is owned and run by Matthew Benham, and it is his money that pays the bills, and he is a businessman," said Riemer. "I think Brentford is one of the only clubs in England that are run with a solid profit every single year, and I respect that. Football has evolved, and many clubs are now owned by multi-billionaires who throw those billions away every year and compete in getting the best and most expensive players. I really respect how Matthew runs this club. It must be a healthy business, and according to his model, that means buying relatively cheap players with a big potential and selling them at a huge profit, and I firmly believe that has had a positive impact."

Thomas Frank agreed and added that Brentford would definitely not be where they are today without the owner. "I would describe Brentford as one of the top three clubs in the world in terms of leadership, and Matthew as one of the top three owners," he said. "The only reason I won't say number one is I don't know all the owners in the world. I think there is more brains behind this than just his, with people working together in the same direction, but we all know that if Matt hadn't come into the club, we wouldn't be here now. A lot of good people have helped him along the way, but the way he thinks, his strategy and his calmness, I think is essential."

Former Bees midfielder Marcus Bean went one step further, saying Benham had been good for the game as a whole rather than just for Brentford. "Matthew Benham has not just been brilliant for Brentford, but for football in general," said Bean. "He's one of the most revolutionary people in the game, and now everybody is thinking about being sustainable and really paying attention to what he has done. He also stays behind the scenes, and that's how he likes it."

Bean's former team-mate, keeper Richard Lee, takes a real interest in the way Benham operates, having watched him closely while he was at the club, and tried to take life lessons from him, which he still uses in his work life today. "It's been mind-blowing, what they have achieved," said Lee. "I remember when I first joined it was a very different club, and things had just started to get going really. I had a few conversations with Matthew over the years about the way he sees football – so methodical and process driven, and the systems they have put in place to make sure the club recruit the right type of players – I think it's so forward thinking. I reference Brentford a lot when I talk about clubs and how they should build. Brentford have constructed brick by brick – quite literally with the new stadium. To go from being almost non-League to Premier League in the time they have is just phenomenal.

"I took a real interest in what Matthew was trying to do and have taken a few lessons from him in the way he operates – in terms of being process-driven and trying to take the emotion out of what I do. It's a tough thing to do as football is an emotional game and you're emotionally invested in the team you support, but the attention to detail is next-level. It's about constant improvement and continually looking to add to whatever it is you're doing. I go back to that phrase 'process-driven' again, it's not a case of you win some you lose some, you want to better what you do in all departments. If you do that, the sum of all the parts will be stronger, and I think Brentford are the epitome of that. Bit by bit, they are maximising every department, which is why, despite being the smallest club in the Premier League, they're punching above their weight. I was just surprised it didn't happen sooner really! Playing such consistent and positive football, year after year, they were unfortunate not to get there sooner. But they're built on such solid foundations that it hasn't surprised me."

Centre back Ethan Pinnock has played for some interesting clubs in his time – from the sustainability-focused Forest Green Rovers to Barnsley, who experimented with a similar model to Brentford's after former 'Moneyball' baseball coach Billy Beane became a minority owner in 2017 – so Brentford seems the perfect fit for him, and he recognises what the model has achieved. "Everything is strategic and planned," he said. "They've had to go about things a bit differently – there's a lot of clever people working behind the scenes, coming up with new, alternative ideas that have been working well on the pitch."

For Phil Giles, innovation is not something the Bees have a monopoly on, but something, at the moment, which they do well. However, he warned against getting too preachy about their methods, as pride can, as the old saying goes, come before a fall. "I don't think we have a monopoly on running a good football club – there's lots and lots of examples at different levels," he said. "Liverpool and Manchester City may have loads of money but, over a long period of time, they've made good decisions, albeit at a different level to us. Leicester and Norwich have been well run for a long period, so there's lots and lots of examples of clubs who can do things in a certain way and have been very successful. I think the key for us, now we're one level higher, is to make sure we keep our feet on the ground and stay humble about that, not to start thinking we've cracked it, or we do it brilliantly, or we're doing better than anyone. We're not going to start preaching to the Premier League how they should be working, because as soon as you do that, you'll fall flat on your face and everyone will laugh at you."

Andy Scott still looks back in wonder at the difference between the club he rejoined as a manager in 2007 and the one he came back to in a scouting capacity eight years later – and furthermore, the one which beat his Swansea side in the play-offs to finally make the promised land. "It's night and day isn't it?" he said. "You look at when I went back in 2007, the ground was a bit scruffy, crowds were down, there was a general malaise around the place. When I left for the first time (in 2009) the crowds were much bigger, we were in League One and we really had the feeling we could maybe have a chance of making the Championship. Lionel Road had been going on for donkey's years and was a pipe dream, but there was obviously a lot of hard work behind the scenes. Coming back as chief scout I could see the training ground had changed, the whole structure of the football club, the mentality, identity, unity of staff, players, it was a top ten Championship side with aspirations. There's been a continual increase, everything's moved forward, and when I went to Watford (in 2017), I said if Brentford make the Premier League, I fancy them to stay there, because they've got the basis of a strong club. When it starts to go wrong it stays solid, everyone reverts to type, knows what their job is and gets on with it. Most clubs in the Premier League just break and fall apart because they have no depth or knowledge of how to do things better.

"I love the new stadium, and the fans who were watching us in 2007, possibly heading out of the Football League, must be wondering what's going on, sitting in the Premier League and getting ridiculous results. Everyone now talks about Brentford being the club people should look at as the template of how you should do things. But other clubs can't replicate it as they don't have the people within the club who work like that, and don't have the strength to be disciplined about the strategy and the plan Matthew, Phil and Rasmus have. That's the strength of the club, there's a belief in what they do and they give people time. There's trust at both ends, and they trust the plan they have in place. That's to be admired, because when there's so much on the line, it's easy to buckle to fans' pressure or media scrutiny. But they believe in what they do."

Returning to Rasmus Ankersen, Brentford's former director of football was keen to emphasise that there is still very much a human element to the manner in which Brentford operate, and it's not all just banks of computers churning out stats. "Sometimes, when you hear about Brentford, you get the sense that people think there's robots running around the training ground talking in algorithms, but it's more simple than that," he said. "Running a football club should be about making good decisions and if you make a lot of small, good rational decisions every day, that adds up and ultimately you are moving in the right direction. We don't know what goes on at other clubs, so it's difficult for us to say specifically how we are different, but I think one of our strengths is that we are very aligned – from Matthew, down to us, then throughout the organisation – there is alignment in terms of what we want to achieve and how we want to do things.

"We have a style of play and a game model. We make sure we have a head coach that believes in that and can execute it, then we have recruitment that aligns, then find the right players to play that kind of football. It's sometimes as simple as that. Also, I don't think we have much politics. There's a lot of politics in football and football clubs in general, but not at Brentford. We focused on the task in hand. Phil and I didn't fight about who had the most power or were concerned about what Matthew thought about us. Good relationships mean you can just focus on executing the task to the best of your ability. That may all sound simple, but that's how it is, which makes a big difference I think. We redesigned the club based on a question: what would a football club look like if it had no human eyes and ears? Of course, it turns out you need a human element. But if you say from the start that 'Oh, it has to be a combination of stats and humans,' then you won't be radical enough to be able to make a difference."

Jon Varney, meanwhile, was keen to emphasise that the club would be careful not to get smug about the path to success it has chosen, or in any way suggest it should be a template for others to follow. But he insists it can, nevertheless, be held up as an inspirational story for other clubs of Brentford's size, or indeed anyone with a belief in how far hard work, teamwork and togetherness can take you. "I genuinely believe the Brentford story is very compelling," he said. "I also think it's something people can associate with. It's aspirational, it's a happy story, it's about hard work, team work, focus, togetherness, believing in where you want to get to and good execution.

"I think we've got a really clear proposition of what we're about and we've got a really compelling story to tell, and I think that is genuinely down to Matthew's vision and what he's created, as well as surrounding himself with people who can execute that strategy. We've got a clear vision now of who we are, what we're about, what we believe in, how inclusivity is important to us, making our environment as welcoming as possible – I think we've got our story telling bang on, and it's not forced. We're not trying to convince people we're this wonderful organisation that doesn't have any sharp edges and is smooth and sophisticated, that is not what we're selling. What we're selling is that we are a community football club that is doing well, has a good relationship with its local community and supporter base, has good values and which you can learn a lot from, and through an alignment, we can help you achieve some of the things we have achieved.

"I've worked for Coca Cola and other brands that have thousands of core objectives, but ours are three-fold. It's about delivering outstanding fan engagement, whether via their matchday experience or digital experience. We're doing good work on the matchday experience, but we need to do more in the digital space. If you look at the KPIs, we were the number one ranked Premier League club last season for matchday experience, so we're doing all right, but we haven't nailed it. The second is around financial sustainability through growth and cost management, and that is about making sure we have an organisation resourced well enough to take us to the next level. Our turnover is significantly increased, not just by the TV revenues, but those we're now starting to unlock through commercial partnerships and the new stadium.

"Our third objective is providing our people with an environment to succeed, because we've spent a lot of money in the last 18 months in taking our off-field staff from 80 to around 140. We've got the academy now, so we're going to have to increase our resources around Jersey Road. There's absolutely no point bringing all those people in if you don't create the right culture or environment for them to believe in and deliver against. Below that, there are a whole raft of departmental objectives, but our horizon is to keep growing, keep believing in what we're trying to do and don't get deviated by all the inevitable noise that surrounds being a Premier League club. We have to be ruthlessly focused on what we're trying to do and stick to it."

Phil Giles agreed, saying that Brentford's model is not necessarily something which will work everywhere else, and quite possibly won't always keep the club going in an upward trajectory. But if there does happen to be a downturn in fortunes at any stage, where the worst did come to the worst, Giles believes Brentford would fall into the camp of teams well positioned to bounce straight back rather than those that keep dropping like a stone. "Hopefully we're set up right so that if we do go down, we continue in the Championship as we previously did," he said. "It's not like we'd be changing the style or culture of the club. We'd have to sell some players of course, and there's seven or eight players you'd look at and think they'd bring in significant sums. But you'd also like to think that with those players, we won't go down in the first place! It would be disappointing, but manageable. Sunderland went straight down through the divisions, but they had in-built problems, but I'd like to think we're not building those problems and have enough assets in the squad that we can pick and choose where we get funds from, and hopefully keep the players which give us the best chance of going back up."

Ivan Toney's call-up to the England squad – although tinged with the disappointment of not actually making it onto the pitch against either Italy or Germany in the Nations League – was yet another proud landmark in the Brentford Revolution. Bees fans eagerly tuned in hoping to see Toney become the first player to pull on the Three Lions in a full international while contracted to Brentford since Ealing-born Leslie Smith came on to replace Stanley Matthews in a 2-0 win over Romania in May 1939. It was not to be, this time at least, but hopefully Toney's time with the national side will come, and hopefully he will still be a Brentford player when it does.

Toney secured his place following a brilliant hat-trick in a 5-2 win over Leeds United at the start of September 2022. Thomas Frank said of Toney's call-up: "He's a very confident guy who believes in himself, and the journey has not been straightforward for him. He said he has dreamt of being an England international since he was a kid. It took a few detours off the path to get that first call up, but Ivan's potential is still very much not at the top yet. The sky is the limit I'd say."

Toney's selection was also discussed on the BBC Radio 5 Live Football Daily podcast by two former Bees, Adam Forshaw and Clinton Morrison, who featured in a single game together for Brentford ten years earlier, when the Revolution was in its early stages – Morrison was making his debut on loan from Sheffield Wednesday in a 2-0 win over Rochdale in March 2012, while Forshaw was sent back to parent club Everton after breaking his jaw during the game.

Forshaw, who watched from the stands as his Leeds side were destroyed by Toney a few weeks earlier, said: "He was brilliant on the day, never mind the three goals. He's had a great start to the season, and I think (his selection) is probably deserved. The way Brentford play, they can surrender possession a little bit at times, and they're comfortable just sitting behind the ball knowing when they want to go, they can play it off him and have runners in behind, with pace on the counter attack. They're not direct, but they know they can be if they want to be because he's up there. He's really good in both boxes and also gets assists." Morrison, himself a former international striker, added: "Toney holds the ball up so well, he is confident, he can finish and he can bring others into play. He's not only good in attacking areas, but in defending areas as well – he will win most of the first headers. He's in there on merit, and he's got a great chance of making that World Cup squad because he's different to all the strikers they have got (in the frame). He gives you different options, he's good on set pieces. England have struggled over the years with penalty takers, and he never looks like he's going to miss."

Summing up Brentford's approach, Forshaw, an important figure in the early years of the Revolution went on to say: "Matthew Benham is everything mathematical and statistical, but there is just a feeling there – a quiet confidence around little old Brentford. The steps they have taken – they were happy to sell and make a profit when they were in the Championship for a few years – to lose the likes of Maupay and Watkins." Morrison may have been a very minor figure in Brentford's journey, but he is making a good name for himself as a respected pundit and added some good final analysis, saying: "Brentford's recruitment is one of the best I have ever seen. Bigger clubs in the Premier League can learn a lot about how they recruit, they're one of the best at it. You have got to give huge credit to everything that happens at Brentford, from the hierarchy downwards."

The final quotes in this book from a player are handed to a man who has participated in much of the Bees' rise in recent years, as well as announcing Brentford's arrival in the Premier League with a stunning goal against Arsenal... Sergi Canos. Speaking with obvious pride at the way he has continued to play a central part in the Brentford Revolution, playing throughout the most crucial years, he also signed off with a nice summary about what the club has achieved during his time at Brentford. "I feel proud because I'm still here and still playing – every signing we get improves the club and I'm still playing, so I feel privileged," he said. "Normally people who have been at the club four or five years are left behind and can't reach the next level, but I feel amazing because I feel every year I'm better and can give more things to Brentford. What we have created at this small club is something everyone should be proud of."

So, there you have it. From looking like dropping out of the Football League altogether to securing a second season in the Premier League, while often matching, and sometimes embarrassing, the country's elite, in less than 15 years. As we said in the introduction, it's not a unique journey by any means, but whereas others, Bournemouth for example, have climbed the leagues through financial doping and driven a horse and carriage through FFP rules, Brentford chose a different journey. Brighton are arguably the closest comparison – from near oblivion to Premier League respectability through sustainable growth, whilst also building an impressive new stadium. Can it be a coincidence that both clubs have owners hailing from a similar background in sports gambling and analytics? Benham indeed once even worked for Tony Bloom before striking out on his own, and a rivalry remains between the two men to this day.

There are various routes clubs of a similar size to Brentford have taken to get to the top, some less sustainable than others and leading to more troubled times after experiencing the sweet taste of glory. So it's a relief to hear Phil Giles say the club has been set up in such a way that if Brentford were to lose their top flight status at some point, they would be in a better position than most to bounce back, and certainly wouldn't become a basket case club dropping through the divisions, picking up point deductions aling the way. However, as both Giles and Jon

Varney underline earlier in this chapter, it's important not to be smug and preachy, as football club ownership is far from being a "one size fits all" model. Let's instead stay humble and remember where we have come from – values which aren't always easy to stick to in the modern era, and with such elevated status achieved so quickly.

Indeed, the culture Brentford has developed through its growth journey has been just as key as any single statistic, player or staff member. How many teams would have bounced back from the ultimate sporting heartache as experienced against Doncaster in April 2013, to be promoted the following season? And then repeat the trick seven years later after losing what has been called The Biggest Game in Football to your bitter rivals thanks to a freak goal late in extra time? It takes a special kind of philosophy, belief and mental strength – especially when, as pointed out by Uwe Rösler, Brentford's numerous past failures on the big stage would be trotted out whenever they reached another final or secured a play-off place. But a sunny day at Wembley on 29 May 2021 changed all that. This is a new and exciting Brentford – let's see where Brentford's Revolution takes them next.

BRENTFORD FANS ROLL OF HONOUR

Tim Street
David Lane
Seb Lane
Bill Grant
Bella Grant
Greville Waterman
Ken Hart
Matthew Murton
Javier Lopez
Bradley
Lopez-Edwards
Phil Perkins
Liam Gorman
Ken Hart
Roy Henning
David Pulford
Abby Meyer
Sue Horlock
Ian Axbey
Mark Axbey
Daniel Mallett
Richard Parker
Tanya Ensom
Peter Chester
Graham Clifton
Matthew Harris
Dan Ferguson
Sam Ferguson
Robert Lampert
Daniel Huxley
Nigel English
Simon English
In memory of
Mick Cox 1963-2022
Tim Taylor
Richard Evans
David Taverner
Roy Woods
Luke Forrester
Herbie Forrester
Danielle Forrester
Axel Forrester
Luna Forrester
Jordan Forrester
Bob Hooper
James Reed
Kevin Walling
Dave & Harry Smith
Ian Blackham
Simon J Webster
Alex Forbes
Steve Brent
Sebastian Mauer
Ben Thomas
Carl Whitaker
Kieran Ryan
Aidan Ryan
Paul Rogers
Paul Barwell
Danielle Wayne
Robin Burks
Peter Crumpler
Jim Conway
Martin Carter
Stewart Amos
Warren Dean
Max Dyble
Wayne Dyble
Brian Tubb
Michael Tickner
Jon Lys
Stephen Byne
Neil Murrum
Liam Lane
Jack Williams
James Mason
Stephen Houlihan
Terry Collett
Mark Currier
John Scrace
John Stansfield
Sam Puddephatt
Stewart Livingston
Andy Griffin
Melvin Collins
Doug Collins
Rowan Caldwell
Terence Parker
David Thurbon
Michael Page
Adam Page
John Cullinane
Philip Bourne
Mark McCormick
In loving Memory of
Ollie Shilling
Bill Park Weir
Geoffrey Tarr
John Stride
Matthew Stride
Daniel Carey
Paul Fletcher
Richard Rumbold
Nick Carter
Shaun Burch
Steve Paddock
Matthew Cook
Chris Reed
James Cook
Alan Jacob
Cathryn Shilling
Jason Smith
Rob Boyce
Sean Talman
Matt Talman
Tony Waterer
Margaret Hicks
Alan Norcott
Tony Dancer
Allan Finnie
Rob Rutter
Satpal Chatha
Ron Johnson
Robert Nicholls
Mark Skelton
Adrian Maybanks
Lewis Family
Down Under
Romain Lewis
Paul Lusher
Mark Atkinson
Molly Atkinson
Brian Atkinson
Christopher Crain
Colin Penn
Trevor King
Jon Alexander
The Randall Family
Helen Lippell
Jim Marshall
Jay Holt
Adam Hobbs
Stephen Osborne
Andy Griffin
Andy Zajczyk
Malcolm Head
Dave Floyd
Jeremy Depauw
Syd Hayward
Pete Hayward
Chris Hayward
Vince Hayward
Anna Rustad
Mark Newman
Michael Nolder
Eddie Cheung
Keith Chandler
John Wilson
Viv Suh
Love Daddy Dan Suh
Andrew Vickers
Clifford Knowles
Christopher Knowles
Gary Cassar
Jorgen Karlsson
Peter Brown
Daniel Toppin
Aaron Padgett
Laritza Gómez
Rory Carruthers
James Clarke
Andrew Gardner
Simon Gale
Geoff Vial
Leif Pedersen
Wallace Avery
Matt Wilson
Steve Hammond
Gary (Bert) Wheadon
Chris Horder
Andrew Gomez
Daniel Coker
Ian Walker
David Cordery
Ian Venner
James Heneghan
Stephen Cleeve
Pete Gregorowski
Stephen Piper
Chris Mackenzie
Davey
John Bray
Paul Davies
Elijah Pawliw
Simon Johnston
Lewys Johnston

Simon Forrester
Neil Plunkett
Tim Moody
Peter Bailey
David Buckland
Nemone and Nick
Katie Jordan
Tes Stranger
In memory of
Cyril Ilett
Philip McConnell
David Thurbon
Joe Turpin-Antonio
Happy 60th Birthday
Phil King xxx
Sara Loewenthal
Pete Goodchild
Leslie Goodchild
Mick Goodchild
Duncan Holden
Mark Cruse
Mark Walter
Stephen Walter
Peter Walter
Katherine Wiseman
Madelyn Wiseman
Denis Hynes
Oliver Morley
Chris Morley
Tom Harrison
Brian Harrison
Henry Bowley
Peter Gill
Richard Schofield
Roger Hailey
Jim Walsh
Justin Stephens
Lucas Heiker
Steve Smith
Bryan Searle
Alex Lumley
Terry Lumley
Colin Bevis
David Fishlock
Michael Vernon
Daniel Vernon
Mark Turner
GrahamTyrrell
Keith Wallis
John Prior
Chris Abigail
Gary Barrell
David Newlin
Anthony Lock
Kim Alway
Paul Hands-Wicks
David Mildon
Ed Turnill

Matt Turnill
James Fishlock
Alan Wood
Iain Stuart
John Hannon
Ben Moses
The Skinner family
The Caldari family
Jonathan Burdett
Nicholas Smith
Kevin Furlong
David Furlong
Barry Lister
Alan Wheatley
Bill Sandy
Jerome Day
Ian Dawes
Robert Pullen
Lynne Morgan
Robert West
James Huxley
Lee Ashton
Graham & Ellie Wolfe
Paul Corfield
Robin Hesmyr
Howard Bines
In memory of Herbie
& Pat Whitaker
Thanks to my mum
Diane Guilfoyle
Richard Butler
David Bigger
David Brassington
Deborah Oliver
John Habes
Sean Moran
John Tønnesen Ripland
Stephen Grant
Sebastian Downes
Carl Smith
Gregory Smith
Tony Girdler
Clive Foskett
Philip Mooney
Richard Nobbs
Brian Prince
Bruce Muni
Julian Mann
David Uren
In memory of
Joseph Prince
Jon Restall
Brian Bowley
Ed Gore Browne
Thomas Gore Browne
Stephen Higgs
Claiden family
Happy 60th Birthday

Phil King
Aaron Leech
Robert Chessher
Keith Piggott
Dave Piggott
John Abbett
Chris Neal
Robert Trand
Kevin Fancourt
Trevor Lancaster
Peter Robinson
Russell Probert
Rob Davies
Steve Davies
Wayne Dickson
Carl Smith
David Ohl
Joe Carr-Hill
Ruzzler Bees
Neil Murrum
Richard Lozinski
Hilesh Radia
Peter & Seth Watkins
Andrew Harris
Kyle Kogge
Barry Mingard
Lewis Byrne
Peter Hills
Shaun Carter
Stuart Hatcher
Roy Hatcher
Roy Woolsey
Rod Woolsey
Tom Baldassari
Richard Peskett
Nigel Doherty
Jeff Owen
David Cordery
John Palman
Jack Holloway
James Dempsey
Dustin Senor
Oscar Thompson
Russell Wallman
Keith Macinnes
Jonathan Burchill
John Hood
Clive Brooks
David Hambidge
Alan Winter
Robert Chamberlain
Chris Chamberlain
Georgina Newton
Caroline Chamberlain
Kevin Jones
Stuart Hughes
David Thurbon
David Ashton

John Mulrooney
Andrew Sage
David Guilfoyle
Paul Reddick
Paul Haines
Nicholas Maniatakis
Gary Reilly-Vince
Tony Aubrey Day
Adrian Mann
Paul Humphreys
Alan Maskell
Alan Westcott
Neil Westcott
John Bennett
Ranjit Singh Jutley
Keith Mosdall
Richard McDougall
Roy East
Malcolm Smith
Alan Maskell
Nigel Phillips
Mark Turner
Carl Stenbäcken
Jacki Woolmington
Simon Radford
Bronislaw Zolyniak
Jim Priest
Mark Chapman
David Wilsdon
Graham Sandys
Stephen Boyce
Dan Wilson
Fintan Murray
Jamie Greenhill
Keith Piggott
Gary Piggott
Alba Siletti
Calvin Woods
Dermont Robinson
Gary Stenning
Les Spink
Jim O'Reardon
Robert Hewett
Harry Benham
Siobhan Dagge-
Benham
Richard (John)
Dearden
Theo Byrne
John Sear
Peter Clements
Darren Kirk
Hugh Dresser
Graham Trueman
Alan Murphy
John Murphy
David Roe
Keith Riley

Ian Westbrook
Saul Westbrook
Dinesh, Leo,
Bethany & Rory
Nirgunananthan
Michael Eivers
Max Lindberg
Brian Martin
Jonathan Foy
Stuart Foy
Joe Thompson
Gary Enstone
Pauline Griffiths
Ian Watson
Alfie Connole
John Pratt
Peter Furness
Richard Lawrence
David Holmes
Darryl Truefan Howell
Mark Fairweather Bluck
Eunice Leech
Robert Harrison
Robert Whale
David Samuels
John Simpson
Derrick Horsley
Siobhan Collins
Richard Bartram
Robyn Bartram
Mark Bluck
Helen Cox
Bill Knutson
Mark Sears
Leon Moore
Jonathon Wiles
Mike Lumley
Peter Skeggs
Stuart Nute
Andrew Martin
Gemma Connoley
Matthew Lister
Richard Lefley
Andrew Prickett
Steve Ramnarain
Neil Shears
Ollie Shears
Paul Sherwood
Paul Minkkinen
Daniel Powell
Kaine Powell
Luna Powell
Ken Powell
Jamie Powell
Jackson Powell
Frankie Powell
Frank Barry
Keith Sansom
Paul Honhold
Barry Barthorpe
Ernie Braithwaite-Smith
Richard Drake
Tom & Elissavet Drake
Huw Davies
Taylor Dawson
David Legg
Philip Rawlings

Thanks to everyone who pre-ordered the book and supported this project.

THANKS & ACKNOWLEDGEMENTS

We would like to thank the following people for their help during the production of this book: Chris Wickham, Chris Deacon, Paul Morrisey, Rasmus Ankersen, Phil Giles, Jon Varney, Beryl Bevan, Trevor Inns, Mark Chapman, Mark Fuller, Greville Waterman, Bill Grant, Andy Scott, Mark Warburton, Uwe Rösler, Thomas Frank, Marcus Bean, Charlie MacDonald, Sam Saunders, Richard Lee, Alan McCormack, Sergi Canos, Rico Henry, Ethan Pinnock, Jim Levack, Martin Holland, Matt Allard, Andy Cooper, Jon Restall, Andy Watson, Lou Boyd, Donald Kerr, Sarah Loewenthal, Jacob Murtagh and Tom Moore.

The authors would like to acknowledge the use of the following resources:
Sporting Intelligence interview with Matthew Benham 2015, De Correspondent article on Marinus Dijkhuizen 2015, TV3 Sport Denmark documentary on Emiliano Marcondes' transfer 2017, Brentford FC programme interview with Romaine Sawyers 2019, London News interview with Ryan Woods 2020, Mediano podcast with Brian Reimer February 2021, Ted Knuston StatsBomb podcast June 2021: Brentford and Tuchel Tales, Bees United interview with Matthew Benham 2022, BBC Monday Night Club interview with Christian Norgaard 2022, BBC Radio 5 Live Football Daily podcast 'Toney Time' - September 2022, Hounslow Chronicle/Get West London – various articles, Beesotted – various articles and podcasts, The Price of Football – various podcasts.

"I THINK EVERYTHING IS POSSIBLE AT BRENTFORD."
THOMAS FRANK
JULY 2022